Split

Class and Cultural Divides
in American Politics

Mark D. Brewer
University of Maine

Jeffrey M. Stonecash
Syracuse University

CQ PRESS

A Division of Congressional Quarterly Inc.
Washington, D.C.

CQ Press
1255 22nd Street, NW, Suite 400
Washington, DC 20037

Phone: 202-729-1900; toll-free, 1-866-4CQ-PRESS (1-866-427-7737)

Web: www.cqpress.com

Cover design: www.archeographics.com
Cover photos: Getty Images

☺ The paper used in this publication exceeds the requirements of the American National Standard for Information Sciences—Permanence of Paper for Printed Library Materials, ANSI Z39.48-1992.

Printed and bound in the United States of America

10   09   08   07   06   1   2   3   4   5

ISBN-10: 0-87289-298-0

ISBN-13: 978-0-87289-298-9

Library of Congress Cataloging-in-Publication Data

Brewer, Mark D.
    Split : class and cultural divides in American politics / Mark D. Brewer, Jeffrey M. Stonecash.
        p. cm.
    Includes bibliographical references and index.
    ISBN-13: 978-0-87289-298-9 (alk. paper)
    ISBN-10: 0-87289-298-0
    1.   Class consciousness—Political aspects—United States.   2.   Social conflict—United States.   3.   Culture conflict—United States.   4.   United States—Social conditions—21st century.   5.   United States—Politics and government—2001-   I.   Stonecash, Jeffrey M.   II.   Title.   III.   Title: Class and cultural divides in American politics.

    HN90.S62B74 2006
    324.273'13—dc22
                                                                2006021812

To Megan
—Mark Brewer

To Lindsay, Cassie, and Maggie
—Jeffrey Stonecash

CONTENTS

TABLES AND FIGURES

FIGURES

PREFACE

Talk of a culture war—conflict over social and moral issues—is virtually inescapable in contemporary American society. The media is awash with references to the battles raging over cultural issues. Stories about conflict over abortion, same-sex marriage, and God's proper place in public life saturate the printed pages, airwaves, and cable and broadband connections throughout America. It doesn't matter if one's taste in reading material runs more toward *Reader's Digest, Playboy,* or the *American Political Science Review,* or if one is more likely to tune in to FOX News, CNN, or NPR. In recent years, discussions about cultural conflict are everywhere.

Agreements about the existence, nature, and impact of a culture war, however, are far less ubiquitous. Almost from the moment James Davison Hunter first introduced the idea of a culture war into scholarly debate in 1991, academics and other political observers have rushed to position themselves as proponents or skeptics of the existence of a moral battle raging within the United States. The only thing that is clear from all of these various contributions is that no consensus has emerged about the existence or impact of a cultural war.

Two recent books on politics—both quite popular and influential—illustrate perfectly this lack of agreement. The first work, *Culture War? The Myth of a Polarized America,* by Morris P. Fiorina and his colleagues, argues that claims of a culture war in the United States are greatly exaggerated. For Fiorina, it is only political elites and a handful of activists at each end of the ideological spectrum who are really at odds over cultural issues. The vast majority of Americans are somewhere in the middle on cultural concerns, and largely in agreement with each other. To most Americans, talk of a culture war is inapplicable and irrelevant, Fiorina posits. Thomas Frank, the author of *What's the Matter with Kansas?*, dramatically disagrees with such a perspective. For Frank, the culture war is a very real phenomenon within American society and is the driving force in contemporary politics. All Americans, from those in the highest public offices to the most average of citizens, fight over abortion, homosexuality, religion, and other cultural issues on a day-to-day basis. Perhaps most important, the culture war is swamping other issues. All other divisions in American society, especially class divisions, are overshadowed if not eliminated all together by the culture war. Frank is particularly agitated that less affluent Americans now regularly act contrary to their economic interests because of their conservative views on cultural issues.

This lack of agreement surrounding the existence and impact of a culture war is what initially led us to pursue this project. Fiorina and Frank could not both be right. But we also had a suspicion that both were not entirely wrong either. We knew through some of our previous research that contrary to the conventional wisdom, social class continues to affect Americans' political behavior. Yet we also had conducted research that clearly indicated the growing impact of such cultural concerns as abortion and religiosity. Does one issue area trump another in the national consciousness? The purpose of *Split* is to determine the extent to which cultural issues and class concerns shape contemporary American politics. How significant are cultural and class conflicts in the United States and what is their relationship to each other?

The short answer is that class concerns and cultural issues both matter. Conflict occurs on both fronts, with neither cleavage overshadowing or displacing the other. For class concerns, the division is centered on issues of opportunity. Growing inequality in the United States has exacerbated differences in income in recent years. This has given new relevance to the old divide between the haves and the have-nots as differences in income create dramatically different opportunities in the areas of education, health care, housing, and overall quality of life. How, or even if, government should address these differences in opportunity is at the heart of class conflict. For cultural issues, the conflict is driven by different ideas of what constitutes appropriate behavior, different views of morality, and ultimately different views on right and wrong. Again, the proper role of government in settling these disputes is key to the cultural divide. Both cleavages involve issues of fundamental importance. Both are important to American citizens. Both shape our politics. We have two splits at work simultaneously—one centered on class, and one centered on culture.

The question of class versus culture is often presented as an either/or situation—one must displace the other. Such a presentation conflicts with reality, and we think it is important for Americans to understand that both sets of concerns are crucial to understanding our country's politics. This understanding is particularly important for students taking political science and government courses across the nation. *Split* highlights many of the central topics and issues in introductory American government courses, as well as more focused courses on parties and elections, electoral behavior, public opinion, and other areas of American politics. We hope that students and instructors will find our examination of the class and cultural divisions in the United States informative and lively.

This book could not have happened without the assistance and support of a number of individuals and institutions. Mark Brewer would like to thank his colleagues in the Department of Political Science at the University of Maine for providing the supportive and collegial work environment in which this work came to fruition. He would also like to thank Courtney Hagenaars for his assistance with the references and his students in his courses on parties and elections and religion and politics for their often insightful discussions of many of the ideas examined in this book. Finally, he would like to thank his wonderful wife Tammy and beautiful daughter Megan for their love and support, and for understanding that sometimes Sundays are for writing. Jeff Stonecash would like to express his thanks for the wonderfully supportive environment of the Maxwell School.

Last, but certainly not least, we acknowledge our debt of gratitude to the staff at CQ Press. Charisse Kiino's enthusiastic support made the book easier to complete, and Michael Kerns's deft editorial guidance significantly improved the final product. Anna Socrates did a wonderful job copyediting, as did Belinda Josey with production and Erin Snow with marketing. We also thank the reviewers whose comments, suggestions, and critiques made this a better book: Scott Adler, University of Colorado; Ted Brader, University of Michigan; William Claggett, Florida State University; John C. Green, University of Akron; Jeffery Jenkins, Northwestern University; and Katina Stapleton, Institute of Education Services. We close with the traditional caveat that any and all errors and weaknesses that remain are solely our responsibility.

DIVISIONS IN AMERICAN POLITICS

Understanding American politics—why Democratic and Republican politicians take certain positions and oppose each other's policies—requires knowing what issues dominate political debate and how the electoral bases of the parties differ. Who does each party represent and what are their concerns? What are the partisan arguments about? Figuring out these differences has not been easy in recent years. Politicians articulate very different views about what is central to our politics. During the 2004 campaign, Democratic vice presidential candidate John Edwards shared the following story:

> I grew up in a small town in rural North Carolina, a place called Robbins. My father, he worked in a mill all his life, and I can still remember vividly the men and women who worked in that mill with him. I can see them. Some of them had lint in their hair; some of them had grease on their faces. They worked hard, and they tried to put a little money away so that their kids and their grand-kids could have a better life.... My mother had a number of jobs. She worked at the post office so she and my father could have health care. She owned her own small business. She refinished furniture to help pay for my education. I have had such incredible opportunities in my life. I was blessed to be the first person in my family to go to college. I worked my way through, and I had opportunities beyond my wildest dreams. And at the heart of this campaign—your campaign, our campaign—is to

make sure that all Americans have exactly the same kind of opportunities that I had no matter where you live, no matter who your family is, no matter what the color of your skin is.... And we have much work to do, because the truth is, we still live in a country where there are two different Americas—one for all those people who have lived the American dream and don't have to worry, and another for most Americans, everybody else who struggle to make ends meet every single day. It doesn't have to be that way.[1]

To Edwards, the important divisions are class divisions. For a long time academics defined class in terms of socioeconomic status or in terms of how voters saw themselves. For the first approach, academics would devise combinations of income, education, and occupation, and then group the combinations into working class, lower-middle class, middle class, etc. The other approach was to ask survey respondents to identify themselves as middle or working class.[2] Class as defined in this book refers not to the status of a person's job, but that person's income level. A family's location within the income distribution is critically important in terms of both the options that are available to them and the economic fears and pressures they face. The less money a family has, the fewer opportunities and greater economic vulnerability it faces. Edwards identifies a crucial political battle over whether we will use our resources to protect the vulnerable and provide more equality of opportunity.

To others, however, the real battle is about which values we should support. Pat Buchanan, former aide to President Nixon, past Republican presidential candidate, and current cable television commentator, places primary importance on cultural issues—what behaviors our society should value and what values our government should discourage or encourage:

The agenda Clinton and Clinton would impose on America— abortion on demand, a litmus test for the Supreme Court, homo- sexual rights, discrimination against religious schools, women in combat—that's change, all right. But it is not the kind of change America wants. It is not the kind of change America needs. And it is not the kind of change we can tolerate in a nation that we still call God's country.... My friends, this election is about much more than who gets what. It is about who we are. It is about what we believe. It is about what we stand for as Americans. There is a religious war going on in our country for the soul of America. It is a cultural war, as critical to the kind of nation we will one day be as was the Cold War itself. And in that struggle for the soul of America, Clinton and Clinton are on the other side, and George Bush is on our side. And so, we have to come home, and stand beside him.[3]

Edwards asks how to increase equality of opportunity, how to treat individual initiative and accomplishment, and how much of our tax resources should be used to help the less affluent. Buchanan asks what values should our society support, what behaviors should government allow or prohibit, and proper definitions of right and wrong.

It's not easy to sort out which of these divisions dominates politics. Some assert class divisions are important while others assert that cultural issues are dominant. Still others argue that the central concern is not whether class or cultural issues dominate, but whether cultural issues have displaced class issues. Finally, some say there really is no "culture war"[4] within the public, but rather only the elites in Washington are divided and caught up in an "inside-the-beltway" debate over morality.

Sorting out the divisions—which groups support Democrats and which support Republicans and why—is central to understanding American politics. Politics is fundamentally a fight over resources and values,[5] and we can't understand what the fight is about if we don't know who is on each side and what motivates them. If Republicans receive strong support from the more affluent and little support from the less well-off, the party will be a strong advocate for lower taxes and fewer government services, particularly services that benefit the less affluent. If Democrats derive much of their support from the less affluent, they will oppose Republican efforts to cut taxes and government programs, and instead call for increased taxation (particularly on the wealthy) in order to fund programs focused on improving the situation of America's economic have-nots.

But the basis of partisan conflict could be very different. If Republicans express their opposition to abortion and receive strong support from pro-life individuals and groups, while Democrats advocate for the right of women to decide about abortions and receive support from those who regard themselves as pro-choice, a different set of policy battles will occur. Republicans will seek to restrain the right to choose, require parental notification for minors seeking abortions, and oppose the use of public funds to pay for abortions. Democrats will oppose these policies. In this situation, public policy on abortion in the United States will be dramatically different based on which party gains control of government.[6]

Understanding what set of issues, if any, are dividing the public and the parties will help us comprehend what motivates politicians to act the way they do. We will understand why some issues dominate the political agenda while others are ignored, what future policy fights might be about, and ultimately what the laws of the nation might look like. The problem for students of politics is that contemporary interpretations of current American politics present very divergent explanations of the divisions dominating the process. The basis of these differences will be presented in later chapters, but a brief summary here may help.

THE CENTRAL ISSUES—CLASS AND CULTURE

Those who see class as primary argue that America gives high priority to the American Dream—defined by Jennifer Hochschild as "the promise that all Americans have the chance to achieve success as they define it... through their own efforts"—and that the central issues of equality of opportunity divide the public politically.[7]

On one side of the class divide are those who see differences in opportunity and advocate using the power of government to increase equality of opportunity, such as providing federal aid to equalize expenditures across school districts, health care for children whose parents do not have it, and more accessible childcare for lower income workers. The advocates of equal opportunity want to provide college grants that do not require repayment rather than loans that create debt for less-affluent students, more generous unemployment and retraining benefits for workers who lose their jobs, and financial assistance for families that have difficulty making ends meet.

Those on the other side of the equality of opportunity debate put much more emphasis on rewarding individual initiative and accomplishments and less emphasis on redistributive efforts. They believe that all Americans have the opportunity to succeed, and that differences in economic success reflect discrepancies in talent, hard work, and perseverance. They oppose higher tax rates for those who are the most successful because they do not think those who have succeeded should be forced to subsidize those not doing as well. They want any federal programs that do exist to focus more on encouraging individual responsibility and initiative, and less on what they see as government hand-outs to the undeserving.

Cultural issues are rooted in different concerns, involving questions of what values and accompanying behavioral practices should be encouraged in society. Money and opportunity are far less central to these disputes over cultural issues, which are focused on what role government should play in identifying, encouraging, and in some cases enforcing appropriate personal practices.

Those on the conservative side of this divide believe strongly that there are proper ways for people to behave and that government should seek to support and enforce such behaviors. Abortion is murder and should not be allowed; homosexuality is wrong and should not be condoned and protected by law. Pornography is immoral and dangerous and, therefore, should be banned. Government should actively seek to support those practices valued by society. For example, marriage between a man and woman is a good thing and, thus, divorce should be more difficult to obtain; religion is highly beneficial to society and, therefore, religious organizations should find it easier to become involved in government and public life. Perhaps most important of all, supporting the institution of the family should always be the government's first priority.

In contrast, those on the liberal side of this cleavage think government should simply provide freedom for individuals to pursue their own preferred lifestyles, without judging those practices. The decision to have an abortion should be left to women without government involvement. The decision to view obscenity and pornography should be left to adults without government interference. Gays should have the same rights as others in society, and single individuals should enjoy the same benefits and priority as families. Church and state should be strictly separated. In short, the government should provide a wide berth to individual choice in the area of personal behavior.

Each of these sets of issues creates politics with very different conflicts, policy proposals, debates, and in the end very different policies and laws. Disputes about class and equality of opportunity create conflicts over the sources and levels of taxation; the design, recipients, and types of government programs; and the extent and nature of benefits provided. Cultural issues create conflicts over what role government should play in personal lives, what role religion should play in government, and what values and behaviors the state—through its coercive power—should encourage or discourage, allow or prohibit. What we are fighting about depends on which set of issues is dominant.

WHY INTERPRETATIONS MATTER

Whether class concerns or cultural issues dominate American politics is an important question. Understanding which set of issues is primary is crucial for politicians, the press, interest groups, and ultimately the public. Politicians who want to keep their jobs try to understand what motivates the public when it comes to politics. If they believe that the public is motivated by class issues, then elected officials will worry about the class composition of their district and consider how policy on class-related issues affects their electoral base. A member of the House of Representatives from a middle-class district who thinks that her constituents resent tax cuts for the affluent will worry about how a vote for such tax cuts will affect her reelection chances. But if she is convinced that her district is inflamed over abortion and gay rights, she may vote as she wishes on tax cuts and worry more about her positions on cultural issues. This congresswoman's behavior is determined by her sense of what motivates the public at the polls. Once elections are over, politicians review election results and form judgments about what got them votes from specific groups and areas. If politicians think issues of class or culture are dominant, and they won by stressing their commitments to one of these, they can then claim a mandate to pursue and enact certain policies.

The press also weighs class versus culture when it decides which events are important, what should receive priority in coverage, and how explanations should be framed. The media in the United States are a for-profit enterprise, and the larger the audience an outlet achieves the more money it makes. One way to attract a large audience is to present people with information they deem to be interesting and important. The news media are continuously focusing on what voters care about and what motivates them to vote Democratic or Republican. Should the media cover claims about class-specific tax cuts or should they devote attention and resources to culture war conflicts, such as school prayer or gay marriage?

Interest groups, particularly those on one side or another of the class and cultural divide, are also searching for the most important issues. The concerns driving American politics affect goals and tactics, and ultimately the success or failure of these groups within the policy arena. Labor unions, long-standing central actors on class issues, are trying to understand if anyone cares about tax cuts and the increase in the numbers of workers without health insurance. The unions must decide if calling attention to such issues will be effective, or if greater public concern about illegitimate births, abortion, and gay rights issues makes such class-based debates unlikely to get on the agenda. Conversely, groups supporting cultural conservatism must determine if the public cares about their causes, and more specifically which issues will mobilize the public to act politically in such a way that will support a conservative cultural agenda. Is the public more likely to respond to sex in the media, gay teachers in public schools, or some other issue? The same types of concerns of course apply to groups advocating for socially liberal causes or for policies benefiting the affluent. Each issue advocate, no matter which side it takes, must understand what concerns the public, how best to appeal to the masses and to public officials, and in the end what will move election outcomes and public policy formation.

Ultimately, understanding what shapes American politics matters to the American public. If politicians misinterpret what concerns voters and mistakenly claim mandates for certain policies, voters do not get a responsive government. If the press misunderstands what concerns voters, it doesn't cover topics that matter to people. If the media, interest groups, and politicians misperceive public preferences, the public doesn't get the policies it wants. In the end, a proper understanding of what drives American politics is crucial for a properly functioning representative democracy.

THE PUZZLING STATE OF INTERPRETATIONS

Despite the fact that interpretations are central to understanding, it would be easy to become confused about what currently shapes American politics. We have two common and dramatically different interpretations with regard to class and culture, and it is difficult to know if accepting one interpretation means rejecting the other or whether both might be accepted. One view is that class divisions have declined in relevance and have been replaced by passionate division over cultural issues. The contrasting view is that class issues are rising in importance and are forcing all other issues to play a secondary role at best in structuring political conflict. There are, of course, also the possibilities that both class and cultural issues are relevant sources of division, with neither displacing the other, or that neither class nor cultural issues matter in American politics. Which are we to believe? Some brief background on these interpretations will help us understand what is shaping current American political divisions.

The Great Depression and Class Divisions

The "decline of class" argument has become a widely stated view of American politics. But how did class concerns come to dominate in the first place? The stock market crash of 1929 and the Great Depression set the stage for social class to structure American politics. During the Depression, unemployment reached 25 percent nationally and higher in some areas, both bank foreclosures and failures were common, and poverty and suffering became commonplace.[8] Herbert Hoover, the unfortunate Republican president in office at the onset of the Depression, chose to do nothing since federal government involvement in the economy went against the *laissez faire* principles of the Republican Party. Franklin Delano Roosevelt, the Democratic presidential candidate in 1932, did not share this disinclination for government activism and promised Americans a "New Deal" using the power of the national government to tackle the economic situation. Whether based on fear or agreement with his policies, the American public voted overwhelmingly for FDR in 1932.[9]

Roosevelt's successful coalition consisted of Northern urban ethnic groups, union members, the working class, blacks migrants from the

South, and white Southerners from all classes. Most of these groups were the have-nots in American society, and thus the New Deal coalition was seen as class-based or as relying heavily on less affluent voters.[10] This collection of have-nots elected Roosevelt three more times, and remained largely intact as the dominant power in American electoral politics through the 1960s. And the coalition did not just win elections—it produced policy results. It provided the basis for legislation during the 1930s that, among other accomplishments, created Social Security, unemployment compensation, multiple public works programs, and laws to improve the situation of labor, such as guaranteeing the right to strike and to bargain collectively.[11] In the first half of the 1960s the New Deal coalition was still going strong, electing Democrats John F. Kennedy and Lyndon Johnson as president, and either creating or increasing funding for programs such as AFDC (Aid to Families with Dependent Children), food stamps, Medicaid (health insurance for the poor), Medicare (health insurance for the elderly), public housing funding, and federal aid for low income schools.[12]

The Great Depression and the widespread poverty it created gave birth to the New Deal coalition. Economic conditions change, however, and there was considerable evidence by the 1960s that such changes were making class a less relevant basis for political divisions. From the late 1940s through the 1960s everyone seemed to become better off as incomes generally increased and inequality among classes declined.[13] The general increase in affluence after World War II appeared to reduce material conflicts within American society.[14] These changes led to the emergence of the decline-of-class interpretation as researchers reported that class-based political divisions were steadily declining.[15]

Race Eclipses Class?

As class seemed to decline in importance, there was a sense that new issues were emerging, dividing the electorate along different lines. These newer issues, involving race and cultural concerns, were seen as fundamentally different and powerful enough to displace the economic issues that solidified the New Deal coalition. Race emerged first as a great "transforming issue" in American politics.[16] The civil rights movement of the 1960s made Americans acutely aware of the racial injustice present in their country, and placed the issue of racial equality on the national agenda. Southern blacks had largely been prevented from registering to vote—much less actually voting— ever since the institution of the post-Reconstruction Jim Crow laws, a situation which changed with the enactment of civil rights laws in the mid-1960s. Among other things, the policy victories of the civil rights activists meant that many more African Americans were suddenly on the registration rolls in the South. As Southern blacks began to vote, they gained electoral importance they had not previously possessed.[17]

The vast majority of these newly enfranchised African Americans threw their support behind the Democratic Party, due in large part to 1964 Republican presidential candidate Barry Goldwater's vehement opposition to the Civil Rights Act of 1964 and support of states' rights in general. This increase in the support of blacks for the Democrats had significant effects on the party. The party became more responsive to their concerns and passed several civil rights laws during the Johnson Administration. The increased presence of African Americans within the party also expanded the Democrats' liberal base.

But events in the larger society involving blacks also created problems for the party. When the 1960s began, blacks were largely seen as sympathetic figures, having borne the brunt of past discrimination. However, numerous urban riots involving mostly African Americans during the latter half of the1960s generated a good deal of unease and anger among many whites.[18] The riots were soon followed by charges that too many blacks were on welfare. Some whites argued that welfare and redistribution programs were largely benefiting undeserving blacks.[19] There were complaints that the Democratic Party leaders, largely affluent and untouched by crime and racial integration issues, were more sympathetic to blacks than to the white working class that had been the party's traditional backbone of support, and that they were willing to tolerate questionable behaviors so as not to alienate their newly acquired black constituency.[20] The result, at least according to some, was the beginning of a political division revolving around race, the alienation of the white working class, and the demise of class discussions in American politics.[21]

Displacing Class Issues?

In short, greater affluence appeared to have reduced the relevance of class divisions and the race issue was dividing blacks and the white working class, pushing the latter away from the Democratic Party. The party had retained its affluent liberals, but lost much of its primary base. The result was an increasingly prevalent argument that the importance of class in American politics had significantly declined, and that racial issues were the hammer that smashed class-based politics. Indeed, many commentators argued that a reversal of the role of class had occurred:

> There has been an inversion of the old New Deal relationship of social class to the vote. In wide sectors of public policy, groups of high socioeconomic status are now more supportive of equalitarian (liberal) change than are the middle to lower socioeconomic cohorts (within white America); and as a result liberal (often, although not always, Democratic) candidates are finding higher measures of electoral sustenance at the top of the socioeconomic ladder than among the middle and lower rungs.[22]

Journalists, relying on the analyses of academics, advisors, and commentators, have come to treat these conclusions as accepted wisdom. In the 1990s and after it was common to read that class was no longer a driving force in American politics:

> The overlapping issues of race and taxes have permitted the Republican party to adapt the principles of conservatism to break the underlying class basis of the Roosevelt coalition.... [R]ace has become a powerful wedge, breaking up what had been the majoritarian economic interests of the poor, working and lower-middle classes in the traditional liberal coalition.... Working-class whites and corporate CEOs, once adversaries at the bargaining table, found common ideological ground in their shared hostility to expanding government intervention.[23]

> ... [O]ne of the defining traits of American politics over the [last] 25 years has been the defection of working-class, white voters, especially men, from the Democratic Party.[24]

...[C]lass alignments in politics have become jumbled. In the 1950s, professionals were reliably Republican; today they lean Democratic. Meanwhile, skilled labor has gone from being heavily Democratic to almost evenly split.... Increasing affluence plays an important role. When there is not only a chicken, but an organic, free-range chicken, in every pot, the traditional economic appeal to the working class can sound off key.[25]

All of the above quotations point to the same conclusion: the class cleavage rooted in the New Deal was dead.

The Emergence of Cultural Issues

While race-based issues seemed at first to have displaced class concerns from political primacy, it now appears that race-based issues have been replaced in recent years by a new set of non-economic disputes.[26] This new set of issues, generally lumped together as "cultural" issues, involve a much broader group of questions and concerns. What values will be honored and recognized as legitimate within society? Which behaviors will be encouraged or allowed by government and which will be discouraged or banned? What is the proper interaction between religion and the government? What is the proper use of government power in dictating fundamental questions of right and wrong?

Sometimes these issues are entangled with race, for example, when blacks are blamed for increases in crime and illegitimate births.[27] But in most instances race-based issues are not prominent in the debates over cultural issues, at least not on the surface. Most of the time, the fundamental concern is about behaviors and practices that are seen as undermining traditional values. Questions of morality dominate, and in many ways all of the cultural debates boil down to the relatively simple question: "Are we as a society living the way that we should be?" Of course the simplest questions are often the most difficult to answer, and generate the most contentious and acrimonious discussions. Contention and acrimony are two words that can certainly be seen as accurately describing the politics surrounding cultural issues in contemporary America.

The heated nature of this debate is more easily understood when one looks at the specific subjects that together make up the cultural issues category. Opinions about abortion, homosexuality, and gay marriage all involve fundamental disputes about morality. Other cultural issues, such as sex and violence in the entertainment media, obscenity, and pornography, fall along similar lines. Other "life" issues such as embryonic stem cell research and euthanasia garner a good deal of attention. Prayer in public schools and other questions about the proper role of religion in government and public life are important for those concerned with cultural issues. Religious perspectives affect whether people support a curriculum with the theory of evolution or the possibility that intelligent design (God) created the universe. The place of women in American society is a rallying point in the culture debates and almost all of those on the conservative side of the cultural divide place the health of the American family as perhaps the biggest umbrella concern of all. Fundamentally the conflict comes down to a dispute over right and wrong.

These cultural issues are, for the most part, relatively recent additions to the American political agenda. This does not mean that the issues themselves are new, or even that their importance to Americans is a recent development. What is true is that, with the exception of women's rights, most of the issues included in the cultural debate were widely perceived as socially and politically settled for most of American history. It is only in the last forty to fifty years that these subjects have even become open for discussion in the policy process. Prior to the 1960s, it was taken as a given that prayer, most likely of a Christian variety, would be present in public schools. Before *Roe* v. *Wade*, a legal abortion was extremely difficult to obtain, and was available in only a few states. Well into the late twentieth century homosexuality was—and for many still is—somehow considered less than normal, if not outright wrong, mostly hidden from public view, and certainly not a legitimate candidate for state protection. Today, much of what we can view on television or hear on the radio, to say nothing of the material available on the Internet, simply would not have been available even ten years ago.

Pick almost any cultural issue, except possibly the place of women in society, and it is quite likely that similar statements can be made. But the conditions indicated by such statements obviously no longer hold. A number of changes, including technological changes, political changes, and most important, societal changes, have brought cultural issues to the forefront of the American public dialogue. Sociologist James Davison Hunter, was one of the first to link the cultural issues coming out of these societal changes to the political realm. "America is in the midst of a culture war that has and will continue to have reverberations not only within public policy, but within the lives of ordinary Americans everywhere."[28] Labeling the two sides in the conflict orthodox and progressive,[29] Hunter argued that the opposing groups were separated by dramatically different views of moral authority, and different views on what the "good" community should look like. For Hunter, these differences were now being played out in the context of American politics. "The nub of political disagreement today... can be traced ultimately and finally to the matter of moral authority. By moral authority I mean the basis by which people determine whether something is good or bad, right or wrong, acceptable or unacceptable, and so on."[30] In Hunter's view, the cultural issues that first appeared on the radar screen in the early 1960s were dominating American politics by the early 1990s.

Displacing Class Issues (Again)

Much as with race, those who see cultural issues dominating American politics argue that these issues are dividing people along new lines, making class divisions less relevant, and appeals to class less effective in influencing voters. The issues agitating voters now are cultural in nature. Those who are pro-choice, tolerant or supportive of gays, and detached from religion are on one side of the dominant political cleavage, and opposed by those who are pro-life, opposed to homosexuality, and desire a larger place for religion in public life, including a more intimate relationship between church and state. As with race-based issues, the argument is that the working class is particularly troubled by the developments associated with cultural issues—the rising number of abortions, greater acceptance and protection of homosexuality, and so forth— and they are abandoning the Democrats because of the party's willingness to accept and defend abortion and homosexuality.

> *"I'm not happy with the moral issues at all with the Democrats. The Republicans will hurt me in the long run in providing for my family, but it's probably more important to watch out for the unborn and that kind of stuff."*[31]

People in both parties have attributed the shift [away from class issue] to the rise of social issues, like gun control and same-sex marriage, which have tilted many working-class voters rightward and upper-income voters toward the left.[32]

The essence of this argument about the displacement of economic class as a dividing line is that conservatives have been able to redefine the substance of class divisions. "The Republicans have often managed to convince Joe that in America, class is not a question of money but of values."[33] According to this view, class conflicts that were previously about opportunity and the distribution of income have been transformed into battles over lifestyle issues and the role of religion in day-to-day life. Conservatives have come along and made the case that cultural elites— usually residing in East and West coast urban centers —scorn the values of working and middle class America—usually populating the Southern and Midwest rural heartland. The cultural elites are described as secular-ists—discounting religion as a source of rules to live by—and rela-tivists—holding there is no absolute truth— and not very respectful of those who are religious and who adhere to traditional values.[34] The con-servatives argue that working and middle-class Americans need to stand with the Republican Party which will advocate for the traditional lifestyles, beliefs, and values. One of the most popular books on politics in the past few years, Thomas Frank's *What's the Matter with Kansas?* devotes a tad over 300 pages to the argument that less affluent Americans now regularly vote against their economic interests because of their views on cultural issues. According to Frank, the current conservatism "mobi-lizes voters with explosive social issues—summoning outrage over every-thing from busing to un-Christian art—which it then marries to pro-business economic policies. Cultural anger is marshaled to achieve economic ends."[35] It is because these traditional values are presumed to be held more by working-class individuals that class divisions are dimin-ished. [36] The common thread in these arguments is that culture now trumps class in American electoral politics.

As confirmation of the new dominance of cultural issues, the National Election Pool's national exit poll from the 2004 presidential election reported that 22 percent of all respondents chose "moral values" as the most important issue in casting their vote, the highest percentage received by any category. Though this was the first time such a response option had been presented to voters and there was considerable dispute about what the category meant, political observers across the printed pages, airwaves, and cable/broadband connections of America seized on this as evidence that cultural issues were now dominant in American politics. Political commentators continue to regularly pronounce that cultural issues are at the heart of contemporary American politics and many of these same observers believe that the dominance of culture has resulted in class concerns being ignored. Some liberal analysts, frustrated that class issues get less attention than they think they should, have almost pleaded for Americans, particularly less affluent Americans and those who seek to advocate for them, to wake up and pay attention to class issues before it is too late. Consider the following excerpt from Paul Krugman, liberal opinion columnist for the *New York Times* and professor of economics at Princeton University:

> *It may sound shrill to describe President Bush as someone who takes food from the mouths of babes and gives the proceeds to his millionaire friends. Yet his latest budget proposal is top-down class warfare in action. And it offers the Democrats an opportunity, if they're willing to take it. First, the facts: the budget proposal really does take food from the mouths of babes. One of the proposed spending cuts would make it harder for working families with children to receive food stamps, terminating aid for about 300,000 people. Another would deny child care assistance to about 300,000 children, again in low-income working families. And the budget really does shower largesse on millionaires even as it punishes the needy. For example, the Center on Budget and Policy Priorities informs us that even as the administration demands spending cuts, it will proceed with the phaseout of two little-known tax provisions ... that limit deductions and exemptions for high-income households.*[37]

Much Ado about Nothing: The "Myth" of a Culture War

Finally, as if sorting out arguments surrounding the respective roles of class and cultural issues, and the relationship between them, is not enough of a puzzle for those attempting to make sense of American politics, an argument has recently emerged that the relevance of all these disputes for the American public has been overblown. In a book that has garnered as much if not more attention than Frank's portrait of a culturally-based duping of the American working class, political scientist Morris Fiorina and his colleagues argue that talk of a culture war in America is bunkum:

> The simple truth is that there is no culture war in the United States—no battle for the soul of America rages, at least none that most Americans are aware of. Many of the activists in the political parties and the various cause groups do, in fact, hate each other and regard themselves as combatants in a war. But their hatreds and battles are not shared by the great mass of the American people.
>
> There is little evidence that Americans' ideological or policy positions are more polarized today than they were two or three decades ago, although their choices often seem to be. The explanation is that the political figures Americans evaluate are more polarized. A polarized political class makes the citizenry appear polarized, but it is only that—an appearance.[38]

Fiorina and his coauthors ask if states won by Bush (red) or Kerry (blue) differ, and come away skeptical that there are large differences. They ask whether Americans have changed their opinions about issues like whether abortion should be allowed, and find little change. They conclude the presence of a cultural war is overrated and their arguments add further confusion to the question of what divisions are shaping political debates. Those looking for answers as to what is driving American politics are often left scratching their heads in uncertainty.

THE CONCERNS AND PLAN OF THE BOOK

To sort out these various claims, then, we need to address several issues. Is class relevant as a source of divisions in American politics, and has it declined in relevance? Have cultural issues emerged as a source of political divisions? If so, has their emergence suppressed the extent of class divisions? Are divisions over class and culture confined only to elites or do they exist within the public and do they affect the political behavior of the public?

Our analysis will demonstrate that there is considerable evidence that class still matters in American politics. A number of studies show that the dominant images of the parties held by the public are economic in nature. When the American public thinks about the Republicans and the Democrats, they are—as they have been since 1952—most likely to think about them in terms of how they benefit the haves and the have-nots in society.[39]

There is also evidence that class differences remain an important factor when it comes to party identification and vote choice in the United States. Looking at party identification and voting in presidential and House elections, Jeffrey Stonecash found that rather than fading over the last twenty years, class divisions in electoral politics have increased and play a significant role in the partisan behavior of voters.[40] Further, class divisions have the potential to continue to increase as inequality in the distribution of income and wealth in the nation continues to grow at a rapid pace.[41]

In addition, the same 2004 exit poll cited earlier for the importance of cultural issues also presented results that suggest the need to reconsider the decline-of-class view of American politics. Table 1-1 presents some results from that poll. While 22 percent chose moral values as the most important issue, 32 percent chose bread and butter opportunity issues such as the economy, health care, and education. While Republican George W. Bush won handily among the moral issues voters, Democrat John Kerry won easily among those voters who chose the more class-related issues as most important. As the table also shows, the division in vote by family income is significant, and as we will indicate later, it is by no means a fluke. Indeed, this division has been gradually growing over the last several decades. The recent economic experience of voters also has a powerful effect, with those who see themselves as better off voting strongly for Bush and those who see themselves as worse off voting strongly for Kerry. In short, while many argue that class and issues of equality of opportunity are of declining importance in American politics, a good deal of evidence seems to indicate otherwise.

TABLE 1-1	Dissecting the 2004 Presidential Election

SURVEY QUESTION	Percentage with Vote Choice of:	
	Bush	Kerry
Most important issue		
Economy / jobs (20%)	18	80
Health care (8%)	23	77
Education (4%)	26	73
Iraq (15%)	26	73
Taxes (5%)	57	43
Moral values (22%)	80	18
Terrorism (19%)	86	14
Family income		
Under $15,000 (8%)	36	63
$15–30,000 (15%)	42	57
$30–50,000 (22%)	49	50
$50–75,000 (23%)	56	43
$75–100,000 (14%)	55	45
$100–150,000 (11%)	57	42
$150–200,000 (4%)	58	42
$200,000 plus (3%)	63	35
Family financial situation		
Better (32%)	80	19
Same (39%)	49	50
Worse (28%)	20	79

Note: Percentages next to each response are the percentages of all respondents offering that response, (i.e., 20 percent indicated the economy/jobs is the most important issue).

Sources: Data are taken from the national exit poll conducted by Edison Media Research and Mitofsky International for the National Election Pool (a consortium of ABC News, The Associated Press, CBS News, CNN, FOX News, and NBC News), as reported by CNN at www.cnn.com/ELECTION/2004/ pages/results/states/US/P/00/epolls.0.html.

Our emphasis on the continuing relevance of class does not mean that cultural issues don't matter. Quite to the contrary, there is also considerable evidence that cultural issues have become more important in affecting political behavior. Conflict over subjects like abortion and homosexuality is very real and increasingly influential in American politics. Cultural issues are important; yet so too are class concerns. Evidence indicates that both cultural issues and class issues are important in American politics, and both sets of issues are in play simultaneously. For example, in 2001 and again in 2003 President Bush and Congress—with mostly Republican support—enacted large tax cuts. Liberals and Democrats criticized these cuts as benefiting the rich, while Republicans disparaged talk of "class warfare" and argued that taxes were too high and lower taxes would stimulate the economy. At the same time the tax-cut discussions were raging, many officials on both side of the partisan aisle were arguing strenuously about cultural issues such as abortion rights and same-sex marriage, giving the impression that these issues are what really matters, both to political elites and to the average American citizen.

OUR PLAN

We seek to explain the development of both class and cultural issues in American politics. For each set of issues we will review the social trends making it a concern, the response of the parties, and then the response of voters. Our focus on the issues of class and culture does not mean that we think that these are the only subjects that matter in contemporary American politics. Additional concerns—such as national security, energy dependence, and foreign policy—are clearly high salience issues. On the domestic front another such prominent concern is race, which is of course in many ways intimately connected to the class and cultural concerns we spotlight. For example, it is impossible to fully understand economic inequality in the United States without accounting for the effects of racial and ethnic discrimination.[42] Similarly, any explanation of the decline of the Democratic party in the South and the realignment of evangelical Protestants that fails to include race would be incomplete. So race is important and clearly tied up with many of the phenomena and developments that we discuss throughout this book. Because we cannot be encyclopedic, however, race will not be a central focus. Class concerns and cultural issues—their respective impacts on American politics and their relationship with one another—are what this book is about, and therefore will occupy center stage.

Both class concerns and cultural issues have an interesting and lengthy history over the last several decades. Our first focus is a brief explanation of the history of class concerns and cultural issues over the last few decades and what social trends brought them to the forefront. Then we examine how the parties made these issues more prominent—through the role of politicians, public comments, legislative proposals, party platforms, and votes in Congress. Finally, the voters, especially their responses and party alignments, are crucial to making issues a source of political division. If politicians clamor about the unfairness of tax cuts or the impropriety of same-sex marriage and voters with differing views do not align themselves with the opposite parties, the issue is unlikely to become a source of division. It is only when those opposed to tax cuts support Democrats and those opposed to same-sex marriage support Republicans that an issue becomes a source of political division. We look at how broad issues of class and culture have become sources of political division.

We then move to the relationship between these two sets of issues. Many of those who presume that class divisions have declined in relevance and have been replaced by cultural issues also presume that one displaces the other. The basis of this conclusion is the presumption that the working class is more religious and less tolerant of abortion, homosexuality, and more diverse roles for women. Drawing upon theories of the authoritarian personality type from the 1950s, it was widely presumed that working class voters were uncomfortable with and resistant to social change.[43] Theorists presume that Republican appeals to the working class voters about abortion, gay rights, and religion in society overwhelm their concerns about opportunity in America and pull them away from concerns about the fairness of tax cuts, lack of health care, reduced enforcement of worker safety rules, limited grants for their children to attend college, and weakened rules about protection of their pensions. As the truck driver quoted on page 14 stated, "The Republicans will hurt me in the long run in providing for my family, but it's probably more important to watch out for the unborn and that kind of stuff."

The second major concern, then, of this book is whether class concerns are actually being swamped by cultural issues. We explore the relationship between the class and cultural issues and ask whether cultural issues are really displacing or suppressing class issues. There is strong evidence that displacement does not occur and that both sources of division coexist in American politics. Any explanation focusing on one and excluding the other interpretation of contemporary American politics is incomplete and inaccurate, therefore, both class and culture are crucial for understanding the current American polity.

The question of class versus culture is not merely an academic exercise. Which explanation is accepted as accurate will have real consequences in American society, since competing interpretations filter through commentators and journalists to average Americans, and become feedback about our reality. The accepted interpretations tell us what matters within our society and what the public cares about. Is same-sex marriage more important than who bears the tax burden? Is access to health care more relevant than abortion? The accepted interpretations tell us what issues are likely to dominate the political agenda and what politicians are likely to argue about. What the politics of the future—at least the near future—will be about depends, at least in part, on the interpretations of what is most important in American politics right now.

CHAPTER 2

INEQUALITY AND OPPORTUNITY IN AMERICA: GROWING DIFFERENCES

Political analyses presume that economic and social conditions create the basis for political issues to emerge. When the recession dragged on in 2002 and 2003 and unemployment was high, more people needed unemployment compensation and food stamps and wanted government to promote economic growth to increase jobs. The large number of people without health insurance either want government to provide some minimal coverage or a government mandate that employers must provide it. Those with lesser incomes want more aid for their children to attend college. Those with higher incomes are concerned that their taxes are too high.

These situations reflect differences in vulnerabilities and opportunity, both strongly associated with income. Those with lower incomes are likely to be more economically vulnerable. Paying bills and avoiding layoffs and health problems are central to the lives of those with lower incomes. They have more problems providing opportunities for their children that higher income families provide without much difficulty. They face greater risk of encountering economic problems.

Income levels and the distribution of income over time provide rough indicators of how differences in vulnerabilities and opportunities are evolving in our society. Inequality in the distribution of incomes is not itself a central issue in American politics—there is not strong support for a simple redistribution of incomes. Rather, this inequality reflects differences in vulnerabilities and opportunities, which can and do become political issues.

Inequality of income and opportunity in the United States has a varied history over the last century that has been interpreted quite differently by various commentators. In the next several chapters we turn to matters of class, first summarizing the history of economic inequality in America and the different historical interpretations, then discussing how the parties and electorate have reacted to issues of inequality.

BY THE NUMBERS: TRENDS IN INCOME AND WEALTH INEQUALITY

The income distribution trend is one of high inequality in the first forty years of the twentieth century, followed by a significant decline in mid-century and then a gradual increase beginning in the 1970s. One way to measure inequality in the distribution of income is the Gini index. The logic of this index is to set perfect equality as a baseline and then measure divergence from that. If every one percent of the population had one percent of income we have perfect equality. If we were to plot this geometrically, every percentage increase in the percentage of the population would be matched by an equivalent percentage of income. In contrast, if there is inequality and 50 percent of the population has only 25 percent of income, a discrepancy from that baseline develops. The greater this discrepancy, the greater the inequality, and the higher the Gini index.

Figure 2-1 presents the Gini index over the past century. The index, which usually ranges from 0 for no inequality to 1 for complete inequality, is multiplied by 100 here, to allow for a comparison with growth in incomes. From 1913 through 1940 there was significant inequality in the distribution of income in American society. The Great Depression made this inequality worse. Then the onset of World War II and the sustained postwar growth significantly reduced inequality.

This post–World War II decline in inequality occurred because real incomes (removing inflation, or general price increases) were increasing and lower income groups were experiencing the greatest increases in income. Figure 2-1 also includes median family income in $1,000 increments. In 1947 the median (if all incomes are arrayed from highest to lowest, the median is the one in the middle) family income (expressed in valued 2004 dollars) was almost $20,000. Over the next 30 years the median family income increased to $40,000. What was significant was that all income strata were experiencing significant increases. Table 2-1

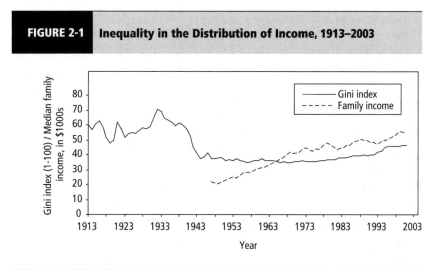

FIGURE 2-1   **Inequality in the Distribution of Income, 1913–2003**

Note: The index measures how evenly incomes are distributed and runs from 0 to 1. A score of zero indicates there is no difference between the percentage of the population and the percentage of income received by that population. High scores indicate that a small percentage of the population has a large percentage of income. Robert Plotnick and his associates use the Gini index for family incomes from the Bureau of the Census for 1947–1996. To estimate scores for 1913–1964 they first fit an equation to estimate the Gini index for 1947–1996 using several independent variables. They then use the parameters derived from the 1947–1996 equation results and data on the same independent variables from 1913–1946, and estimate a Gini index for 1913–1946.

Sources: The Gini index is taken from Robert D. Plotnick, Eugene Smolensky, Eirik Evenhouse, and Siobhan Reilly, "The Twentieth Century Record of Inequality and Poverty in the United States," Institute for Research on Poverty, Discussion Paper no. 1166–98, 1998, at www.ssc.wisc.edu/irp/. The Gini index from 1997–2001 is taken from U.S Census Bureau Historical Income Tables at www.census.gov/hhes/www/income/histinc/ie1.html. Median family income data are taken from www.census.gov/hhes/www/income/histinc/f05.html.

indicates how income gains were distributed during those 30 years. All incomes were arrayed from top to bottom in 1949 and then again in 1969. The array is then divided into tenths. The same people are not in each group in the different years since people move in and out of groups over time, but it does allow us to compare how the 1949 bottom tenth compares with the bottom tenth 20 years later. Over that time period all income groups experienced gains, with those at the bottom experiencing the greatest gains. Everyone was doing well and the greatest gains were at the bottom. The result was a general decline in inequality in the distribution of income.

While inequality was declining, government was also enacting policies designed to create a safety net and reduce economic risk for those economic problems. During the decade from 1963 through 1973 the federal government enacted increases in welfare benefits and made access to these benefits easier. A food stamp program, which provided stamps that could be redeemed at grocery stores for food, was dramatically expanded from its previous incarnation as a small pilot program and extended nationwide. Funds were provided to create more public housing for low-income citizens. Medicaid, a program to provide health care for less affluent individuals, and Medicare, a program to provide health care for senior citizens, were enacted. Pell grants—federal grants to help pay college tuition that did not have to be paid back—were established, along with a federally subsidized student loan program. There appeared to be a new era in American politics. The private sector was generating less inequality and government was enacting programs that responded to vulnerability and differences in opportunity among Americans. It was not uncommon during that era to hear comments such as "a rising tide lifts all boats" and that class divisions were declining.[1]

Then, fairly abruptly, inequality in the distribution of income began to increase. The right half of Table 2-1 compares the years of 1973–1991 with the earlier period. Inequality began to increase because the affluent began to experience significant growth in their incomes while those at the bottom of the income strata were realizing no growth. Table 2-2 provides information on more recent changes in the distribution of incomes. From 1979–2003 those in the highest strata received considerably greater increases in income than those in the lower quintiles, creating greater inequality. The impact of these changes is shown in the trend in the Gini index for more recent years, shown in Figure 2-1. Over the time period of 1970–2003 there has been a slow but unmistakable rise in the index, and an increase in inequality.

Perhaps more important than current income is accumulated wealth, or assets such as property, savings, and stock accounts. Inequalities in the distribution of wealth are much greater than for those for income, with some families having very little in the way of wealth while others have substantial assets. While the Gini index for the distribution of income has recently ranged around .45, the recent index for wealth ranges from .8 to .85.[2] Keeping in mind that an index of 1.0 represents complete inequality, these figures show that wealth is distributed very unequally and it has become more unequal.[3] Figure 2-2 presents the percentage of all wealth

TABLE 2-1	Percentage Change in Income by Income Groups and Era

INCOMES GROUPED BY TENTHS	Era and Percentage Change	
	1949–1969	1973–1991
Lowest	457.1	-19.0
Second	168.4	-8.1
Third	130.8	-1.1
Fourth	114.6	4.1
Fifth	106.3	9.6
Sixth	102.2	12.7
Seventh	99.8	15.6
Eighth	94.9	17.8
Ninth	92.8	20.8
Highest	102.2	21.5

Note: Incomes are first grouped from lowest to highest, and then broken into groups of tenths. The percentage increases in incomes within each category, from the beginning to the end of the era, are then computed. In this case, they also divided incomes by the poverty line to provide an index of how incomes compare to the poverty line. The percentage increases still provide a valid measure of income growth within each income category. The same differences were reported when the years of 1947–1979 and 1980–1997 were compared (Allen, 1999: 57).

Source: Sheldon Danziger and Peter Gottschalk, *America Unequal* (Cambridge: Harvard University Press, 1955), 53.

TABLE 2-2	Average Pre-Tax Income by Income Group (in 2003 dollars), 1979–2003

INCOME CATEGORY	1979	1990	2003	% Change 1979–2003	Dollar Change 1979–2003
Lowest fifth	14,700	14,400	14,800	.7	100
Second fifth	31,900	31,900	34,100	6.9	2,200
Middle fifth	47,800	48,600	51,900	8.6	4,100
Fourth fifth	64,600	68,700	77,300	19.7	12,700
Highest fifth	123,700	149,800	184,500	49.2	60,800

Source: Congressional Budget Office, *Effective Federal Tax Rates, 1979 to 2003*, Table 1C, December 2005.

held by the top 1 percent of all households. As with income, there was high inequality during the 1920s and 1930s, and then a gradual decline in inequality. By the mid-1970s the top 1 percent held 20 percent of all wealth, compared to the 35–45 percent held during the 1920s and 1930s. Since the 1970s inequality has increased and the top 1 percent now holds

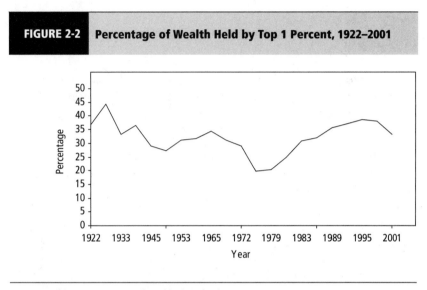

FIGURE 2-2   **Percentage of Wealth Held by Top 1 Percent, 1922–2001**

Source: www.faireconomy.org/research/wealth_charts.html.

33 percent of all wealth.[4] In contrast, the top 1 percent holds about 17 percent of all current income.

INEQUALITY AND THE LIVES OF AMERICANS

While the trends of increasing inequalities in the distributions of income and wealth are significant, more important is what they show happening to people's lives and opportunity. As the old saying goes, differences in income have consequences from "cradle to grave." Children from less affluent homes have poorer nutrition and get less health care. Families with higher incomes live in neighborhoods with more expensive homes, higher tax bases, and more locally generated property tax revenues to support neighborhood schools. These schools provide more academic and extracurricular opportunities for children. Students from these schools, on average, do better on standardized tests and have a greater chance of attending college.[5] Parents who are doing well are able to provide their children with more opportunity than the parents with lower income levels or without much in terms of accumulated wealth.

An Education Divide

These differences have been further accentuated by several changes during the last few decades. There has been a consistent movement of population to suburbs, with most of the movement occurring among those who are more affluent.[6] Their movement, combined with zoning laws that restrict higher density rental units and low-income housing in many of the areas where the better-off are relocating to,[7] has created greater class segregation within metropolitan areas.[8] There are now greater differences among school districts in the wealth of their populations and tax bases.[9] This in turn creates dramatic variations in the resources and programs of schools. Students in central-city schools have more run-down schools, far fewer academic and extracurricular programs, fewer resources, and more students from less affluent families. In short, students in public schools in low-income areas have much less opportunity than their counterparts in more affluent school districts. Students in poorer schools do not do as well on standardized college entrance tests such as the SAT and lower percentages of these students go on to college. Students from schools in more affluent areas are generally better prepared by their schools for such tests, combined with the reality that their families can hire tutors to better prep them for the SAT or the ACT.[10] The bottom line is that the general increase in income and wealth inequality influences the distribution of wealth across communities and school districts within metropolitan areas.

Differentials in access to education become even more important when we consider the effects of higher education. It has been true for a long time that those with greater education earn more money over their lifetimes. In 2003 those with a college degree were likely to earn 1.73 times as much over their lifetime as those with only a high school degree. Those with a professional degree were likely to earn 3.36 times as much.[11] Figure 2-3 indicates for 2003 the average earnings of those with different degrees who were 25 to 34 years old. We see that education and race both have an effect on earnings in American society. Those with a master's degree earn over twice as much as those with a high school education. In recent years these differences in earnings have increased.[12] Those with less education are experiencing declining incomes while

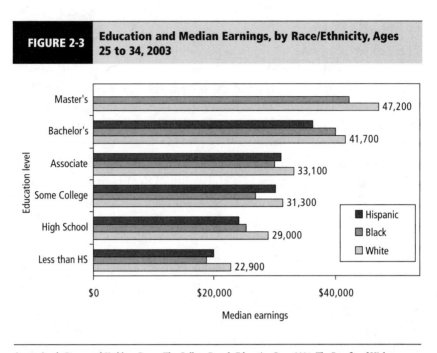

FIGURE 2-3 | **Education and Median Earnings, by Race/Ethnicity, Ages 25 to 34, 2003**

Source: Sandy Baum and Kathleen Payea, The College Board, *Education Pays, 2004: The Benefits of Higher Education for Individuals and Society,* available at www.collegeboard.com/prod_downloads/press/cost04/ EducationPays2004.pdf, Figure 4, 13.

those with more education are experiencing growing incomes. Race becomes an issue because blacks and Hispanics at every education level make less than whites. A college education is increasingly the ticket to higher income.[13] Inequalities in access begin in elementary and secondary schools and continue through to higher education, and they have very significant impacts over a lifetime. When we examine not just those 25 to 34 years old but the entire population over 25, the differences in income due to education are even greater.[14]

The ability to pursue the benefits of education—to attend *and complete* college—is affected by the costs of attending (tuition, room and board, and books), and the availability of aid to help pay these costs. Over the last thirty years, tuition charges have increased at a rate faster than inflation, pushing up the real cost of attending college.[15] At the same time, support from government has declined. State governments now provide less tax revenue support and devote smaller portions of their budgets to higher education than they did thirty years ago.[16] Federal government support has declined as well. The Guaranteed Student Loan Program was established in 1965 and the Pell Grant program was instituted in 1972.[17] During the 1970s these federal Pell grants, which provide aid to a student that does not have to be paid back, covered a substantial portion of the costs of attending college. Since its initial establishment, amounts granted have not increased with inflation, which means they now cover less of the cost of attending college. In 1985 Pell grants covered 57 percent of the cost of attending public schools and 37 percent of the cost of private schools. In 2004–2005, these grants covered 26 percent and 6 percent, respectively, of college costs.[18] The federal government has shifted to an emphasis on loans, altering the composition of student aid. Government grants provided directly through educational institutions have also declined substantially.[19] The result is that more students are now borrowing to attend college.

The policies of the last thirty years have effectively shifted more and more of the burden of higher education away from government to the individual.[20] The trends of the last twenty years have, in effect, resulted in "privatizing" the cost of higher education. From 1985 to 1991 the average cumulative student loan increased from $6,488 to $16,417,[21] and an increasing percentage of students worried about having enough money to finish college.[22] By 2004–2005 students were leaving college with an average debt of approximately $20,000, with some students having very large loans to pay back.[23]

Figure 2-4 indicates how enrollment rates have changed over time by family income levels.[24] Those with higher incomes are more likely to attend college, but over the last several decades the participation rate among all income groups has increased. The combination of these changes—education becoming more important, greater availability of loans, but higher costs and less access to grants, coupled with the growing inequality of income—has produced two contrasting trends. An increasing percentage of society is able to enroll in college, which most would agree is a good thing. But inequality in completion rates by income categories is also rising.

There is still the problem of needing enough money to complete college. Students from lower income families run into more financial problems

FIGURE 2-4	Percentage Enrolling in College, by Family Income and Year, 1970–2003

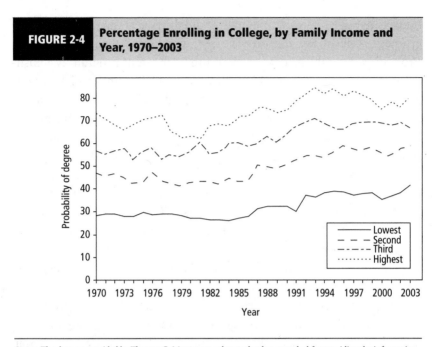

Source: The data are provided by Thomas G. Mortenson, who we thank a great deal for providing the information. He used data from Table 14 in the Census Bureau's annual report on school enrollments at www.census.gov/population/www/socdemo/school/cps2003.html.

and routinely have to interrupt their study. Many struggle to finish. This is much less common for students from more affluent families. Figure 2-5 presents trends of success rates in obtaining a degree—who actually graduates—by income groups.[25] The probabilities present the estimated chances of achieving a BA by age 24 for each family income quartile. For the least affluent, these trends indicate little change over 25 years in the chances of achieving a college degree. More affluent students, on the other hand, have seen their likelihood of successful completion dramatically increase. For those in the top quartile of family income, the probability of completion has risen from approximately 40 to 70 percent, an increase of 30 percentage points. Students in the second quartile have gone from 10 to 13 percent, for a gain of only 3 points. For those in the third quartile the gain has been from 14 to 28 percent, or a gain of 14 percentage points. In the lowest income quartile, the change has been from 6 to 8 percent, or a gain of 2 percentage points.

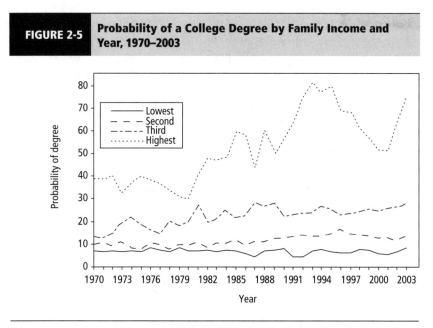

| FIGURE 2-5 | Probability of a College Degree by Family Income and Year, 1970–2003 |

Source: The data are provided by Thomas G. Mortenson. We thank him for sharing his data with us.

The differences in college completion rates have important consequences for how inequality evolves in American society and who ends up being vulnerable and having less opportunity. Those from affluent families have a greater chance of obtaining a degree. Students from lower income families are more likely to run into financial obstacles and less likely to finish in four to six years. They are also more likely to end up with loans and no degree, a situation that limits their future ability to buy a home and build equity, thus creating wealth, rather than rent. Initial differences in opportunity play out over a lifetime and have cumulative consequences. While higher education is becoming more important, it is not an easy route for many students in American society. The way college educations are financed—a combination of family income, loans, and grants—also contributes to unequal access and completion. Not only are less affluent students much less likely to enroll in college than higher income students, but those who do enroll are less likely to finish than their better off counterparts. Black and Hispanic families generally make less money and students from these families have lower chances of finishing college. Not finishing means a lifetime of lower incomes. In addition, these lower income students will also accumulate far more debt over the course of their college experience—whether they finish or not—which will make it that much more difficult to save money or otherwise accumulate wealth.

Health Care and Pension Divides

The consequences of inequalities continue to play out once people enter the labor force. Two crucial consequences involve health insurance and pensions.[26] Inequalities in access to health insurance, of course, are not new. In 1954 only 64 percent of the population had hospital insurance, 54 percent had surgical insurance, and 30 percent had general medical insurance.[27] By 1963 the percentage with hospital and surgical insurance had increased to 70, but there were still significant variations in coverage by family income.[28] By 1972 the percent of *workers* with some sort of group coverage had increased to 74 percent, with the percentage covered ranging from 59 percent for the lowest income group (0–$4,999) to 90 percent for the highest income group (above $25,000).[29] For those unemployed and poor, Medicaid surely provided some additional coverage, but there were still significant variations in access to health insurance within the electorate.

Access to health insurance and health care began to erode during the 1980s. The percentage of people without health insurance increased from 14 percent in 1987 to 16 percent in 2003. Of those making less than $25,000, 23.5 percent were without insurance, while 8.2 percent of those making above $75,000 were without insurance.[30] With incomes for most workers declining or stagnating, many have chosen not to enroll in an insurance program because of the costs.[31] In addition, provision of health insurance is strongly associated with the size of a company and the permanence of a job. Many small businesses do not provide coverage, and the growth of employment in small businesses has left many workers without coverage.[32] Finally, there has been a trend toward hiring more temporary workers who typically do not receive coverage.[33] These changes have reversed the trend toward wider health insurance coverage. Those who make less money remain less likely to be covered,[34] and many with coverage may worry about retaining it.

The trend in access to pensions is much the same as that for health care. The percentage of the public with private pensions increased after the 1940s. In 1940 only 15 percent of private sector workers were covered by pension plans. That percentage rose to 25 percent by 1955, to 41 percent by 1960, and to 45 percent by 1975. Since then there has been little change.[35] In addition, as with health care, there are significant variations in who has private pensions.[36] Participation in private pension plans is higher for those in larger companies, those who are full-time workers, and those who earn higher hourly wages.[37]

If there has been a significant change in recent decades, it has been in how worker pensions are structured. More and more companies are changing from a defined-benefit to a defined-contribution plan.[38] In the post–World War II era most companies granted pensions largely based on the number of years worked and the average salary of an employee. A worker might get 1 to 2 percent for each year worked (30 years multiplied by 2 percent equals 60 percent; 30 years multiplied by 1 percent equals 30 percent) multiplied by the average of the last three years pay. This commitment by a company could be very large if workers live longer over time.

Both employers and employees began to see problems with this arrangement. To employers, with employees living longer, these future, open-ended commitments could become enormous. This demographic situation prompted many companies to move to a system where the company makes its contribution on an ongoing basis—a defined contribution—with no obligation after retirement. A company might contribute 5 to 10 percent a year and tax laws may allow a worker to contribute the same amount, with the worker contribution tax deductible. In these cases it is up to the worker to exercise enough discipline to make contributions. Defined contribution plans shift the burden of planning and setting aside money onto workers and away from the company.

It was not just companies that saw benefits in this plan. In the 1950s and 1960s a worker might work for the same company for an entire career so he or she would build up enough years to qualify for a relatively good pension. With workers staying fewer years at any company, many workers would leave a company before they qualified to receive a pension, so they would not accumulate any retirement savings. Many wanted a portable pension plan (called 401k plans), or one in which the contribution from a company remains theirs even when they leave and go to another company.

While these portable 401k plans have grown, inequities in access go along with them. Those in higher income jobs are more likely to participate in such plans.[39] Those with higher incomes are able to put away more money, such that their pensions will cover a larger percentage of the income they had before retiring.[40] Lower income workers find it harder to find money to contribute, which is creating greater anxiety about having sufficient retirement funds for those with lower incomes.[41]

Once workers enter the labor force, differences in income continue to have considerable impact on their economic situations, and inequality in the distribution of income continues to increase in America. The incomes of those in the bottom 40 percent of the income distribution are not increasing much while those in top category are increasing significantly. Not only are those with lower incomes not making much progress, but their economic vulnerability has increased because they are now experiencing greater year-to-year fluctuations in income than was the case thirty years ago. We have studies that track the same people over time. They show that in the 1970s families in the bottom fifth used to fluctuate up or down by 25 percent from one year to the next. Now they experience swings of 50 percent from year to year.[42] This greater volatility accentuates the patterns just reviewed. It becomes harder to cope with bills, rent, house payments, college tuition payments, and many other demands when incomes fluctuate significantly.

INTERPRETING INEQUALITY

While it is clear inequality in the distribution of income is increasing, not everyone sees this trend as a serious social problem. The liberal view is that the general increase in inequality and the concentration of increases in the upper income strata over the last thirty years reflects a serious problem in American society. Differences in income create differences in opportunity. Blacks and Hispanics, with lower incomes, experience more of these problems. This inequality is increasing even as more and more families have both parents working. In the 1960s about 20 percent of women were in the labor force. The number of women in the labor force is now almost 70 percent.[43] Most families now have two income-earners, yet even with this additional income, many of these families are not experiencing income gains.

There are also many who acknowledge growing inequality, but do not see it as any sort of crisis. Conservatives argue that recent trends reflect the idea that our capitalistic society is working as it should. They have several arguments. First, they note that inequality, despite the recent increase, has not approached the levels that prevailed from 1900–1940, as Figure 2-1 shows. Second, they note that real median family income is increasing steadily over time, and as Table 2-2 shows, they note that those in the lower income strata are experiencing income growth, but the increases are just smaller. While some are gaining more than others, all strata are doing better. As long as everyone is doing better, there should be some restraint in characterizing the situation as a serious problem that requires more government programs that create redistribution of incomes.

Third, and perhaps most important, there are serious and fundamental differences of opinion about what income inequality reflects.[44] To critics inequality means there are growing differences in opportunity in our society. To others this inequality could well be a reflection of the very much desired social mobility that should occur if the American Dream is alive and well.[45] The crucial question is whether inequality reflects a rigid social stratification or a fluid movement of individuals through the income distribution as a reward for their efforts. It could be that those who work and achieve are those being rewarded.

Bill Clinton, president from 1993 to 2001, expressed the American Dream succinctly:

> The American Dream that we were all raised on is a simple but powerful one—if you work hard and play by the rules you should be given a chance to go as far as your God-given ability will take you.[46]

The important question is whether this version of the American Dream is occurring. Is there mobility across generations and during a lifetime and is it associated with hard work and achievement? Do individuals who started in the lower strata but who work hard and achieve move up the income ladder and do individuals who start in the upper strata, but who do not work hard, move down the income ladder over their lifetime? Or do children born into poor families largely stay poor and do children born into rich families stay rich regardless of their efforts and achievements? In general, is there upward and downward social mobility and is it associated with hard work and achievement? If these conditions do not exist, there are reasons to worry a great deal about potential for inequality to translate into serious class conflict. If the conditions do exist, then there is a state of "healthy inequality,"[47] which reflects the market rewarding some skills more than others, and, arguably, no efforts should be made to intrude on the processes creating inequality.[48]

The reality is that we know much less about social mobility than we would like. We do know there is social mobility across generations and across lifetimes. There are, however, serious differences of opinion about what constitutes enough mobility within society. There is also not much data on why mobility occurs and how much of the change that does exist is due to the all-important matter of hard work and achievement.

Table 2-3 presents data from studies which follow the situations of a set of people over time and assess whether they have moved up or down over time. Changes from 1969 to 1979 for a constant set of people are presented followed by their changes from 1988 to 1998.[49] In general, those from well-to-do families end up well-to-do and those from poorer families end up poorer.[50] But there is also movement, with some ending up better off than their parents and some worse off.

The data indicate change, but they also provide the basis for different interpretations of what is occurring in American society. Individuals are first grouped by where they were in the income distribution in the initial year. The left column indicates the quintile, or fifth of the income distribution, that someone was in as of 1969. The row next to each quintile of 1969 indicates where individuals in the 1969 situation were in 1979, ten years later. Starting with the lowest quintile, 49.4 percent were in the same (the lowest) quintile ten years later. At the same time 24.5 percent moved up to the next quintile, while 3.3 percent moved from the bottom to the top group over ten years. Upward mobility does occur. The issue is whether the glass is half full (more than 50 percent were able to advance) or half empty (about 50 percent did not change). There is also evidence of downward mobility. Of those in the top quintile in 1969, 49.1 percent

TABLE 2-3	Percentage Moving from One Quintile to Another: 1969 to 1979 and 1988 to 1998				

| | Income Quintile in 1979 | | | | |
1969 QUINTILE	First	Second	Third	Fourth	Fifth
First (lowest)	49.4	24.5	13.8	9.1	3.3
Second	23.2	27.8	25.2	16.2	7.7
Third	10.2	23.4	24.8	23.0	18.7
Fourth	9.9	15.0	24.1	27.4	23.7
Fifth (highest)	5.0	9.0	13.2	23.7	49.1

| | Income Quintile in 1998 | | | | |
1988 QUINTILE	First	Second	Third	Fourth	Fifth
First (lowest)	53.3	23.6	12.4	6.4	4.3
Second	25.7	36.3	22.6	11.0	4.3
Third	10.9	20.7	28.3	27.5	12.6
Fourth	6.5	12.9	23.7	31.1	25.8
Fifth (highest)	3.0	5.7	14.9	23.2	53.2

Source: Katharine Bradbury and Jane Katz, "Women's Labor Market Involvement and Family Income Mobility When Marriage Ends," New England Economic Review, Quarter 4, September 2002, www.bos.frb.org/economic/neer/neer2002/neer402c.pdf.

stayed there, but 23.7 percent dropped one quintile and 5.0 percent dropped to the bottom quintile.

While there are arguments about whether this is enough mobility, it should be noted that we know very little, if anything about the central issue of whether these changes reflect "just rewards." We do not know how much talent these people had, how hard these people worked, or how many personal or family crises,[51] or "lucky breaks" occurred in their lives. The American Dream is that talent and hard work should result in success. Amid the arguments about how much change is occurring, we don't know very much about what the change reflects about initial talent and effort.

The data on 1988 to 1998 reflect a similar pattern, but they also reflect another aspect of the debate about mobility. From 1968 to 1979, 49.4 percent stayed in the bottom or top quintile, which means more than 50 percent moved. From 1988 to 1998, 53.2 percent of those in the bottom quintile stayed there over 10 years, and 53.3 percent of those in the top quintile stayed there over 10 years. Those who are less troubled about the degree of mobility point to the continued upward and downward economic mobility at the same time that inequality is increasing. Those who are critical of the degree of mobility point to the fact that from 1988 to 1998, as compared to 1969 to 1979, a higher percentage within the bottom and the top strata stayed in their strata, suggesting a decline in mobility.

CONCLUSION

The trend toward greater inequality in America is clear and consistent. Income and wealth are more unequally distributed than thirty years ago. The divides in income, wealth, and opportunity—in short, the class divides—are widening. Those inequalities have consequences across a lifetime. Those with lower incomes are more vulnerable to economic problems and their vulnerability appears to have increased in recent decades. Those with lower incomes also face more challenges in acquiring the opportunity to get out of their situation. These differences in vulnerability and opportunity have the potential to become a central concern in political debates. The important matter is just how central they have become.

CHAPTER 3

PARTIES AND POLICY PROPOSALS ON CLASS ISSUES

With inequality increasing, are political parties responding by making inequality a political issue? Washington think tanks may disseminate studies about inequality trends and the media may cover the issue, but for things to change, issues like the minimum wage, food stamps, health insurance, education, or taxes have to get on the agendas of politicians and parties. If the elected representatives of one party continually push for policies in response to an issue such as taxes and they meet opposition from the other party, the chances of an issue emerging on the agenda are much higher.

Politicians push for policies on class issues for several reasons. They may strongly believe in the issues. They may also have an electoral base that would benefit from the policies they are advocating and they want to establish that they are working for their constituency. Or they may believe that taking action on an issue will help create a clear policy identity for their party and attract constituents the party wants as supporters in future elections. The dynamic of the relationship between a party and its constituents, therefore, is complicated. A party may respond to its current supporters, but it also may seek new supporters from those who identify with another party or neither party. The attempts to win over new supporters are particularly interesting. Some initial success encourages the party to continue to pursue the same groups to increase their electoral base, which results in a gradual transformation in their electoral base.

A note of caution is in order about elite-mass interactions. Just because our discussion of party positions begins with a focus on elites does not mean that we presume that the political parties' issue stands originate only with elites. While individual citizens respond to the parties based on cues from party elites,[1] these same elites react to changes at the mass level as they formulate their party's positions.[2] If party elites want to achieve and maintain majority status, they need to monitor and listen to the concerns that citizens are expressing. There is, then, an ongoing dynamic between mass and elite preferences that determines a party's issue positions. We begin with elites solely for analytical ease.

INCREASED PARTY DIFFERENCES

Over the last several decades partisan divisions within Congress have increased and the electorate is seeing parties with very different agendas.[3] This general divergence of the parties reflects, in large part, growing differences on economic issues. Republicans have long been more conservative on economic issues. They have more faith in the private sector and in the outcomes of free markets. They are less likely to support interventions to regulate businesses or markets and more likely to accept the inequalities that follow from the workings of the private sector. Democrats have long been more liberal on economic issues. They are less likely to trust the private sector and more likely to want government to regulate markets. They are more likely to enact legislation to address inequities, often by some combination of imposing higher taxes on the more affluent and instituting programs to expand equality of opportunity.[4]

While the parties have always differed on class issues, they have grown further apart in recent years. In the 1960s the differences in the parties were less pronounced than they are now. There was enough of a consensus between the two parties that Congress was able to pass a remarkable number of new programs that increased the role of the federal government in our society and economy: civil rights laws, expanded welfare eligibility, a food stamp program for those with lower incomes, an expansion of public housing programs, and Medicare and Medicaid.

While these changes seemed to represent a consensus, they heightened the differences between the parties and triggered reactions that are still playing out.[5] The enactment of numerous new redistributive social programs alarmed fiscal conservatives, who began to mobilize with renewed vigor to oppose the growth of government and the extent of such programs.[6] Republicans increasingly took more economically conservative positions, advocating limits on spending and redistributive programs and cuts in tax burdens.[7] At the same time there was an increase in funding for conservative think tanks, which began to produce sustained arguments about the harmful effects of federal programs on the incentive for individuals to work.[8] While liberals saw welfare as supportive of those in need, conservatives saw it as undermining the inclination to join the workforce and exercise the discipline necessary to succeed in life.[9] Fiscal conservatives supported deregulation and cuts in taxes and as they gradually gained control of the party, the party itself attracted more and more conservatives within the electorate.

The Democrats were also changing. The civil rights legislation of the 1960s and the social and economic transformation of American society significantly altered the party's base. The civil rights bills dramatically increased the registration of black voters in southern states. Districts that previously had an almost all white constituency and elected conservative southern Democrats suddenly became much more racially diverse and began to elect moderate or liberal Democrats. In other southern districts with fewer African Americans, conservative Republican representatives replaced conservative Democrats.[10] The replacement of conservatives with moderates in some cases and the elimination of conservatives in other districts altered the composition of the Democratic Party.

At the same time, the composition of American society was undergoing a significant transition. Congress changed the immigration laws during the 1960s, allowing a significant increase in the immigration of Hispanics/Latinos, who are on average less affluent and tend to be more supportive of the Democratic Party. The result has been an increase in the presence of those who identify themselves as non-white in census reports. In the 1960s 64.8 percent of House districts had less than 10 percent of non-whites and only 12.6 percent had 30 percent or more non-whites. By 2002, only 23.2 percent of House districts had less than 10 percent non-whites, while 30.1 percent had 30 percent or more of non-whites. As Democrats were losing conservative southern Democrats, they were gaining seats in districts with substantial percentages of non-whites,[11] and these districts were electing liberal House members.

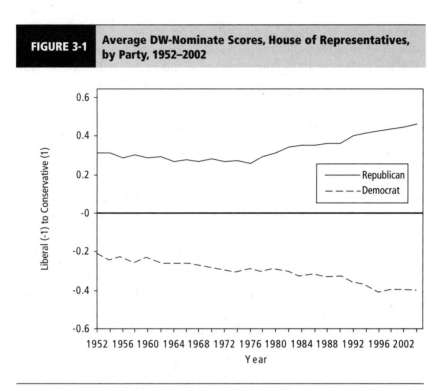

FIGURE 3-1 Average DW-Nominate Scores, House of Representatives, by Party, 1952–2002

Source: Data from Keith Poole, taken from voteview.com/dwnl.htm.

As these changes have unfolded the parties have gradually drifted further apart in their policy stands. Republicans are winning more seats in districts that tend to be conservative and Democrats are winning more seats in districts that tend to be liberal, and the voting behavior of members reflect these differences in their districts. Political scientists have taken the votes of members of Congress and developed measures of how conservative or liberal each member is.[12] Scores range from 1 (more conservative) to –1 (more liberal). Using these DW-Nominate scores it is possible to calculate the average score of Republicans and Democrats in the Congress over time. Figure 3-1 presents some evidence of this, using results for the House. Since the 1970s there has been a steady drift of Republicans to more conservative positions and a steady drift of Democrats to more liberal positions. The difference between the parties is now greater than at any time in the last fifty years and growing steadily.

The gradual drift apart of the parties is evident in the party platforms. Table 3-1 presents a comparison of some of the language of the 1960 and 2004 platforms. In 1960 the Democrats presented a fairly liberal set of proposals, expressing concern for full-employment and good jobs, and promising to raise the minimum wage and do more to improve benefits such as food stamps, public housing, and unemployment compensation. Republicans offered some differences, but they were modest. They also pledged to increase the minimum wage and unemployment compensation and made general references to private-sector jobs being better than government jobs.

By 2004 the differences in the language and emphases were greater. Democrats made repeated reference to inequality and unfairness in how success was distributed in American society, while Republicans expressed strong support for the private sector and individual solutions to problems. They did not support using government as a solution to problems. One party's concern with inequality was countered with the other party's testimony to the virtues of free markets and individual responsibility.

TAXES: BATTLES OVER REVENUES AND WHO PAYS

The battles between Republicans and Democrats about specific class-related policies begin with taxes, which provide the revenue for programs. Tax policies involve issues of who makes what money, which tax rates should be applied to income levels, and who ultimately bears the burden of funding government. If there is an issue that highlights the class-related differences between the parties, it is taxes. Republicans and their conservative allies have made this a central issue in recent years.[13]

Conservatives argue that taxes in general are too high and that the current system punishes and discourages achievers. They advocate that overall tax levels be reduced, that there should be reductions in the tax rates on top income earners and on those who realize capital gains, and that the estate tax should be reduced, or even better, abolished. Capital gains occur when the value of an investment in a business or in stocks, for example, increases over the amount originally invested. Conservatives believe these investments should be encouraged because they ultimately help the economy grow and that taxing them at the same rate as normal income deters growth. The estate tax—called the "death" tax by many

| TABLE 3-1a | Class/Economic Equality Material Contained in the Platforms of the Democratic and Republican Parties, 1960 |

DEMOCRATIC PLATFORM	REPUBLICAN PLATFORM
• reaffirmation of FDR's "Economic Bill of Rights," including "the right to a useful and remunerative job in the industries or shops or farms or mines of the nation."	• statement that economic growth is created primarily by the private sector, not government.
• support for a policy of full employment.	• call for tax reform to make it easier for businesses to expand and create jobs.
• pledge to "create new industry in America's depressed areas of chronic unemployment."	• statement that wages must be tied to productivity.
• pledge to strengthen the Fair Labor Standards Act, including a promise to "raise the minimum wage to $1.25 an hour and to extend coverage to several million workers not now protected."	• statement that labor and management must work together to meet "their mutual public obligation."
• pledge to "use the food stamp programs authorized to feed needy children, the aged and the unemployed. We will expand and improve the school lunch and milk programs."	• pledge to further increase the minimum wage and extend unemployment benefits.
	• pledge to support job training for displaced workers.
• declaration of "the right to every family to a decent home" including a "low-rent public housing program."	• statement that "our tax structure should be improved to provide greater incentives to economic progress, to make it fair and equitable."
• pledge of greater federal support for state public assistance programs.	• call for "adequate authority for the federal housing agencies to assist the flow of mortgage credit to private housing, with emphasis on homes for middle- and lower-income families."
• promise to "establish uniform standards throughout the nation for coverage, duration, and amount of benefits."	
• support for "a program of loans and scholarship grants to assure the qualified young Americans will have full opportunity for higher education, regardless of the income of their parents."	
• pledge to "close the loopholes in the tax laws by which certain privileged groups legally escape their fair share of taxation."	

TABLE 3-1b	Class/Economic Equality Material Contained in the Platforms of the Democratic and Republican Parties, 2004

DEMOCRATIC PLATFORM	REPUBLICAN PLATFORM
• support for a policy of full employment.	• "as Republicans, we trust people to make decisions about how to spend, save, and invest their own money. We want individuals to own and control their income... we want more people to own a home... we want more people to own and control their health care, people to own personal retirement accounts."
• "a strong America keeps promise of opportunity for all and heeds the warning of special privileges for none. In President George Bush's America, unfortunately, too often you need special privileges if you want opportunity."	
• "we believe in progress that brings prosperity for all Americans, not just for those who are already successful."	• "we believe that good government is based on a system of limited taxes and spending.... The taxation system should not be used to redistribute wealth or fund ever-increasing entitlement and social programs."
• "we will ensure that the right to organize a union exists in the real world, not just on paper, because that's how we create more jobs that can support families."	• "personal retirement accounts must be the cornerstone of strengthening and enhancing Social Security.... Assets in personal accounts should belong to each individual. Every American should have the opportunity to build a nest egg for the future and pass along that money to their children or grandchildren."
• "we want a tax code that rewards work and creates wealth for more people, not a tax code that hoards wealth for those that already have it."	
• promise to expand child care credits for low-income families.	• "Health Savings Accounts allow people to own and control their health care. They are an important step toward creating a system of consumer-driven health care that puts patients and doctors at the center of decision-making—not government bureaucrats."
• "we believe that health care is a right and not a privilege."	
	• "we know what brought us this success [a growing economy]—the hard work of the American people and the Republican commitment to low taxes."

Note: The platforms of all parties whose presidential candidate received at least one electoral vote can be found at www.presidency.ucsb.edu/platforms.php.

Republicans—is a tax imposed on the value of someone's estate when that value is received as income by another individual. Currently a certain amount of the estate is excluded from consideration for taxes—roughly one million dollars in 2005. Conservatives argue that estate holders paid taxes during their lifetime and the value of their estates should not be subject to further taxes for those who receive this value. They also argue that the estate tax may require the sale of a family-owned business to be able to pay the estate tax. Liberals argue that the heirs are receiving income and should have to pay taxes on this income just like any other income they receive.

Who Pays What?

While specific taxes draw strong reactions, the central issue in all tax debates is who makes what money and who should pay how much in taxes. Table 3-2 presents data central to this issue and that provokes strong reactions from conservatives and liberals. The top section of the table summarizes data from the Internal Revenue Service on the distribution of incomes in the nation since the 1960s. The table indicates the percentage of adjusted gross income grouped by percentiles of filers, which are ranked from the highest incomes to the lowest. For example, the 1 percent of filers with the highest incomes is considered as a group, the top 5 percent is considered as another group. Adjusted income refers to all income received after subtracting expenses experienced in the process of making the money.

Since 1960 those in the top percentiles are receiving a larger percentage of all income in the nation. For example, the top 10 percent of filers have increased their share of income from 30.6 percent in 1960 to 41.7 percent in 2002. At the same time, the bottom 50 percent of all filers has seen its percentage of income decline from 20.5 percent to 14.2 percent of all income.

These trends provoke strong reactions from liberal elites troubled by the growing inequality. They charge that "the rich are getting richer" and that, as the beneficiaries of the capitalistic system which our government protects and our society supports, the affluent should be required, in turn, to contribute significantly in the form of taxes. Liberal elites also point out that the bottom 50 percent earns a small percentage of the total

TABLE 3-2	Distributions of Income, Tax Rates, and Percentage of Personal Income Taxes Paid, 1960–2002, by Groupings of Income Tax Filers

	Percentile of Income Distribution					
YEAR	Top 1	Top 5	Top 10	Top 25	Top 50	Bottom 50
Share of Adjusted Gross Income						
1960	8.6	20.5	30.6	53.4	79.5	20.5
1970	8.0	20.2	30.8	54.5	80.9	19.1
1980	8.5	21.0	32.1	56.7	82.3	17.7
1990	14.0	27.6	38.8	62.1	85.0	15.0
2002	16.1	30.6	41.7	64.4	85.8	14.2
Δ 60-02	7.5	10.1	11.1	11.0	6.3	-6.3
Income Tax Rates per Income Filing Group						
1960	30.0	22.0	19.4	16.1	14.0	6.6
1970	30.0	22.5	19.6	16.6	14.7	7.1
1980	35.1	27.1	23.7	19.8	17.4	6.1
1990	23.3	20.5	18.5	16.1	14.4	5.0
2002	27.3	23.0	20.5	17.0	14.7	3.1
Δ 60-02	-2.1	1.0	1.1	.9	.7	-3.5
Percent of Taxes from Income Filing Group						
1960	20.8	36.2	47.6	68.9	89.2	10.8
1970	18.3	34.3	45.6	68.3	89.9	10.1
1980	19.3	37.1	49.5	73.2	93.0	7.0
1990	25.1	43.6	55.4	77.0	94.2	5.8
2002	33.7	53.8	65.7	83.9	96.5	3.5
Δ 60-02	12.9	17.6	18.1	15.0	7.3	-7.3

Source: The Tax Foundation, www.taxfoundation.org/publications/show/250.html.

income and how important it is to create programs to increase their opportunity if there is to be any equality of opportunity in this society. Liberal elites argue that the affluent are the least likely to need tax cuts and that most cuts should go those in the middle-class and below.

Conservative party elites interpret the trends of recent years very differently. They argue that our economy is changing and the greater growth of incomes by some reflects rewards for desired talents. They cite clear differences in tax rates by income group, shown in the middle section of the table, whereby those earning the most pay much higher income tax rates than those at lower income levels. Indeed, critics of the current income tax system point out that the top 1 percent pays rates almost 10 times that of those in the bottom half. Their most serious complaint, however, involves the information in the bottom section of the table. Over the last several decades the percentage of total federal income tax revenue provided by the most affluent has steadily increased. From 1960 to 2002 the percentage of all income tax revenues provided by the top 10 percent of income earners has increased from 47.6 percent to 65.7 percent. Conservative elites argue that the affluent appear to carry the bulk of the income tax obligation, and that they deserve the tax cuts, otherwise the achievers and entrepreneurs, who create jobs and wealth, are being penalized for their accomplishments.

Figure 3-2, which is key to the conservatives' argument, takes the percentage of all income tax revenue derived from each quintile of income level and divides it by the percentage of income the group receives. If the top quintile pays 50 percent of all taxes raised and receives 50 percent of all income, then its ratio is 1. If a group provides a higher percentage of taxes than it receives in income, the ratio is over 1. The figure tracks the ratio by income quintiles over a twenty-four year period. Those in the top income group provide a percentage of taxes higher than their percentage of income. That is to be expected with a progressive tax system, which taxes the more affluent at a higher rate.

What is important to conservatives is how the trends differ by income group. For quintiles 1—the bottom—through 4—the second-highest—these ratios have declined over the past twenty-four years. That is, each of these income quintiles is now providing less tax revenue relative to the percentage they earn. As a result of the redistributive effect of the earned income tax credit which gives a refund to people who work and do not earn very much, those in the bottom quintile receive more money back than they pay, so their ratio is negative. The ratio for the middle quintile dropped from .68 to .32. The top quintile, on the other hand, was at 1.43 in 1979 and in 2003 it was at 1.63. Conservatives interpret this as indicative of a tax system in which the highest earners and achievers are increasingly carrying more than their fair share of the tax burden.

Democrats respond with two counterarguments. First, they note that the affluent are the only group experiencing significant increases in

FIGURE 3-2	Ratio of Percentage of Income Tax Obligations to Percentage of Income, by Quintiles, 1979–2003

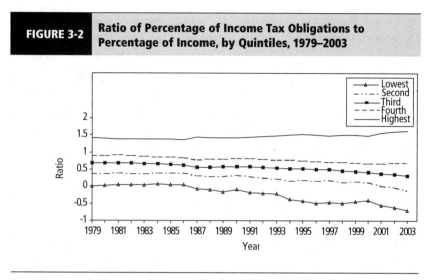

Source: Congressional Budget Office, *Effective Federal Tax Rates, 1997 to 2001*, Table 1C, April 2004.

income, thus the increase in the percentage of tax revenue derived from them just reflects that trend. Because the rich earn more they should pay more. Second, liberals argue that the focus on the income tax system distracts from the larger issue of all taxes, including Social Security and Medicare taxes, which taken as a whole are far less progressive. Social Security and Medicare taxes are imposed on wages and incomes, with a cap at income below about $90,000 for the former and no cap on the latter. The Social Security tax on all employees is a little over 7 percent, while the Medicare tax is about 2 percent. The liberal argument that the overall tax system is much less progressive than the income tax alone would indicate is met with skepticism from many conservatives, who argue that the Social Security and Medicare taxes fund specific programs—which benefit the less affluent far more than those who are better off—and thus should not be seen as part of the general tax system.

Fighting Over What Taxes Should Be

Needless to say, these very different views of the current tax system have generated major conflicts over taxes during the last two decades and heated battles in recent years. Republicans increasingly advocate tax cuts while Democrats oppose them on equity grounds and because they want to protect government revenues for programs they support. In 1993, Democrats supported and Republicans opposed President Clinton's proposed tax increase on the affluent to generate more revenue to reduce the federal deficit. Following the 1994 elections Republicans acquired majorities in both houses of Congress and vowed to cut taxes. In 1997, 1999, and 2000 Republicans proposed significant tax cuts, but Clinton vetoed the bills. The parties again divided significantly.

The tide turned after the 2000 presidential election. With Republicans in control of the presidency and both houses of Congress, President Bush proposed large tax cuts in 2001, 2002, 2003, and 2004. The proposed tax cuts (eventually largely enacted) and the ensuing debate illustrate how differently the two parties approach the issues of who should pay and how tax burdens should be distributed.

President Bush proposed cuts that reduced income taxes at all levels of income. Perhaps most important was how his office presented the cuts and how Democrats viewed them. Bush's 2001 "President's Jobs and Growth Plan" presented the following explanation of the tax cuts:

- "Under President Bush's plan, Americans in the lowest tax brackets receive the largest percentage reduction in their tax burden."

- "Three million moderate-income families will see their income tax burden eliminated entirely."

- "Treasury Department estimates show the share of income taxes paid by high-income Americans will actually rise."[14]

Figure 3-3 shows the percentage of the reduction by income level for the Bush tax cuts.[15] These percentage reductions are calculated as follows. If someone was paying $2,000 in taxes, and the plan would reduce their taxes to $1,500, then their reduction is $500, or 25 percent less in taxes. If someone was paying $20,000 in taxes and received a cut of $4,000, then their reduction is 20 percent less than what they were paying.

Not surprisingly, Democrats and liberal groups did not agree with Bush's explanation of his tax cuts. When liberal groups, such as the Center on Budget and Policy Priorities, assessed these cuts, they saw a very different picture of who benefited the most from the tax cuts. Table

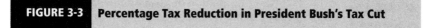

FIGURE 3-3   **Percentage Tax Reduction in President Bush's Tax Cut**

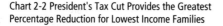

Chart 2-2 President's Tax Cut Provides the Greatest
Percentage Reduction for Lowest Income Families

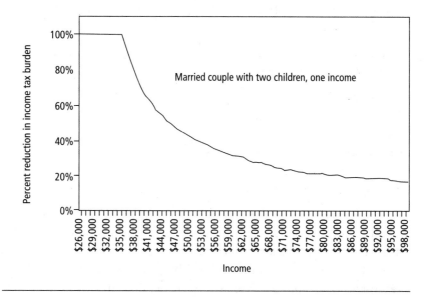

Source: A Blueprint for New Beginnings, IV, "Major Policy Initiatives Provide Tax Relief for American Families,"
35 (February 28, 2001) see www.whitehouse.gov/news/usbudget/blueprint/bud02.html.

3-3 summarizes their 2004 intepretation on how the benefits of the cuts
were distributed, which the liberal groups calculated very differently
from the administration.[16] While the White House focused on the percentage reduction compared to taxes paid, this group focused on the distribution of the overall tax cut. Their analysis focused on the larger dollar reductions and the bulk of tax savings that went to the that higher
income groups. In assessing the cuts enacted over the prior three years,
they found that 59 percent of the reductions went to those in the top 20
percent of the income distribution.

TABLE 3-3	Who Benefits? Distribution of Bush Administration Tax Cuts in 2004 (excluding the effects of corporate and estate tax cuts)			
INCOME GROUP	Average Income (in dollars)	Average Tax Cut (in dollars)	Percentage of Share of Tax Cut	Percentage of Change in After-Tax Income
Lowest 20%	16,600	-230	2.8	1.5
Second 20%	38,100	-720	8.3	2.2
Middle 20%	57,400	-980	11.5	2.0
Fourth 20%	84,300	-1,520	17.7	2.3
Highest 20%	203,700	-4,890	59.9	3.3
All	80,100	-1,680		2.7

Source: David Kamin and Isaac Shapiro, "Studies Shed New Light on Effects of Administration's Tax Cuts," Center on Budget and Policy Priorities, revised September 13, 2004, 5.

Differing Party Interpretations

This tax debate is not easy to sort out. In reality, both sides are right. The different interpretations are not just cases of politicians twisting and distorting facts.[17] Republicans are correct that the lowest income groups got the greatest percentage cut in their tax obligation. To return to the earlier example, $500—or 25 percent— is a greater percentage of $2,000 than $4,000—or 20 percent— is of $20,000. It is also accurate to say that the actual cuts in dollar amounts are much higher for those with higher incomes and that the bulk of actual tax reductions go to those who make the most money. All these facts were correct, with an obvious difference in emphasis. What is interesting are the parties' reactions to these facts and their justifications for how to interpret them.

Members of the Democratic Party have leveled numerous criticisms at the cuts, focusing on who benefits and the consequences for other programs. In 2001 Senate Minority Leader Tom Daschle, D-S.D., claimed that with the first tax cut, "earners making about $300,000 would get enough of a tax break to pay for a Lexus, while people making $50,000 a year would see only enough tax savings to buy a muffler for a used car," and for good measure he posed with a Lexus for TV. Richard Gephardt, D-Mo., then House Minority Leader, said "America should not spend all of its national resources on a massive tax giveaway for the wealthiest

Americans."[18] During the 2004 presidential campaign Democratic candidate John Kerry continually criticized the tax cuts as unfair. Kerry's running mate John Edwards also regularly criticized changes in tax laws, which resulted in lower tax rates for dividends and capital gains. During a debate among Democratic candidates in 2003, before he received the vice-presidential nomination, Edwards said, "Everyone on this stage is against Bush's tax cuts for the rich, but there's something more radical than that going on here. What this president is doing is trying to shift the tax burden in America from wealth to work."[19] He later reiterated that point in a televised debate with Richard Cheney, the Republican vice-presidential candidate:

> ... talking about tax policy, the country needs to know that under what they [the Republicans] have put in place, a millionaire sitting by their swimming pool, collecting their statements to see how much money they're making, making their money from dividends, pays a lower tax rate than the men and women who are receiving paychecks for serving on the ground in Iraq.[20]

The Democrats emphasized "fairness" and continued criticism of doing too much for "the rich."

Republicans expressed very different views of the cuts. A debate on the floor of the Senate about a 2003 tax bill illustrates the Republican faith in individual choice, private markets and economic growth from the efforts of private entrepreneurs. The first comment is from Sen. Charles Grassley, R-Iowa, and the second is from Robert Bennett, R-Utah.

> There is the difference between one party that believes money in the pockets of 110 million taxpayers is going to do more economic good if the 110 million taxpayers spend it or invest it than if I, Senator Grassley, and 534 others here in DC are going to make that decision. We have to believe that if the money is in the pockets of 110 million taxpayers it is going to do more good. It is going to turn over more times in the economy. It will respond to the dynamics of our free market economy rather than a political decision being made about what to do with it.[21]

... This is not a debate about whether Bill Gates should get a tax cut. This is a debate about whether small businessmen and small businesswomen all across this country should get an incentive to hire, an incentive to invest, and incentive to build for the future, whether to plant seeds of growth which will yield a significant harvest for us later on.[22]

Republicans also expressed very different reactions on the fairness issue. As Representative Thomas Petri, R-Wisc., put it:

As you've probably heard, a lot of the President's critics blast the new tax law for being a "tax cut for the rich." And, yes, the people who pay the most taxes will get significant cuts. It's worth noting that in 1979 the richest 10 percent of Americans paid 41 percent of federal taxes, but now they pay over 50 percent. Nobody's sorry for the rich, but wealthy Americans have not been getting a free ride.[23]

As the above quotes clearly show, the parties' views on fairness—who is being treated well and who is not—were far apart. From the 1950s to the 1970s this difference was not quite as sharp. Republicans were different from Democrats, but two things have changed in recent decades. During the 1950s–1970s a major focus in discussions of tax bills was how changing the tax laws would affect economic growth and job creation. While the effects on the economy are still very significant considerations, distributional debates—which income groups get what— have been added as a central and recurring part of the discussions. And the parties differ not only in their rhetoric—they now vote very differently on tax legislation as well. While in the past some Democrats voted with Republicans and some Republicans voted with Democrats on tax bills, there is much less party line-crossing now. Voting patterns in the House of Representatives on tax bills illustrates how the differences between the parties have increased. During the 1950s–1970s there were twelve major tax bills, and the average difference in party support for the bills was 25.9 percent. That is, when the percentage of Republicans voting for a bill is subtracted from the percentage of Democrats voting for a bill, and this difference is averaged, the result was 25.9 percent. In the 1980s there were four major tax bills and the difference was 26.3 percent. In the 1990s there were five major bills and the difference was 79.8 percent. From 2000–2004 there were three major tax bills with recorded votes and the average difference was 93.4 percent.[24] Tax policy has gone from being an issue with some agreement to a highly divisive issue. With all the accusations about unfairness and the treatment of "the rich," it is likely that voters will see a greater split between the parties on class issues than they did thirty years ago.

BATTLES OVER PROGRAMS

Taxes are only the beginning of party battles. The parties also increasingly differ over whether government should intervene through programs and policies to affect society and the economy. Party stances are evident for policies such as welfare and unemployment compensation, which largely benefit those making less money, and policies to help business. During the 1960s and 1970s, welfare rolls expanded as government made it easier for people to get welfare. While Republicans never enthusiastically supported expanding this program, their resistance was not intense. As the 1980s evolved, the Republicans began to see opposition to welfare as a stand they should take. They opposed the principle of unlimited government support of recipients. They also decided to make this position a defining trait of the party and in the 1994 campaign the party published the Contract with America and promised to dramatically change welfare. In 2003 the Republicans pushed to increase the hours per week that recipients had to work from 30 to 40. Democrats, while uneasy defending welfare to the American public, strongly opposed these changes.

The growing differences between the political parties are evident in the votes on welfare bills in the last two decades. Table 3-4 presents party voting for some of the major bills in recent years. In 1988 a welfare reform bill was negotiated between President Reagan and congressional Democrats, which gave each some of what they wanted. Democrats got more education and job training and other benefits for recipients while Republicans, for the first time, got a requirement that recipients find employment. The parties differed but were able to forge a compromise and the result was bipartisan support for the bill. By 1996 Republicans, seeking to fulfill their Contract with America promise, pushed a welfare bill that limited benefits to two continuous years at any one time and five years over a lifetime and required states to have a steadily rising percentage of beneficiaries working more hours. Republicans voted strongly for the bill, while Democrats split in the Senate and House Democrats voted strongly against it. In 2003 the legislation had to be renewed. President Bush and congressional Republicans insisted that the work requirements be increased, and the bill passed with a significant split between the parties. Over time, welfare benefits and regulations have become a more partisan issue.[25]

Another indicator of policy differences between the parties is unemployment compensation, a federal program managed by the states after the federal government provides federal aid to match state revenues. The program normally provides for a number of weeks of benefit payments after someone is laid off, with the number varying with the program each state establishes.[26] This program is also used more by people with lower incomes than those with higher incomes.[27] The state unemployment compensation programs run into critical problems when a recession drags on and individuals find their benefits exhausted. This generally results in bills in Congress to extend the number of weeks in which the federal government helps fund extended benefits. Support for these bills is another indicator of how the parties differ. Table 3-5 indicates how divisions about this program have evolved. In 1991, with a recession occurring, Democrats and Republicans in both houses agreed to extend benefits. In 1993, with the economy still somewhat weak, the efforts to extend eligibility for program benefits produced a division between the parties, with Republicans opposing an extension. The same situation occurred in 2003. The economy was recovering slowly from a recession and Democrats wanted to extend benefits for twenty-six weeks rather than thirteen. Republicans opposed and defeated the bill proposing the longer extension, and they then passed a bill extending benefits for thirteen weeks.

Economic differences between the parties are evident in other policy areas as well. For example, the federal government regularly issues regulations specifying safety conditions, disposal procedures for environmental wastes, and what information a business must disclose. When

TABLE 3-4	**Congressional Votes on Welfare Bills, Selected Years**

	HOUSE		SENATE	
	For	Against	For	Against
HR 1720, October 1988				
Democrats	205 (86%)	34 (14%)	52 (98%)	1 (2%)
Republicans	142 (88%)	19 (12%)	41 (95%)	2 (5%)
HR 3734, August 1996				
Democrats	30 (15%)	165 (85%)	23 (50%)	23 (50%)
Republicans	226 (98%)	4 (2%)	51 (98%)	1 (2%)
HR 4, February, 2003				
Democrats	11 (6%)	189 (94%)	Passed by voice vote	
Republicans	219 (99%)	2 (1%)		

Sources: 1988 votes taken from 1988 *CQ Almanac,* 23; 1996 summary and votes from 1996 *CQ Almanac,* 6-13-21, H-108 and S-42; 2003 vote from 2003 *CQ Almanac,* 16-3-4 and H-14.

TABLE 3-5	**Congressional Votes on Unemployment Compensation, Selected Years**

	HOUSE		SENATE	
	For	Against	For	Against
HR 3575, October 1991: Adds 13–20 weeks of additional support				
Democrats	260 (99%)	4 (1%)	40 (98%)	1 (2%)
Republicans	135 (84%)	26 (16%)	51 (98%)	1 (2%)
HR 3167, November 1993: Extends time period for eligibility for benefits				
Democrats	226 (92%)	20 (8%)	56 (100%)	0
Republicans	27 (16%)	141 (84%)	10 (23%)	33 (77%)
HR 2185, May 2003: To add 26 weeks of benefits instead of 13 weeks				
Democrats	204 (100%)	1	Failed; did not go to Senate	
Republicans	1 (0%)	222 (99%)		

Sources: Votes for 1991 and 1993 taken from 'thomas.loc.gov'. Votes for 2003 were taken from the *2003 CQ Almanac,* H-74.

Republicans won the presidency and maintained control over Congress in the 2000 election, George W. Bush proceeded to significantly cut regulations imposed on business, which Democrats strongly criticized.[28] These actions create an impression of a Republican Party that is more sympathetic to business interests.

Republicans also took advantage of their control after 2000 to enact other policies that provide benefits to business. President Bush proposed and Congress passed legislation in 2005 making it harder to file class-action suits, which are used by large groups of people with grievances against an industry or company. Their argument was that lawsuits against businesses were increasing because lawyers, who get a percentage of settlements, were pursuing personal gain, and increasing the cost of doing business.[29] Most Democrats opposed the law. Nancy Pelosi, D-Calif., the House Minority Leader, said it was "an injustice to consumers and a windfall for irresponsible corporations."[30] Representative James McGovern, D-Mass., said the bill "limits the rights of low-wage workers to seek justice from employers who have cheated them out of their wages."[31]

Then Republicans passed legislation to reduce the ability to declare bankruptcy. Business groups, and particularly credit-card companies, complained that existing laws were too lenient and allowed people to abuse bankruptcy law and avoid paying their credit-card bills. Democrats opposed the change in the law, arguing that most people who declare bankruptcy are in that situation because of a combination of limited assets and medical emergencies or short-term crises and the law would make it harder for these people to get out of these situations.[32] Democrats in turn sought to make the issue one of fairness by seeking to remove language that shielded trust funds or expensive homes as claimable assets if someone declared bankruptcy.[33] Republicans defeated that amendment. President Bush also wants to limit medical malpractice suits.[34] Doing so would benefit more affluent elements in American society, such as physicians, the health care sector, and the insurance industry.[35]

With all these disputes about how legislation affects groups, sorting out the facts is a complicated and demanding task. What is important for voters is to see which groups both parties defend or attack. In the cases of class-action lawsuits, bankruptcy law, and medical malpractice lawsuits, Republicans were conveying their faith in the private sector and their hostility to the personal-injury lawyers who they saw as bogging that system down. Democrats were expressing their unease about some outcomes heavily weighted toward the private-sector and their concern for those they portrayed as vulnerable. The parties were projecting different images of the groups they felt merited the most concern in a way that it would be hard for voters to miss.

SOCIAL SECURITY, PRIVATE MARKETS, AND REDISTRIBUTION ISSUES

Social Security, a pension program established in the 1930s, further highlights the differences between the parties. Workers contribute a percentage of their wages to the Social Security Trust Fund, and employers contribute an equivalent percentage. This required percentage has risen steadily over the history of the program, and is now a little over 7 percent for both. Periodically, concerns that there may not be enough revenue from these taxes to pay for future benefits have sometimes led to increases in the Social Security tax.

The Social Security issue emerged again in recent years because George W. Bush decided in 2005 to push for major changes in the program. There were occasional efforts to discuss changing Social Security in prior years, but politicians usually quickly backed away because there are so many recipients, and almost all of them are seniors who vote. Politicians were reluctant to propose changes that might be seen as a cut in benefits because of the large number of active voters who might vote against them. The program also enjoys wide public support, another reason for elected officials to be wary of altering it.

While that anxiety to alter the program existed, conservatives had been developing an argument against the Social Security system for some time.[36] Conservatives complained that the system was compulsory, provided a low rate of return on the money contributed, and creates an entitlement (a guaranteed benefit) that does not encourage people to save and plan for their future. Further, it provided more revenue to government and created more federal bureaucrats who could intrude into people's lives. Many conservatives much preferred letting the program be voluntary and letting people retain and invest their own money.[37]

While conservatives had been criticizing the policy for some time, it took until the early 2000s for a major Republican figure to forcefully advocate these positions. President Bush advocated that some portion of each individual's Social Security tax contribution be assigned to a private account designated by the individual. The funds would become the property of each individual, rather than part of a pool of government funds. As a member of the White House staff put it,

> [This effort is] one of the most important conservative undertakings of modern times.... We have it within our grasp to move away from dependency on government and toward giving greater responsibility to individuals.[38]

While most Republicans embraced Bush's efforts to change the system, though with varying degrees of enthusiasm, Democrats saw the issues involved very differently. They perceived Social Security as a safety net program, intended to pool society's resources and cover as many people as possible. While conservatives saw people who did not plan for their futures, Democrats saw people who had encountered difficulties and were being helped by the safety net provided by the system. Democrats saw vulnerable people who needed the assurance of Social Security coverage.

While it is not often discussed in these terms, Social Security acts as a redistributive program. A worker need only accumulate forty quarters of work (ten years) and contributions to the system to qualify for benefits. The program establishes a minimum set of payments, so even if someone has only worked 10–20 years over a lifetime, they will qualify. The result is that those who make less get back more than they put in. Figure 3-4 indicates the typical ratio, over a lifetime, of total benefits received relative to taxes contributed for different income groups.[39] Those who end up with the lowest incomes as seniors receive about twice what they contribute. Those with higher incomes receive about what they put in. The emphasis of Democrats is that this is not just a retirement program, but a safety net designed to provide security of income in old age to everyone so that no seniors are poor in old age.

The role of Social Security benefits in helping those with lower incomes is evident in Figure 3-5, which indicates reliance on Social

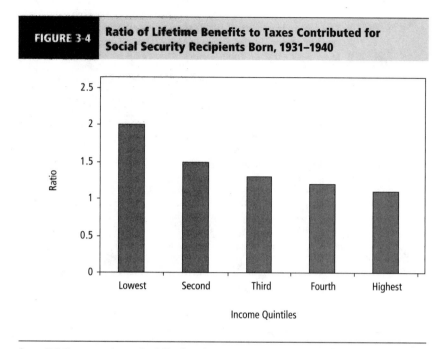

| FIGURE 3-4 | Ratio of Lifetime Benefits to Taxes Contributed for Social Security Recipients Born, 1931–1940 |

Source: U.S. Government Accounting Office, "Social Security and Minorities," GAO-03-387, April 2003, 10.

Security funds by income level of seniors.[40] The graph presents the percentage of all income, within income quintiles, that is derived from Social Security funds.[41] For those in the bottom quintile, or 20 percent of the population, Social Security provides 90 percent of all their income. The elderly in the next income group derive 76 percent of their income from Social Security. Those in the top quintile derive only 20 percent of their income from this source. Battles over Social Security, while often couched in terms of maintaining the soundness of the system, or restraining its proportion of the federal budget, are also battles with strong class implications.

The party stances on proposed changes were again indicative of the differences between the parties. Republicans, again with varying degrees of enthusiasm, supported exploring President Bush's proposal of private accounts. Democrats refused to participate in discussions that included proposals to create private accounts. They were aware that a plan that involved workers setting aside part of their wages would tie benefits to earnings levels. Lower income workers would put away much less than

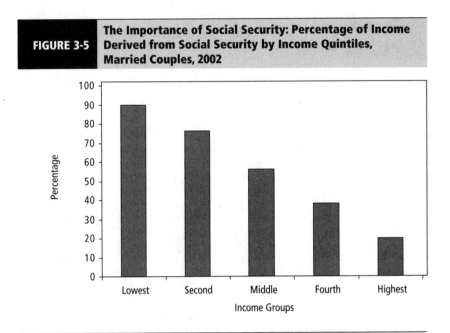

FIGURE 3-5 The Importance of Social Security: Percentage of Income Derived from Social Security by Income Quintiles, Married Couples, 2002

Sources: Income of the Population 55 or Older, Social Security Administration, SSA Publication No. 13-11871, March, 2005. Table 1.6, 26–27. The report is available at www.ssa.gov/policy/docs/statcomps/income_pop55/2002/incpop02.pdf.

higher income workers, and their benefits would be less. Those who worked fewer years in the labor force would get less. The result would be that the redistributive, collective safety net, nature of the program would be less. While those with lower incomes now get less in retirement benefits than those with higher incomes, these differences would increase.

SUMMARY

While the parties have always differed in their support for private markets and the role of government in the economy, these differences have increased in the last several decades. Republicans have become more concerned that government is taking too much of people's income, playing too much of a role in our society, and imposing too many regulations. They have sought to reverse many of these policies. Many of their concerns have redistributive consequences and have created a party that may well be seen as more sympathetic to business and the affluent. Democrats have responded by opposing many of the changes, such as tax cuts and deregulation, and defending many of the programs that exist. Now more than ever, the Democrats clearly demonstrate their concern for those less well off in American society, while the GOP has perhaps never been more open about their support for the economic winners. The important matter for political discussions is how the public responds to the differing class orientations of the parties. Do the voters perceive them? And if so, do they align themselves by class interest such that the electoral bases of the parties differ?

CHAPTER 4

CLASS DIVIDES IN THE AMERICAN PUBLIC

Inequality may be increasing, but whether that trend becomes a politically divisive issue depends on several matters. The issue must first register as an important issue with the public. Then the political parties must adopt opposing policy positions that reflect the different views in the society. If voters choose which party to support based on the party's policy position, then a partisan division over the issue will develop. This chapter considers whether the trends of increasing inequality and differences between the parties have resulted in those with different incomes dividing politically such that class political cleavages are increasing.

While the process by which such divisions emerge sounds relatively simple, voter reactions develop slowly over years. Most voters do not follow politics closely.[1] Given this relatively distracted and intermittent engagement, for the public to become aware of differences the parties must consistently adopt positions in opposition to one another. If this happens, and it is regularly covered by the media, then voters will gradually perceive differences and align themselves with the party they see as best representing their concerns.

Perceiving the differences between parties is not always easy for voters. Even when the parties differ, they may engage in activities that somewhat blur these distinctions and make it harder for voters to see them clearly. Party members generally represent their policy proposals as broadly beneficial, which may obscure differences in effects. Both parties engage in these practices. To return to taxes, Republicans generally present their tax cuts as benefiting everyone equally, and portray Democrats as standing in the way of changes benefiting a wide array of people. In an attempt to structure how the public sees the tax cuts, Republicans focus on the percentage cut in taxes for each income level. They compare proposed taxes to prior tax obligations, and note the reduction, rather than present the cuts in dollar terms. Affluent individuals may get large dollar cuts, but these cuts may be relatively small as a percentage of their total tax obligation. A lower income individual may get a small dollar cut, but it is a significant percentage of the total they were previously paying. Republicans also tend to focus on the average tax cut, which serves to hide any big differences that might exist between income categories. While their figures are accurate, the GOP's approach makes it difficult for many to sort out the distribution of benefits by income level and harder for voters to assess which constituents the party is seeking to benefit.[2]

Likewise, Democrats represent their party as champions for the less affluent, who need a tax break, and argue that Republicans are just enacting tax cuts for the rich. In doing so the Democrats may misrepresent the extent to which the tax burden in recent decades has shifted to the top quintile, as shown in the prior chapter. This positioning has been important with regard to the estate tax.[3] Democrats have argued that the tax should be retained since it affects only the very rich, and the revenue goes for programs that benefit all members of society. The average voter listening to Democrats would probably think the most affluent are providing less tax revenue now than they did twenty years ago. With both parties taking positions that portray themselves as concerned with the interests and well being of the majority of the population, voters often are left unsure of just how the parties differ in whom they represent.

Parties engage in these presentation practices to some extent because voters do not pay much attention. Parties simplify messages and policy images in hopes that their message gets through. These practices help the two parties criticize and characterize each other, but voters may find it hard to understand specific public policy situations and the effects of party proposals. Perceiving the stances of a particular party, then, can potentially take a while.

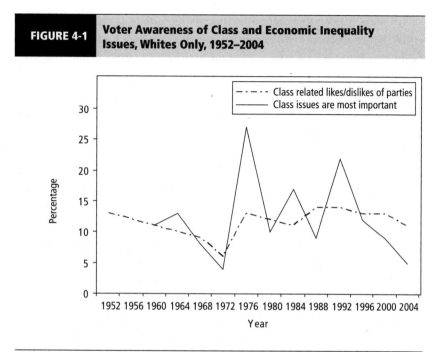

FIGURE 4-1   **Voter Awareness of Class and Economic Inequality Issues, Whites Only, 1952–2004**

Notes: Results are for whites only. There are two possible reasons besides real opinion change for the decrease in class issue mentions in 2004. The first is a change in question wording. Prior to 2004, the question asked respondents to identify the most important problem facing the country. In 2004, the question asked respondents to identify the most important issue facing the nation over the past four years. Not surprisingly, mentions of 9/11, al Qaida, terrorism, and the war in Iraq dominated in 2004, accounting for 57 percent of the total mentions.

Sources: For the most important problem: 1960–2000, *NES Cumulative Datafile, 1948–2004*, vcf0875a and vcf0875b; 2004, NES 2004, v045238. For likes/dislikes: *NES Individual Year Studies.* Full coding schemes are available from the authors on request.

THE PUBLIC'S PERCEPTIONS OF INEQUALITY

For matters of class to become an issue, voters must see such matters as relevant and recognize the trend of greater inequality in the distribution of income. Do voters express any concern about issues of class and inequality? Surveys by the American National Election Studies (NES) provide some information about how much these matters register with voters. Figure 4-1 indicates trends in two reactions of voters about class issues. Voters are regularly asked what they like and dislike about the parties. Their responses can be coded as to whether they mentioned issues of class or inequality. To the extent the voters mention them as either something they like or dislike about the major parties then we can assume that such issues matter to voters and that they connect the parties to these issues. The percentage of respondents mentioning such matters has been fairly steady in recent years, varying between 11 and 15 percent since 1976. Voters were also asked in the same study what is the most important national issue. The percentage of respondents that mentioned class or economic inequality issues has been fairly high, except during the 2000 and 2004 presidential elections, a matter that will be discussed later.

Do Americans recognize that inequality is increasing? The responses to poll inquiries indicate that they do. When asked if they agree or disagree with the statement: "Today it's really true that the rich just get richer while the poor get poorer," polls conducted over the last twenty years indicate that 70 percent or more agree and 30 percent or less disagree.[4] There is also a sense that inequality is increasing. When asked whether America is "becoming a society of haves and have-nots," in the 1980s roughly 30 percent agreed with the statement and in 2001, 44 percent agreed. In a 2004 poll by the Maxwell School of Syracuse University, 68 percent agreed with the statement.[5] In the same 2004 poll 46 percent thought inequality had increased and 24 percent thought it had decreased.

There is also a sense that not everyone has the same opportunity to succeed. When asked if "everyone in American society has an opportunity to succeed, do most, or do only some have this opportunity," 29 percent say everyone, 48 percent say most, and 22 percent say only some.[6] There is also concern that something should be done about inequality. The same Maxwell Poll in 2004 found that 41 percent think "the current extent of inequality is a serious problem."[7] Another poll found that 65 percent of Americans think that "money should be more evenly distributed among a larger percentage of the people."[8]

THE PUBLIC'S PERCEPTIONS OF THE PARTIES

If the public thinks that inequality exists and that it is a matter of concern, do they also see a difference between the parties when it comes to this matter? We have survey results over a lengthy period of time about whether voters see the parties as different—just generally and not with regard to specific issues—and whether they care which party wins the presidential race. These questions have been asked since the 1950s, and Figure 4-2 shows the trends for the survey results.

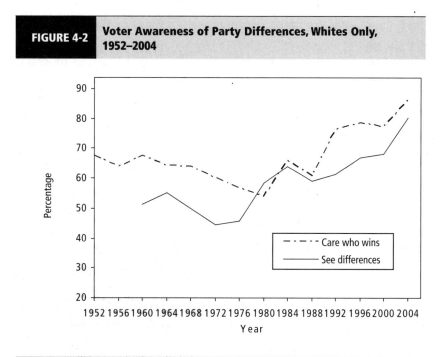

FIGURE 4-2 **Voter Awareness of Party Differences, Whites Only, 1952–2004**

Source: NES Cumulative File, 1948–2004.

Our subsequent analysis will generally be limited to whites only because our primary subjects of interest—the supposed decline of class-based voting and the asserted rising importance of cultural issues in electoral behavior—are almost always portrayed as relating to whites only.[9] The consistent argument over the last several decades is that the white working class has defected from the Democratic Party partly out of concern that the party is too sympathetic to blacks and "cultural diversity,"[10] and that the party does not respect the work ethic so appreciated by the working class.[11] Further, African Americans overwhelmingly support the Democratic Party (at least since 1964), regardless of other factors that sometimes affect electoral behavior, such as income, education, church attendance, gender, area of residence, etc. African Americans seem to strongly support the Democrats because they believe the party is more clearly aligned with their interests as blacks, to the exclusion of other factors.[12] African Americans also continue to exhibit much lower income levels than whites,[13] and they are also among the most highly religious of the demographic groups present in American society.[14] Given these matters, including blacks might lead some to say any class divisions that exist are just because blacks are less affluent and overwhelmingly Democratic. Therefore this chapter will generally focus on whether class political divisions among whites have declined or increased over the last several decades. Chapter 7, which assesses cultural divisions, will also focus largely on whites.

In the 1960s roughly 50 percent of all whites saw a difference between the parties. That percentage has been steadily rising and in the 2004 election it reached 80.3 percent. Among those who vote in presidential elections the percentages are even higher. The other indicator of whether voters see a difference between the parties is whether they care which parties win. That percentage, again for all whites, has also increased steadily in the last 30 years. Both figures reached their high points for the entire series in 2004.

When we move to views of the parties on specific issues, there is also evidence that voters perceive growing differences. Beginning in 1972, respondents were asked in the biennial NES national survey to place the Democratic and Republican Parties on a liberal–conservative scale, with 1 as very liberal and 7 very conservative. Figure 4-3 indicates the differences between the two parties in perceived ideological placement. In 1972 the average difference was 1.85 and by 2004 it was 2.75. Again, voters take a while to perceive differences, but the trend is important. Voters are gradually seeing larger differences between the parties. Voters were also asked about the placement of parties on the issue of whether government should guarantee jobs. The question presented is not ideal because government rarely directly provides jobs anymore, but the question still captures perceptions of concern with jobs and their availability, and the proper role of government in addressing these matters. There is also an increase in perceived differences on this issue. In 1972 the differences were 1.50 and by 2004 the difference was 2.30.

We also have very recent survey results about perceptions of who each party favors. A 2002 NES survey asked respondents to identify "which party is better for poor people" and "which party is better for the rich." In response to the first question, 53 percent of all respondents said the Democratic Party, 9 percent the Republican Party, and 37 percent said

| FIGURE 4-3 | Voters' Sense of Differences between Parties, Whites Only, 1972–2004 |

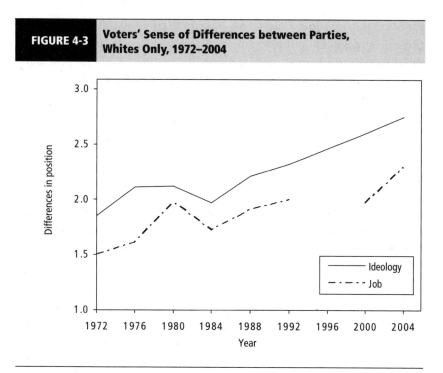

Note: The question regarding jobs was not asked in 1996.

Source: NES Cumulative File, 1948–2004.

there is not much difference between the two parties. In response to the latter question, 56 percent said the Republican Party, 5 percent the Democratic Party, and 37 percent said there is not much difference between the two.[15] These reactions do not vary much by income. There is considerable clarity about which party is perceived as best for the poor and which as best for the rich.

THE EMERGENCE OF CLASS DIVISIONS

If the public recognizes differences in the constituencies the parties care about, are partisan divisions by income growing among voters? The simplest way to assess this is to examine the partisan choices of citizens by income levels. The NES surveys are useful for assessing whether partisan divisions by income are increasing. Since 1952, the NES surveys have asked respondents their family income, how they have voted in the presidential and House elections, and their party identification. Using these results, we can group respondents into roughly thirds of the income distribution—high, medium, and low. We can then examine how party support varies by income group and how that difference has changed over time.

Table 4-1 presents those results with respondents grouped by decades for ease of presentation and interpretation. For this table, only those who identify themselves as white are included.

The data in Table 4-1 show two important trends. First, while many political scientists argue that class divisions are now less than in prior years, Table 4-1 shows that class divisions in the 1950s and 1960s were not very large. In the 1950s, for example, 42 percent of whites in the bottom third of the income distribution voted for the Democratic presidential candidate and 38 percent of those in the upper third voted Democratic, for a difference of only 4 percentage points. The differences by class in partisan voting for House candidates and in party identification were small as well. The "past"— at least the 1950s and 1960s—were not times of significant class divisions in American politics.[16]

Second, compared to the 1950s–1960s, the differences between the bottom and top thirds in the income distribution have increased in recent years. The differences are not large—an issue to be discussed later—but are clearly greater now than before. While there can be disputes about how big a division has to be before it is significant, the evidence indicates that class political divisions have gotten larger over time. Recent decades show an increase, not a decline, in class divisions in American politics.

This increase in class divisions is not just a result of analyzing whites. When those who identify themselves as non-white are included, as they are in Table 4-2, the divisions are slightly greater than when just whites are considered. Non-whites, on average, make less money, and are more likely to be in the middle or bottom thirds of the income distribution. They are also much more likely to vote Democratic. The result is greater divisions in presidential vote, House vote, and party identification for every decade.[17] Including non-whites in the analysis only increases rather than decreases evidence of a class cleavage in electoral behavior.

TABLE 4-1	Democratic Support by Income: Percent Voting for and Identifying with Democrats, by Decade, Whites Only, 1950s–2000s								
DECADE	Presidential Voting			House Election Voting			Party Identification		
INCOME	Low	High	Diff	Low	High	Diff	Low	High	Diff
1950s	42	38	4	56	48	8	51	43	8
1960s	49	47	2	56	52	4	50	41	9
1970s	42	33	9	61	49	12	44	32	12
1980s	46	30	16	62	48	14	42	30	12
1990s	54	38	16	52	41	11	39	27	12
2000s	51	41	10	53	41	12	35	25	10
Change	9	3	6	-3	-7	4	-16	-18	2

Notes: Decades are defined here and for Table 4-2 as follows: 1950s: 1952–1958, 1960s: 1960–1968, 1970s: 1970–1978, 1980s: 1980–1988, 1990s: 1990–1998, 2000s: 2000–2004. The percentages for voting are the actual Democratic percentage of the total vote, not just of the two-party vote. For party identification, the percentages are for those who strongly or weakly identify as Democrats, or who lean to the Democratic Party. Results are the averages of different years within each decade. All years are used, which means the 1990s consist of 1992 and 1996 for presidential results and 1990, 1992, 1994, 1996, and 1998 for House elections and party identification.

Numbers are the percent indicating they either voted for Democrats in the presidential (vcf0705) and House elections (vcf0707), or identified with the Democratic party (vcf0303).The percentages for each year within a decade are averaged. To derive the groupings of low and high (bottom and top third) of income groupings, the groupings of family income for each year were recoded so that those in the 0–33 percentile were in the bottom third, and those in the 66–100 percentile were coded as top third. The 2002 survey did not provide detailed groupings similar to those used in previous years. The variable recording income for 2002 provides groupings very similar to the 1948–2000 grouping. Only whites are included because for the last several decades their behavior has been the primary concern. To derive the ideology response groupings, scores of 1–3 were grouped as liberal, while those 5–7 were grouped as conservative. Those with a score of 4 are coded as moderate.

Sources: The data are taken from the National Election Studies files for 1952–2002. The American National Election Studies (www.electionstudies.org). The 1948–2004 NES Cumulative Data file [dataset]. Stanford University and the University of Michigan [producers and distributors], 2005.

LIMITS ON CLASS DIVISIONS IN AMERICAN SOCIETY

While class divisions are greater now than they were in the 1950s–1960s, two questions persist about the extent of class divisions in American politics. The first question is why class divisions are not greater than they currently are. Why doesn't the bottom third of the income distribution support the Democratic Party at even higher levels than it presently does? In recent decades inequality has grown and the parties are further apart on economic issues, yet many would regard the class divisions shown in the 1990s and 2000s as modest, especially given the

TABLE 4-2	Democratic Support by Income: Percent Voting for and Identifying with Democrats, by Decade, 1950s–2000s (All Respondents)								
DECADE	Presidential Voting			House Election Voting			Party Identification		
INCOME	Low	High	Diff	Low	High	Diff	Low	High	Diff
1950s	44	38	6	57	49	9	53	43	10
1960s	54	49	5	60	53	7	53	42	11
1970s	52	36	16	66	52	14	49	34	15
1980s	56	34	22	68	51	17	48	33	15
1990s	65	42	23	66	44	22	45	29	16
2000s	59	44	15	60	44	16	40	29	11
Change	15	6	9	3	-5	7	-13	-14	1

Notes: See notes to Table 4-1.

Source: The data are taken from The American National Election Studies (www.electionstudies.org). The 1948–2004 NES Cumulative Data file [dataset]. Stanford University and the University of Michigan [producers and distributors], 2005.

trends just mentioned. The second question is why, given the general trend toward greater divisions, has the extent of the class division been so erratic from election to election? As will be shown later, the division fluctuates. Both questions raise issues about the importance of any existing class division.

With regard to the differences in Democratic support between those with low and high incomes, individualism in American culture is key. Surveys indicate that many in our society believe that individual effort largely influences whether or not someone succeeds. In a 2004 poll, respondents were asked what factors affect what people achieve and whether hard work can overcome initial disadvantages.[18] The results, presented in Table 4-3, indicate just how much people believe that individuals create their own fate. Only 7 percent responded that "what you achieve in life depends largely on family background," while 61 percent say abilities and hard work are dominant. In addition, 82 percent agree that "hard work and perseverance can usually overcome differences in opportunities."

People not only believe that hard work can overcome disadvantages, but they are generally optimistic about how much mobility is possible and actually occurs. As Table 4-4 indicates, 35 percent believe there is a

TABLE 4-3   **Individualism in American Culture**

Do you think what you achieve in life depends largely on your family background, or on your abilities and hard work?

Family background	7.4
Both	29.6
Abilities and hard work	60.8
No opinion	2.2

Would you agree or disagree with the following: While people may begin with different opportunities, hard work and perseverance can usually overcome those disadvantages.

Agree	82.4
Disagree	13.1
No opinion	4.5

Source: Maxwell School Poll on Inequality and Civic Engagement, 2004.

lot of upward mobility, and only 10 percent believe there is not much. In contrast, there is less pessimism about downward mobility. Only 17 percent see a lot. Fifty-seven percent of Americans see themselves as better off than their parents and only 17 percent see themselves as worse off. Finally, 62 percent think their economic situation will be better off in the next several years and only 10 percent think they will be worse off. The public generally believes they are better off than their parents and will do better in the future. Inequality may be growing, but that has not yet dampened optimism about the future. Belief in the continuing existence of the American Dream remains strong, even as reality might suggest otherwise.

While there may be considerable overall support for the view that individual effort determines achievement and future prospects are good, the important matter is whether these views vary by income. If the more affluent are optimistic and the less affluent are not, it could create a basis for significant class conflict.

Table 4-5 presents responses to questions about views about opportunity, inequality, and future prospects by family income levels of

TABLE 4-4	Optimism about Economic Mobility and the Future

How much upward mobility—children doing better than the family they come from—do you think there is in America: a lot, some, or not much?

A lot	34.8
Some	53.0
Not much	10.4
No opinion	1.7

How about downward mobility in America—children doing worse than the family they come from—is there a lot, some, or not much?

A lot	16.9
Some	54.1
Not much	24.9
No opinion	4.2

Compared to your parents, are you better off economically, about the same, or worse off?

Better	57.3
Same	24.1
Worse	16.5
No response	2.1

Over the next several years, do you think your economic situation is likely to improve, stay the same, or get worse?

Improve	61.6
Stay the same	23.3
Get worse	9.9
No response	5.3

Source: *Maxwell School Poll on Inequality and Civic Engagement*, 2004.

respondents. Those with lower incomes are more likely to think just some have the opportunity to succeed, they are more likely to see inequality as a serious problem, and are more likely to believe that family background affects success. They are less likely to say they are better off than their parents and they are less likely to say they think things will be better in the future. But it is just as important to note that those making less than $50,000 in 2004 are not terribly negative about these matters and they are not dramatically different from those making more than $100,000. For example, 74.8 percent of those making $100,000 or more think their economic situation will better, but 56.0 percent of those making less than $50,000 also think this. The difference is almost 19 percent percentage points, which is fairly modest. Most important, all income strata are much more positive than negative about their future situation. If there was a strong sense among the less affluent that individuals do not have much opportunity it might make it easier for Democrats to make an appeal about the need for programs to create more opportunity and attract more of the less affluent, which would create greater class divisions.

The less affluent are not negative about their situation in the American economy. A majority believes that all or most in America have an opportunity for success and that hard work determines success. Most Americans believe they will be better off in the future. While inequality has been growing for over three decades and there is considerable evidence that those in the bottom half are not experiencing income gains, there is still considerable optimism about the prospects for the future within the country. That optimism about future economic prospects tempers, but does not by any means eliminate, class political divisions in our society.[19] If inequality continues to increase, this confidence in the efficacy of hard work and the faith in future prospects may erode in the future.

THE POLITICAL DEBATE ABOUT INEQUALITY

These survey results suggest why some do not see class issues as being of greater relevance in American politics. During the 1980s and 1990s it was common to read analyses arguing that class divisions were declining and less relevant to American political debates.[20] That argument continues, with current commentary suggesting that issues of inequality are not a part of contemporary debates,[21] and that the "cultural wars" have displaced conflicts over class and inequality.[22] These commentators suggest that inequality is not a highly salient issue in American politics and doesn't enter into the political debate over government's role in society.

Despite such claims and the faith in individualism, divisions of opinion about opportunity in America do affect political choices. Liberals and

TABLE 4-5	Family Income and Views of Existence of Opportunity

| FAMILY INCOME | How many have opportunity to succeed? | | |
	Everyone	Most	Just some
Under $50,000	26.4	44.3	27.9
$50,000–99,999	28.8	50.5	20.2
$100,000 plus	23.1	58.5	15.4

| | How much of a problem is inequality? | | |
	Serious	Somewhat	Not much
Under $50,000	46.1	45.7	8.2
$50,000–99,999	33.3	43.1	22.1
$100,000 plus	32.5	38.6	25.4

| | What determines success? | | |
	Family	Both	Hard work
Under $50,000	10.8	22.5	65.2
$50,000–99,999	6.1	25.7	67.4
$100,000 plus	2.0	38.0	59.3

| | Economic situation compared to parents? | | |
	Better	Same	Worse
Under $50,000	46.3	25.0	27.8
$50,000–99,999	51.7	26.2	17.5
$100,000 plus	68.6	18.5	13.0

| | Expected future economic situation? | | |
	Better	Same	Worse
Under $50,000	56.0	23.8	15.4
$50,000–99,999	66.9	24.1	6.1
$100,000 plus	74.8	17.9	5.0

Source: Maxwell School Poll on Inequality and Civic Engagement, 2004. "No opinion" responses not included.

conservatives and Democrats and Republicans differ about how much opportunity there is and those differences have a significant impact on partisan voting. As Table 4-6 indicates, Democrats and liberals see opportunity as less widespread than Republicans and conservatives do. Further,

TABLE 4-6	Political Ideology and Party Identification and View of Existence of Opportunity (Percentages sum across for each category)

POLITICAL IDEOLOGY	How many have opportunity to succeed?		
	Everyone	Most	Just some
Liberal	14.0	43.9	42.1
Moderate	21.1	58.8	18.6
Conservative	43.1	44.2	11.1
PARTY IDENTIFICATION	Everyone	Most	Just some
Democrat	17.9	49.0	33.2
Independent	18.3	56.5	23.5
Republican	42.8	47.3	8.5

Source: Maxwell School Poll on Inequality and Civic Engagement, 2004.

Democrats are increasingly likely to be liberals and Republicans are likely to be conservatives.[23] The concentration of liberals and conservatives in the Democratic and Republicans Parties, respectively, results in parties which present very different arguments about the existence of equality in society and the need for programs to respond to these concerns.[24]

Inequality and Presidential Choices

These differences between Democrats and Republicans also affect partisan voting. In an October 2004 poll respondents were asked which presidential candidate they were planning on supporting. Those results are shown in Table 4-7. Those who did not see inequality as increasing supported George Bush 61.0 percent to 23.5 percent. Those who saw it as increasing dropped almost 18 percent points in their support for Bush. Those who thought America has become a society of the haves and have-nots supported John Kerry 49.6 percent to 32.6 percent, while those who disagree with this view were strong supporters of Bush, 76.9 percent to 10.2 percent. The perception of the opportunity to succeed also affected partisan support. Those with a positive view of the opportunity to succeed supported Bush 65.6 to 16.9, while those who see limited opportunity supported Kerry 60.8 to 23.2. Those who saw inequality as a serious problem were supportive of Kerry, while those not seeing it as a serious

TABLE 4-7	Inequality Issues and Presidential Vote Choice (Percentages sum across, representing choice by indicated opinion)			
	George Bush	John Kerry	Other	No Choice
Changes in income inequality?				
Increased	43.4	42.6	1.9	12.2
Stayed the same	61.0	23.5	3.0	12.5
Have we become society of haves and have-nots?				
Yes	32.6	49.6	4.1	13.7
No	76.9	10.2	0	12.9
Opportunity to succeed in America?				
Everyone	65.6	16.9	3.1	14.4
Most	43.7	40.7	1.9	13.7
Just some	23.2	60.8	5.6	10.4
How serious is inequality as a problem?				
Serious	23.7	57.3	4.3	14.7
Somewhat serious	53.9	31.0	2.6	12.5
Not much of a problem	78.6	9.5	1.1	10.7
Should government do more to reduce inequality?				
Yes	32.6	49.6	4.1	13.7
No	76.9	10.2	0	12.9

Source: Maxwell School Poll on Inequality and Civic Engagement, 2004.

problem were strong supporters of Bush. The result is that a candidate such as George Bush realizes that he has a constituency less troubled by inequality, and the party can propose policies more in accord with an individualistic view of society. Democrats, with an electoral base much more troubled about inequality, continually criticize such policies and charge that the growing inequality is being ignored. The ongoing public dialogue about inequality is organized around parties and ideology.

THE IMPORTANCE OF SHORT-TERM EVENTS

The second issue involves the likely trend in class divisions in the future. While views on inequality certainly affect individual electoral behavior, and class divisions are now greater than they were 30 to 40 years ago, election-to-election variations in class divisions raise questions about

FIGURE 4-4	Class Divisions in Presidential Voting, 1952–2004 (All Respondents)

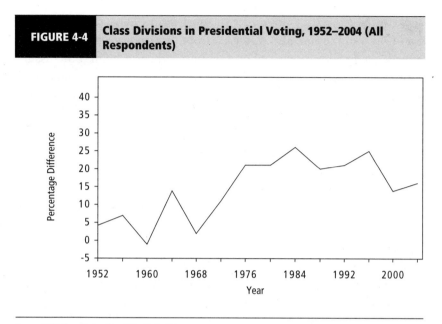

Source: NES Cumulative Data File, 1948–2004.

whether this division will continue to exist. The divisions in presidential elections, shown in Figure 4-4, illustrate these variations. After reaching the level of a 21-point difference between the top and bottom thirds in 1976, there was little further increase from 1980 through 1996. Then in 2000, the difference declined to 14 points and in 2004 it was 16 points. The lack of growth in the class cleavage over the past few years occurred at a time when the press was filled with accusations by Democrats that tax cuts proposed by Bush had provided bigger benefits to the affluent. Does this lack of growth suggest that any conflict surrounding class peaked in the 1990s and has been displaced by other factors, such as cultural issues?

Two responses are relevant here. First, few political trends proceed uninfluenced by external current events, and during the last two elections short-term factors may have intruded. Indeed, we strongly suspect short-term factors—the September 11, 2001, attacks and the ongoing war in Iraq—dampened the extent of the class cleavage in 2002 and 2004.[25] Second, once we examine the role of income while controlling for other matters, there is no decline in the role of income.

With regard to the importance of short-term events, divisions evolve over time, but they are also displaced from time to time by the intrusion of an issue that dominates public attention and overwhelms other issues. In 1998 Republicans chose to impeach and try Bill Clinton. Voters divided sharply on these actions, with some strongly favoring the efforts and others strongly opposing the actions. As a result, voters set aside many other bases of reactions to the parties and voting was driven largely by reactions to impeachment.[26] Class declined significantly in relevance in House elections that year.

Campaigns also can dampen class divisions. When George Bush ran for the presidency in 2000, he consistently presented himself as a "compassionate conservative" and as an advocate of the "No Child Left Behind" Act. Both positions probably reduced the extent to which he was seen as conservative and lowered the extent of class divisions in the election. Other short-term factors affected the 2004 election. George W. Bush had become a polarizing presidential leader, but his positions on class issues were completely overshadowed by the Iraq War. Table 4-8 indicates how much views on the war affected voting. The first column indicates the percentage of whites within each income group who voted for George Bush. The overall difference between the low and high-income groups was 11.2 percentage points. What dominated voter's choices was how they felt about Iraq. Those who disapproved of the war uniformly voted against Bush, regardless of class. Those who approved voted uniformly and overwhelmingly for Bush, regardless of class. The result was a modest overall division by class.

TABLE 4-8	Republican Presidential Vote by Income, and by Reaction to the Iraq War (All Respondents)		
		Reaction to Iraq War	
INCOME THIRD	**Whites**	**Disapprove**	**Approve**
Low	51.2	26.4	96.6
Middle	61.5	30.2	93.0
High	62.4	31.2	98.8
Difference	11.2	4.8	2.2

Source: The National Election Studes. The 2004 National Election Study [dataset]. Ann Arbor, MI: University of Michigan, Center for Political Studies [producer and distributor], 2005.

CONCLUSION

These short-term factors significantly affected the division of partisan support between lower and higher income individuals. Are class divisions still significant after we control for other factors? We will review more detailed results in Chapter 8, when we assess the joint effects of class and cultural issues, we see how, but suffice it to say at this point that the relationships between income and voting for presidential and house candidates and party identification follow the same pattern as shown in Figure 4-2. The relationship is greater in the last two decades than for the 1950s and 1960s. It increases in the 1980s and remains higher than in the 1950s and 1960s, with fluctuations as other issues intrude.[27] To understand this relationship, however, we must first examine the rise and role of cultural issues, which many see as suppressing class issues. We turn to the emergence and effects of cultural issues next.

CHAPTER 5

THE RISE OF CULTURAL ISSUES: TRENDS AND DEVELOPMENTS IN AMERICAN SOCIETY

The previous three chapters have been devoted to class—the developments in American society that have kept class concerns alive and relevant, the response of the political parties to these concerns, and, finally, how voters have reacted to both class concerns and the parties' responses to these concerns. But this book is about cultural as well as class issues, and this chapter reintroduces cultural issues to the analysis. Recall Pat Buchanan's declarations in Chapter 1 that America was in the midst of a "cultural war," a "struggle for the soul of America." Buchanan likely found the rhetoric to express his sentiments in *Culture Wars: The Struggle to Define America*, the now famous book by University of Virginia sociologist James Davison Hunter. Because Hunter's thinking is so important to the debate over cultural politics in the United States, it is useful to once again quote him here:

> *I define cultural conflict very simply as political and social hostility rooted in different systems of moral understanding. The end to which these hostilities tend is the domination of one cultural and moral ethos over all others. Let it be clear, the principles and ideals that mark these competing systems of moral understanding are by no means trifling but always have a character of ultimacy to them. They are not merely attitudes that can change on a whim but basic commitments and beliefs that provide a source of identity, purpose, and togetherness for the people who live by them. It is for precisely this reason that political*

*action rooted in these principles and ideals tends to be so pas-
sionate.... Because this is a culture war, the nub of political disagreement today...can be traced ultimately and finally to the
matter of moral authority. By moral authority I mean the basis
by which people determine whether something is good or bad,
right or wrong, acceptable or unacceptable, and so on. Of course,
people often have very different ideas about what criteria to use
in making moral judgments, but this is just the point. It is the
commitment to different and opposing bases of moral authority
and the world views that derive from them that creates the deep
cleavages between antagonists in the contemporary culture war.*[1]

Hunter, and many other political observers have little doubt that conflict over cultural issues drives contemporary American politics. Just
what is the status of cultural issues in the United States? If cultural issues
are to dominate American politics, cultural issues must first develop
within American society. In other words, societal change leading some
citizens to mobilize politically in response is a necessary precondition.
Cultural conflict cannot become central if there are no cultural issues to
fight over.

We need not worry about such a scenario. The United States has
undergone major social change over the last half century in such central
areas of American life and culture as public education, the media, sexuality and reproduction, gender roles, and family relations. Many of these
changes have unfolded in ways that have made some Americans very
uncomfortable and worried about the future.[2] We note at the outset that
there is no normative component to our discussion of these changes. We
neither applaud nor denounce these developments. We simply present
them to the reader as part of the larger effort to gauge the importance of
cultural issues in American politics.

Look again at the quotation from Hunter that begins this chapter. If he
is correct, then political battle in the United States is currently being
waged over ground that is both basic and profoundly important. Indeed,
for Hunter, as well as other analysts, the culture war is a fight over nothing less than what it means to be American.[3] Given this possibility of
heated conflict over the national identity, it is perhaps surprising that

fifty years ago very few people would have seen this fight coming. Going back to the mid-1950s, the issues at the forefront of today's cultural conflict—abortion, homosexual rights, prayer in public schools, sex in the media, proper models of family life—simply were not on the agenda. Going even further, with the exception of an ongoing, although at that point somewhat quieted, debate over the place of women in society, the vast majority of today's cultural issues were viewed by the bulk of Americans as settled, with little need of revisiting. This is not to say that public discussion over some cultural issues—such as abortion, sex education in public schools, the place of prayer in public schools, or proper models of family life—did not take place prior to the past few decades. We know that these issues were fodder for public debate in the nineteenth and early twentieth centuries.[4] But in much the same way that class concerns were seen as having retreated from the national agenda in the 1950s, cultural issues simply were not on the radar screens of the American public in that decade. This situation has obviously changed.

RELIGION IN SCHOOLS

Prayer in public schools was the first cultural issue thrust into the American political spotlight. Organized religion and education share a long history in the United States, and conflict over the proper relationship between the two goes back to the earliest days of American public schools.[5] However, most of these conflicts involved questions of how religion would be present in public classrooms, not whether it should be present. Most Americans supported prayer and other forms of religious expression in schools, and accepted such practices as givens.

Indeed, the practice of prayer in schools was widespread. Surveying public school elementary teachers in 1964 and 1965, political scientist H. Frank Way Jr. found that 71 percent of these teachers conducted some form of prayer in their classrooms prior to 1962. Other religious practices, such as Bible reading, hymn singing, and the saying of grace were common as well.[6]

This all began to change with the Supreme Court's decision in *Engel v. Vitale* in 1962. *Engel* centered on a prayer prepared by the New York State Board of Regents for discretionary use in the state's public schools. The prayer read: "Almighty God, we acknowledge our dependence upon

Thee, and we beg Thy blessing upon us, our parents, our teachers, and our Country."[7] Complaints about the prayer from parents in one school district eventually resulted in the matter going before the Supreme Court in 1962. In a decision that stunned observers, the Court ruled that prayer in public schools violated the Establishment Clause of the First Amendment, and was thus unconstitutional. Prayer was no longer allowed in public schools. The Court followed a year later with a ruling that also banned Bible reading in the classroom in *Abington School District v. Schempp* (1963).

Disapproval of the Court's decisions on prayer and Bible reading was strong and widespread among both the general public and political elites—especially members of Congress.[8] A solid majority of Americans supported prayer in public schools, a fact that remains true today.[9] But the Court ruled that the practice was out. And despite the widespread public unhappiness and the Court's lack of enforcement powers, prayer in public schools slowly but surely declined.[10] While the practice does still remain today in some locales in the United States,[11] the Court has clearly rendered prayer in the public schools illegal in just about all conceivable circumstances. Even in those classrooms where prayer is still conducted, the reality is that one phone call by an unhappy parent, teacher, or student to the ACLU would likely be enough to stop the practice. Even having a moment of silence in the school day that might allow for private, silent prayer has been ruled unconstitutional.[12] For those Americans who feel that God and religion properly belong in public schools, though, these developments are clearly problematic.

SEX EDUCATION

At the same time prayer and the Bible were being removed from public schools, sex was being brought in. Or at least sex education was. Now, it is true that attempts to include sex education in America's public classrooms were not unique to the 1960s. As far back as the first decade of the twentieth century well-organized efforts to educate public school students in matters of sexuality were underway. In fact, a survey sponsored by the United States Public Health Service found that in 1920 40 percent of the responding public high schools provided at least some kind of sex education to their students.[13] However, the sex education of the 1920s, where it existed, would be considered quaint by today's standards. The most prevalent topics discussed were the biology of reproduction and personal hygiene—especially the dangers of prostitution and venereal disease—and while discussions moved away from sex as somehow dirty, they emphasized remaining chaste until marriage. In addition, support for sex education in the schools declined in the decades after the 1920s, as did its presence.[14]

The sex education that began to appear in classrooms during the 1960s was different from the earlier programs. In 1964, Dr. Mary Calderone, then medical director of Planned Parenthood, and four other prominent family life professionals founded SIECUS, the Sex Information and Education Council of the United States. The primary purpose of this organization, according to its founders, was to responsibly prepare young Americans for their sexual adulthoods.[15] Early support for SEICUS was strong, and sex education programs began to appear in an increasing number of America's public schools. While the curriculum taught varied by individual school, a number of institutions added topics such as homosexuality, masturbation, premarital sex, and contraception to the more standard fare of reproductive biology, dating, and marriage.[16] As Janice M. Irvine points out, the material being presented in most schools was not terribly radical in nature, especially compared to what was transpiring in the larger sexual revolution of the 1960s that was exploding throughout society at approximately the same time.[17] However, the material in question was quite radical in comparison to what had been presented in American classrooms prior to the 1960s, and it wasn't long before sex education made some Americans quite angry.

The protests against sex education started out locally in the late 1960s, but it did not take long for national organizations and figures to get involved, especially once they saw the protestors' depth of emotion. One of the first national actors to join the fray was Christian Crusade, an evangelical organization founded and directed by the Reverend Billy James Hargis. Hargis's organization published a widely popular pamphlet in 1968—*Is the Schoolhouse the Best Place to Teach Raw Sex?*—written by Crusade official Gordon Drake.[18] By the late 1960s a conservative movement against sex education in public schools was well underway, and battles over what should be talked about in school broke out all over the country, with confrontations often getting heated, and sometimes even violent.[19]

These battles continue today, and the question of how—or for some, *if*—sex education should be conducted in public schools remains open. On the one hand, some form of sex education in public schools has become almost universal. According to a series of surveys of students conducted by the Kaiser Family Foundation in 1998 and 1999, 89 percent of public school students say that they receive some form of sex education in school between seventh and twelfth grade.[20] Jacqueline Darroch and colleagues report a similar figure from a 1999 national survey of public school teachers, with 93 percent of respondents saying their school offered sex ed between seventh and twelfth grade.[21] On the other hand, there has been a dramatic movement in recent years away from comprehensive sex education programs to programs that focus exclusively on abstinence.[22] In the same Kaiser Family Foundation report cited above, 34 percent of public secondary school principals surveyed in 1999 said that their school's program was one of abstinence only,[23] while Darroch et al.'s teacher survey revealed that 23 percent of sex education teachers taught abstinence only in 1999, a figure up from 2 percent in 1988.[24] While the increase in abstinence-only programs certainly pleases cultural conservatives, many opponents of sex education in schools remain unhappy, and often argue that talking and providing information about sex to students causes them to actually engage in sexual activity that they otherwise would avoid.[25] The increase in the number of abstinence-only programs seems to indicate that criticisms providing information about sex results in increased sex are having an impact.[26] The fight over sex education in America's public schools is not yet settled, and it has assumed a prominent place in the American culture wars.[27]

SEX IN POPULAR MEDIA

If kids are unable to get enough information about sex from the classroom, they can certainly turn to the media. Anyone who turns on the television or peruses the selections at a newsstand cannot help but recognize the abundance of sexual content in the media. And kids do get a good portion of their sexual information from the media. A Kaiser Family Foundation study of teens aged 13–18 in 1998 found that 40 percent of the respondents got sexual health information from television and the movies, and 35 percent got such information from magazines. These figures were smaller than the percentages for friends (61 percent) and sex education classes in school (44 percent) as sources of information, but larger than the percentage for parents (32 percent).[28]

When Americans of today turn their eyes or ears to the media, what sexual content do they see and hear? The short answers are a lot—and a lot more than even in the recent past. We will concentrate on television, as it remains young people's top media choice.[29] According to a comprehensive study of the entire television landscape conducted during 2004–2005, 70 percent of non-news, non-sports, and non-children's television shows contained some sexual content. Sixty-eight percent of these same shows contained talk about sex, while 35 percent portrayed some form of sexual behavior, including 11 percent of shows where sexual intercourse was "either depicted or strongly implied." Those shows with sexual content averaged 5.0 scenes with sexual messages per hour. In addition, much of the sexual content emphasizes the fun and pleasure in sex, with much less focus on the risks and responsibilities. Programs directed at "teens" were no less likely to contain sexual content, with 70 percent of these shows having some form of sexual language or depiction in them.[30]

So we know there is a good deal of sexual content on TV today, but how does this compare with the past? Unfortunately empirical analyses of this question are scarce.[31] No study of which we are aware goes back to the 1950s, or even to the 1960s. The best data available comes from a 1996 study by Dale Kunkel and colleagues that examined the sexual content of a sample of broadcast network programming during "family hour"—8:00–9:00 p.m. Eastern Time—for the fall seasons in 1976, 1986, and 1996. While the hours of programming analyzed in this study were limited, especially so for 1976 and 1986, the results are still quite telling. In 1976, 43 percent of the shows broadcast during family hour contained some sexual content. In 1986, this figure reached 65 percent, and by 1996 the number had grown to 75 percent. In 1976, the average number of "sexual interactions" per hour was 2.3. In 1996, the figure was 8.5. And while it is true that the most common sexual behaviors shown involved mostly innocuous flirting or kissing, there were 15 instances per hour of sexual intercourse depicted or strongly implied in 1996. There were no such depictions in either the 1976 or the 1986 sample.[32] But do we really need a study to understand how much sex on television has changed over the last 50 years? Consider two of the most popular situation comedies of all time—*The Andy Griffith Show*, which aired on CBS from 1960–1968, and *Seinfeld*, which was broadcast by NBC from 1990–1998. Both shows are still regularly shown, so any readers who are unfamiliar with them can easily sample an episode. As any *Seinfeld* fan will readily tell you, "The Contest," one of the most popular episodes of the show, centered on a wager among central characters Jerry Seinfeld, George Costanza, Cosmo Kramer, and Elaine Benes as to who could last the longest amount of time without masturbating. This contest was the center of the episode, and was frequently discussed throughout. The thought of Andy Taylor, Barney Fife, and Gomer Pyle (central characters in *The Andy Griffith Show*) sitting around Aunt Bee's table and discussing such a wager is unthinkable.

While television is most often the focus when sexual content in the media is discussed, it is, of course, not the only outlet where the amount of such content has increased. Popular music, long a target of those concerned about sexual content, has certainly become more risqué in recent years, in both its lyrics and especially its music videos.[33] Video games, which 92 percent of kids aged 2–17 now play,[34] also sometimes contain sexual content, as evidenced by the recent controversy involving the game "Grand Theft Auto: San Andreas."[35] Magazines, which were already a cause of concern regarding their sexual content in the 1970s,[36] now regularly contain high levels of sexual content. Consider the following titles taken from the August 2005 tables of contents of two magazines popular among teenaged girls, *Cosmo Girl* and *Seventeen*: "Quiz: Should You Ask Him Out?," "FREE 32-Page Horoscope Booklet: Predictions on Love, Lust, Friends, and Money," and "Kissing Secrets: Guys Reveal What They Love." And although Howard Stern moved to satellite radio in January 2006, he previously brought sexual content to the radio airwaves for many years, and spawned a large number of imitators. Even this brief listing only encompasses the mainstream media; it does not take into account more hardcore content that is considered pornography.[37] With its actions since the 1950s, the Supreme Court has removed almost all restrictions on material that can be disseminated,[38] and pornography is now widely and easily available. Walk into many video stores, or easier yet, get onto the Internet and a wide array of pornographic material is instantly accessible. While information on the pornography industry is somewhat difficult to obtain and notoriously unreliable, some estimates place the revenue generated by pornography at between $10 and $14 billion per year, and a recent study puts the number of pornographic websites at 420 million, an increase from 14 million in 1998.[39]

Sexual content is clearly out there in the media. In fact, it would be difficult to avoid. And that, for some Americans, is a problem. Many people who express concern for the amount of sex in the media are particularly concerned about the possible effects of this content on children, worrying either that children may be exposed to something that upsets them, or even more problematic, that exposure to such material might make children more likely to engage in sexual activity themselves.[40] And, indeed, some evidence supports this concern. A study published in the September 2004 issue of *Pediatrics*, the official journal of the American Academy of Pediatrics, found that "adolescents who viewed more sexual content at baseline were more likely to initiate intercourse and progress to more advanced noncoital sexual activities in the subsequent year, controlling for respondent characteristics that might otherwise explain these relationships."[41] Concerns about exactly such effects fuel the anger of many Americans toward the amount of sexual content in the media.

ABORTION

One of the favorite targets of cultural conservatives in the United States is "activist" federal judges in general, and the Supreme Court specifically. The school prayer decision outlined earlier in this chapter is one major cause of such complaints. Recent decisions on homosexual rights are another. No Court action, however, has even come close to sparking the ire and outrage that resulted from the 1973 decision in *Roe v. Wade*. As Hunter noted in his follow up to *Culture Wars*, "Abortion remains the knottiest moral and political dilemma of the larger culture war, contested now for more than two decades with little hope of a satisfying resolution."[42] No cultural issue looms larger.

That abortion is central to cultural conflict is perhaps the least surprising statement in this book. Everyone knows abortion is a hot-button issue in the United States, and has been for some time. However, it is important to remember that the decision in *Roe* was shocking in 1973. With one stroke—really two, if you include the companion decision in *Doe v. Bolton*—the Supreme Court invalidated the abortion laws of all fifty states. Involved parties on both sides of the issue were stunned at the breadth of the decision, as was the nation as a whole. Anti-abortion forces mobilized quickly in response to *Roe* and mounted a strong pro-life movement, and they were met relatively soon thereafter by an equally vigorous and committed pro-choice effort.[43] Abortion soon became a—many would say *the*—symbolic issue to those individuals at the polar opposites of opinion on this issue, making compromise and constructive dialogue nearly impossible.[44] For pro-choice individuals, abortion is about the right of women to make decisions regarding their bodies without outside interference. For those on the pro-life side, abortion is the termination of human life and, therefore, murder. For those at the poles, there is no gray area, no negotiation, and ultimately no compromise.

Just how prevalent is abortion is in the United States? Figure 5-1 presents the number of abortions performed per 100 live births in the United States from 1970–2001. A few caveats about the data. The data prior to 1974 must be taken with a grain of salt. Most the abortions performed prior to *Roe* were illegal and, therefore, not officially recorded. While Figure 5-1 shows only about 5 abortions per 100 live births in 1970, Dallas A. Blanchard reports estimates of at least 1 million illegal abortions per year pre-*Roe*,[45] which, if true, would make the figure for 1970 shown in the graph much higher. It also bears noting that California, among other states, has not reported any abortion data since 1997. Given that California has the largest population of any state in the nation, it is possible that the decline in the abortion rate since 1998 shown in the graph is not real.

With these pieces of information in mind, Figure 5-1 shows that since the decision in *Roe*, there have been approximately 25 to 35 abortions per 100 live births per year in the United States.[46] This is a relatively high figure. Whether or not this represents a dramatic change from the pre-*Roe* years is unclear, and certainly a matter of debate. But

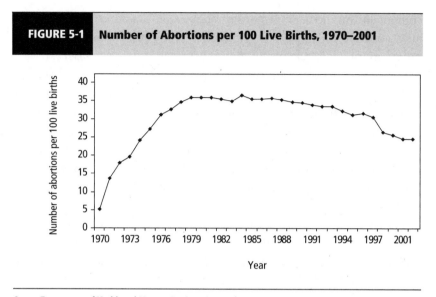

FIGURE 5-1 Number of Abortions per 100 Live Births, 1970–2001

Source: Department of Health and Human Services, Centers for Disease Control and Prevention, *Morbidity and Mortality Weekly Report, Abortion Surveillance—United States, 2001*, November 26, 2004, vol. 53, no. SS-9.

it is true that abortion now is a much more public matter. The Centers for Disease Control and Prevention gather and publish data on the procedure. Anyone who wants to know how many abortions are performed each year simply has to open a book or go to a Web site. There is also no doubt that the *Roe* decision made abortions much safer, easier, and cheaper to obtain.[47] Before 1973, an abortion was very difficult for most women to obtain. That is not true today. Even with the restrictions some states have imposed in the wake of the Court's decisions in *Webster v. Reproductive Health Services* (1989) and *Planned Parenthood v. Casey* (1992), most women can obtain an abortion without great difficulty if they choose to have one.[48] Abortion is a very salient issue, with strong and highly committed activists on both sides. It will not be leaving the public arena any time soon.

THE ROLE OF WOMEN IN SOCIETY

Part of the power of the abortion issue in the United States lies in the multiple ways it links to other issues on the cultural politics agenda. Many abortion opponents see clear connections between some of the issues we have discussed thus far in this chapter—sex education, sexual content in the media, and pornography—and abortion. The view that abortion both opens the door to and results from dramatic declines in sexual morality is relatively common among cultural conservatives.[49] Perhaps the most common connection is between abortion and another issue on the cultural agenda—the proper role of women in American society. Some observers have noted that for many people opposed to abortion, their opposition is about much more than protecting what they see as human life. Abortion also raises questions about motherhood, the traditional division of labor between the sexes, and the proper raising of children. In short, abortion also entails questions about women's place in the modern world.[50]

Perhaps the most dramatic social changes of the twentieth century altered the role of women in American society.[51] Despite the first wave of the American women's movement in the nineteenth century, the successful culmination of the drive for suffrage in the early twentieth century, and the critical role played by women during World War II, in the late 1940s the proper role of the American woman was widely thought to be much the same as it had been throughout the nation's history: wife and mother. Sure, women worked outside the home, but overwhelmingly their jobs took second place to those of their husbands, and work was supposed to be put on hold—if not stopped for good— once children came into the picture.

However, this view began to change in the 1950s. The traditional view of women only as wives and mothers started to decline. A number of developments—such as the introduction of bottle-feeding as an alternative to breast-feeding, increases in the duration of both the school day and the school year, and dramatic improvements in contraception, most notably "the pill"—increasingly freed women from what Ethel Klein has termed "motherwork."[52] With Betty Freidan labeling the traditional American home a "comfortable concentration camp" for women in *The Feminist Mystique* (1963),[53] the second wave of the women's movement began in earnest during the 1960s.[54]

As Figure 5-2 shows, women's participation in the paid labor force began to rise at the same time that the renewed women's movement gained momentum. The 1970s and early 1980s witnessed heated debates surrounding possible ratification of the Equal Rights Amendment

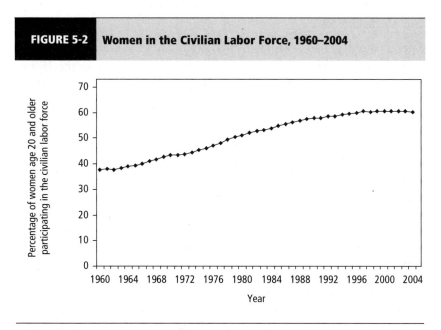

FIGURE 5-2   Women in the Civilian Labor Force, 1960–2004

Source: U.S. Census Bureau, *Current Population Surveys*, reported by United States Department of Labor, Bureau of Labor Statistics, available at data.bls.gov/PDQ/servlet/Survey/OutputServlet. Accessed 7 July, 2005.

(ERA).[55] Soon debates were not about whether women should be working, but rather why were they not earning the same amount as men for the same jobs. Gender roles blurred, and eventually no one was sure whose responsibility it was to make dinner, or wash the dishes, or handle childcare duties. Some women decided that they didn't need men at all, at least not in the long-term, and the number of single-parent (mostly single-mother) families began to rise.[56] Now, not all, or even perhaps most, of this single-parent increase is by choice, but some certainly is. And this "some" has received quite a bit of attention. Who can forget Vice President Dan Quayle's battle with Candice Bergen in 1992 after Bergen's character on the television show *Murphy Brown* chose to have a child out of wedlock?[57] While some questions about the role of women in society have been answered to most everyone's satisfaction, others clearly have not. One thing however is certain: the place of women in the first decade of the twenty-first century is dramatically different than it was in the first, or even fifth decade of the twentieth century.

THE AMERICAN FAMILY

Dan Quayle's above-noted irritation with *Murphy Brown* illustrates a larger concern, perhaps the largest concern, over culture in the United States—the status and health of family life. In many ways, each of the subjects touched in this chapter can ultimately be linked to the family—especially children—and that is in fact precisely what many cultural conservatives do. A common argument is that the removal of prayer and other forms of religion from schools harms the moral atmosphere of the schools, and therefore harms the children who attend the schools. Sex education is problematic because it increases the likelihood that children will have sex. Much of the concern with sex in the media lies with its feared impact on children. In the same way, some pornography opponents are particularly concerned with its threat to children.[58] The link of abortion and concern for family life is obvious—on both sides of the issue—as are the connections between women's role and the family. The grievances of many cultural conservatives boil down to concerns over family life and the well-being of children.[59] Consider Lorraine Fox Harding's description of what she labels "the family values lobby":

> *Broadly speaking, this viewpoint regards recent family changes such as more divorce, cohabitation, lone parenthood, and employed motherhood, as negative, and would seek to reverse such changes if possible. It aims to reinstate what is perceived as a "traditional" family form—the stable married family held together by a breadwinning male head who is also a source of authority, the family form characteristic of the 1950s, which is idealized in this viewpoint. Abortion and contraception may be opposed, as indeed may sex education, because of the freedom they allegedly give to express sexuality outside of marriage. Another element is intolerance of the expression of gay and lesbian sexuality.... A critical view is taken of feminism and its demands. Children are seen as best cared for and socialized within a permanent two-parent unit which should not be disrupted during their childhood. Obligations in families are stressed rather than individual interests or rights.[60]*

Despite the outrage, Harding is largely correct in her depiction of the concerns many cultural conservatives have with modern family life. But are these concerns—whether or not they are justified—rooted in social reality? What does the modern American family look like?

There is little doubt that the structure of American family life has seen dramatic changes over the last fifty years. As Lynne Casper and Suzanne Bianchi state, "In 1950 there was a dominant and socially acceptable way for adults to live their lives, a well-understood road map for successful family life."[61] Such a map no longer exists. There are now a number of different forms of family life in the United States, and while the traditional two-parent, male breadwinner model may in some ways still be offered as the ideal type, it is far from reality for many Americans. Consider the role of women in family life. We have already shown the percentage of women working outside of the home in Figure 5-2. Figure 5-3 provides additional information on this matter, presenting the percentage of women active in the civilian labor force who have infants under one year of age.[62] The increase from 1976, when 31 percent of such women were participating in the labor force, to 2002 when 55 percent of such women were active, is quite large and represents a relatively dramatic change.[63] In 2001, the latest year for which data are available, 61 percent of children age 0–6 not yet in school received some form of non-parental child care on a "regular basis,"[64] and data from 1997—again, the most recent available—show that the preschool child of an employed mother spent on average 30 hours per week in non-parental care of some kind.[65] While no comparable data from the 1950s are available for these last two figures, it probably safe to say that they both represent increases from that time.

Women's presence in the workforce is not the only area where family life has changed. Some of the most basic characteristics of participation in family life have changed as well. Americans are now getting married for the first time later in life. In 1970 the median age at the first exchange of wedding vows was 20.8 years for women and 23.2 for men. By 2003, these figures had increased to 25.3 for women and 27.1 for men. In 2003, a third of all men ages 30–34 had never been married, with the same figure for women being 23 percent. In 1970 these percentages were 9 percent

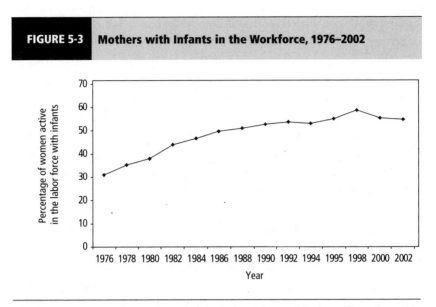

FIGURE 5-3   Mothers with Infants in the Workforce, 1976–2002

Note: The Census Bureau first began gathering these data in 1976. Infants are defined as children under one year of age.

Source: Barbara Downs, "Fertility of American Women: June 2002," U.S. Census Bureau, *Current Population Reports,* P20-548, October 2003.

and 6 percent respectively.[66] The average age of mothers at their first births has increased as well, going from 21.4 in 1970 to 24.9 in 2000.[67]

In addition, these last two characteristics—marriage and birth—do not go together like they used to.[68] As Figure 5-4 shows, the percentage of live births to unmarried mothers increased from 5 percent in 1960 to 35 percent in 2003.[69] This certainly contributed to the increase in single-parent households over time. From 1970 to 2003, the percentage of single-mother households increased from 12 percent to 26 percent, while the number of single-father households went from 1 percent to 6 percent.[70] Meanwhile, the percentage of children under 18 living in a two-parent household went from 88 percent in 1960 to 68 percent in 2004.[71] Other forms of "unconventional" household arrangements for children have also increased. The percentage of children under 18 living in unmarried couple, "cohabitating" households rose from less than 1 percent in 1977 to almost 5 percent in 1997,[72] and the percentage of children under 18 residing in a household maintained by their grandparents went from just over 3 percent in 1970 to 5.5 percent in 1997.[73]

FIGURE 5-4   **The Trend in Births to Unmarried Mothers, 1960–2003**

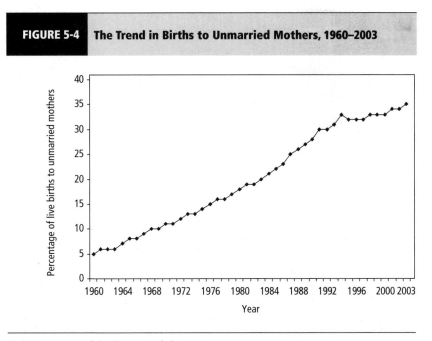

Note: Figures are rounded to the nearest whole percent.

Sources: Centers for Disease Control and Prevention, National Center for Health Statistics, National Vital Statistics System. Data for 1960–1999 are drawn from Stephanie J. Ventura and Christine A. Bachrach, "Nonmarital Childbearing in the United States, 1940–99," *National Vital Statistics Reports*, vol. 48, no. 16 (18 October 2000). Data for 2000–2001 are drawn from Joyce A. Martin, Brady E. Hamilton, Stephanie J. Ventura, Fay Menacker, Melissa M. Park, and Paul D. Sutton, "Births: Final Data for 2001," *National Vital Statistics Reports*, vol. 51, no. 2 (18 December 2002). Data for 2002–2003 are drawn from Brady E. Hamilton, Joyce A. Martin, and Paul D. Sutton, "Births: Preliminary Data for 2003," *National Vital Statistics Reports*, vol. 53, no. 9 (23 November 2004). Data for 2003 are preliminary.

The increase in out-of-wedlock births is another example where race becomes entangled with issues of class and culture, in this case, culture. While it is true that births outside of wedlock have been increasing for all racial and ethnic groups since the 1970s, the percentage of births to single women is much higher for blacks and Hispanics than it is for non-Hispanic whites. In 2003, 29 percent of the live births to non-Hispanic white women were to unmarried mothers. The corresponding figures for blacks and Hispanics, respectively, were 68 percent and 45 percent.[74] Such differences are not a new development, and have long led conservative commentators such as Lawrence Mead and Charles Murray to argue that the decline of family values and the overall collapse of morality are

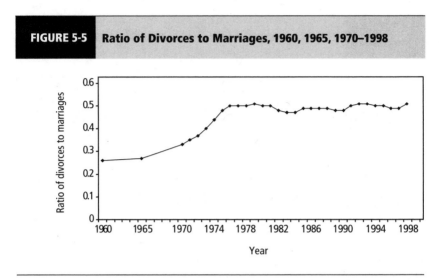

FIGURE 5-5   **Ratio of Divorces to Marriages, 1960, 1965, 1970–1998**

Source: Department of Health and Human Services, Centers for Disease Control and Prevention, National Center for Health Statistics, as reported in U.S. Census Bureau, *Statistical Abstract of the United States: 2003*, 72, Table No. 83.

much more prevalent in minority, particularly African American, communities.[75] But regardless of what racial or ethnic groups are the source for such births, they are extremely disquieting to cultural conservatives.

The biggest change of all is in the number of divorces from 1960 to 1998 (the last year for which data are reported by the United States Census Bureau), shown in Figure 5-5 as the ratio of divorces to marriages.[76] In 1960, there were .26 divorces for every marriage in the United States. That figure increased to .51 by 1998. This is a dramatic change. At the same time, the average length of marriages has been declining.[77] Any way one chooses to look at it, the structure of the American family has been significantly altered over the past fifty years. And in each case, these alterations have been of a nature that could make cultural conservatives quite unhappy.[78]

We will close our discussion of family structure with a brief look at American adolescents. They are, after all, one of the primary reasons cultural conservatives care about such issues as sex education, media content, and family structure. Those who worry about teens having sex apparently have some cause for concern: A 2002 study by the Centers for Disease Control and Prevention found that 46 percent of both females

| FIGURE 5-6 | The Increase in Births to Unmarried Teenage Mothers, 1960–2000 |

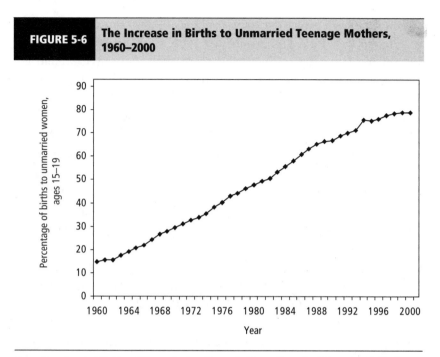

Source: Department of Health and Human Services, Centers for Disease Control and Prevention, National Center for Health Statistics, Stephanie J. Ventura, T. J. Matthews, and Brady E. Hamilton, "Births to Teenagers in the United States, 1940–2000," *National Vital Statistics Reports*, vol. 49, no. 10, September 25, 2001.

and males between 15 and 19 have had sexual intercourse at least once.[79] While these figures actually represent a decline from 1988, they still seem somewhat large. There are no data prior to 1988 with which to compare the 2002 figures, so it is impossible to say if roughly half of 15–19 year olds having sex represents an increase over time. But cultural conservatives certainly believe it does. At least some of this teenage sex is resulting in teenage pregnancies. In and of itself, teenage pregnancy is not all that unusual over the course of American history. In an earlier time when men and women married at earlier ages, teenage mothers were, if not the norm, at least somewhat common. What is different today is the large percentage of births that occur to unmarried female teens. This development is what has fueled concerns over the "crisis" of teen pregnancy in the United States.[80] As Figure 5-6 shows, the percentage of births that occurred to women ages 15–19 who were not married rose from 15 percent in 1960 to 79 percent in 2000. Looking at these same data in a slightly different way, the Census Bureau reported that from 1960–1964 59 percent of women ages 15–19 who premaritally conceived a child got married before the child was born. From 1990–1994, that number had dwindled to 16 percent.[81]

We know from earlier in this chapter that teens watch a good deal of television. We now know that they also have sex, and some have babies. What else do they do? At least some of them get into trouble for some type of delinquent behavior. Of course, concerns over juvenile delinquency are not new. Youth behavior was an important issue for some Progressive Era reformers of the early twentieth century,[82] and talk of an "epidemic" of juvenile delinquency in the United States goes back at least to the 1950s.[83] However, incidents of juvenile delinquency increased from 1960 through the mid-1990s before falling again the past few years. Figure 5-7, which presents the number of juvenile delinquency cases disposed of per 1,000 juveniles from 1960–2000, clearly demonstrates this.[84]

Criminal activity in schools also concerns some Americans. Data on this subject is available for a much shorter period of time, but contemporary figures are available. According to data gathered through the U.S. Department of Education, there were 14 students killed at school during the 2001–2002 school year and 2,001,300 non-fatal crimes committed at or on the way to or from school in 2001. While this is an improvement from the 34 fatalities and 3,409,200 non-fatal crimes from 1992–1993 and 1992 respectively, any parent of a school-aged child—and probably most others as well—would say that these figures are still too high.[85] As was the case with the statistics on family structure, some indicators of adolescent behavior certainly provide the raw material for cultural concern, if one chooses to interpret them in such a fashion.

HOMOSEXUAL RIGHTS

The final issue to discuss in our examination of cultural issue development is homosexual rights. The battle is fierce. If school prayer first put cultural concerns on the agenda in the 1960s, and if abortion fueled the rise of cultural issues in the 1970s and 1980s, then homosexual rights is the hot concern of the past ten years. For most of the country's history, homosexuality was largely hidden from public view. Homosexuality

| FIGURE 5-7 | Juvenile Delinquency Cases, 1960–2000 |

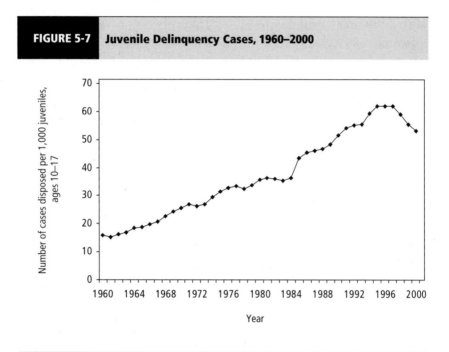

Sources: Data on juvenile delinquency cases disposed taken from A. Stahl, H. Snyder, and T. Finnegan, *Easy Access to Juvenile Court Statistics: 1985–2000* [data analysis and presentation package], Pittsburgh, PA: National Center for Juvenile Justice [producer], Washington, DC: Office of Juvenile Justice and Delinquency Prevention [distributor], 2002. Available online at www.ojjdp.ncjrs.org/ojstatbb/ezajcs. Data on population totals for juveniles are from the population estimates produced by the Population Division of the U.S. Census Bureau. Figures for 1960–1984 were taken from the Population Division's estimate archives (available online at www.census.gov/popest/archives/), while figures for 1985–2000 are taken from the National Center for Juvenile Justice's Easy Access to Juvenile Court Statistics online service.

certainly existed, but was definitely not on the political agenda, nor a meaningful part of public dialogue. The homosexual rights movement exploded on the national scene with the Stonewall riots in 1969 in New York City,[86] but at first was unable to gain much public attention or policy action. Throughout the 1970s and 1980s, large majorities of the American public disapproved of homosexuality.[87]

But public opinion began to shift in the 1990s, as attitudes moved in a liberal direction on at least on some specific elements of the homosexual rights debate.[88] At the same time, gay and lesbian activists began to pursue a more classic and energetic strategy for protection of their civil rights, by using the courts and increased public pressure in the attempt to attain favorable policy outcomes.[89] These new tactics resulted in some important gay rights victories, such as *Romer v. Evans* (1996), a case in which the Supreme Court struck down a Colorado constitutional amendment that voided all existing and prevented all future legal protections for homosexuals, and *Lawrence v. Texas* (2003), where the Court extended the right of sexual privacy to consenting adult homosexuals and overturned remaining state sodomy laws.

But these victories also got the attention of cultural conservatives, many of whom view homosexuality as an immoral abomination prohibited by God. They mobilized against what they saw as government either protecting and sanctioning immorality or according special treatment to a group that did not warrant such treatment.[90] This mobilization has been quite effective, and concerns over homosexual rights—especially gay marriage—have seemingly dominated the culture wars of the past few years. In the 2004 presidential campaign, George W. Bush announced his support for an amendment to the Constitution of the United States that would ban gay marriage. Eleven states had such amendments to state constitutions on their ballots in 2004, and all eleven were approved by voters. Even in Massachusetts, where homosexual marriage was first made legal by the state's supreme judicial body in 2004, there are efforts to amend the state constitution to bar same-sex marriage, efforts supported by the state's Republican governor Mitt Romney. For many cultural conservatives, the issue of gay rights has become a core element in the culture wars, and will not be going away.[91]

SUMMARY

In the America of the 1950s, kids prayed in school and they were not instructed in sex education. When they got home from school in the afternoon they were greeted by their mothers who did not work outside of the home. Later in the afternoon or early evening dad would be home as well, because the overwhelming majority of American households were two-parent households, and divorce was relatively rare. If the children were allowed to watch television before bed, there was practically no possibility that they would be exposed to any sexual content. Outside of the home, abortion was illegal except under very specific circumstances, and while homosexuality most certainly existed, it was neither seen nor acknowledged in public. Fast forward to America, 2006. School prayer, even a moment of silence for optional prayer, is strictly prohibited in the public schools. Sex education, however, is relatively universal, and adolescents are having sex on a relatively frequent basis. When the kids get out of school for the day, chances are good mom will still be at work, so the home will be empty. It is also less likely that dad will be home for dinner, because it is now less likely that mom will be married to dad. For after-dinner television, the difficulty will not be in finding sexual content to view, but rather in avoiding it. The easy availability of pornography on the Internet also beckons. Out in the larger society, abortion is relatively easily available and battles rage over homosexual rights, including gay marriage.

The above comparison is by necessity a simplified one. But it is also a relatively accurate one. For a cultural conservative, the 2006 version of America is, at the very least, cause for concern, and for many, worthy of political confrontation. But to fight such a battle, elites, especially the elites of the political parties, must present different options on cultural issues and themselves be ready and willing to fight over these issues. Does this describe the two major political parties in the United States? It is to this question that we now turn.

CHAPTER 6

PARTY AND POLICY PROPOSALS ON CULTURAL ISSUES

Cultural concerns are clearly poised to become political issues. Over the past half century a combination of social change and government actions—mostly involving the courts—has focused public attention, and in some cases, public unease on a number of cultural topics, such as the place of religion in public education, abortion, sex in popular culture, women's role in society, homosexual rights, and the status and proper composition of the American family. However, public attention by itself is not enough to turn a social issue into a political issue. Entrepreneurs must move an issue onto the political agenda. At the national level in the United States, without such mechanisms of "citizen democracy" as the initiative and referenda, entrepreneurs are usually political elites affiliated with one of the two major political parties. In other words, before a set of issues can fuel the engine of American politics, at least a few partisan elites must put the issues in the tank. The parties must offer citizens clear and different positions on the set of issues in question so that voters can effectively register their preferences. As E. E. Schattschneider reminds us, in America the people are rulers who can only speak two words—"yes" and "no." [1]

Do the parties offer the public clear and differentiated positions on cultural issues? As we discussed in Chapter 3, there is no doubt that the parties have long differed on class issues. From its very inception, the Democratic Party has identified itself as the party of the less fortunate in society,[2] and the cleavage of the Democrats as the party of the have-nots and Republicans as the party of the haves has been firmly in place since the end of the nineteenth century.[3] Does such a stark partisan divide also exist for cultural issues? To answer this question, we analyze the rhetoric and actions of partisan elites with regard to cultural issues. Specifically, we examine party platforms and the behavior of members of Congress, presidential candidates, and presidents for indications of where the parties stand on cultural issues. The Democrats and Republicans now present Americans with very different—indeed, nearly polar opposite—positions on many of the cultural issues present in American society. Over the last thirty years, the Democratic Party has championed cultural liberalism, while the GOP staunchly defended cultural conservatism.[4]

Once again, our focusing first on partisan elites does not mean that we believe they are the only, or perhaps even the dominant actors, in producing political change. The mass public plays an important role here as well. Most new political issues are likely to start at the mass level. As party change theorists such as Key, Schattschneider, Sundquist, and Carmines and Stimson have long pointed out, party elites—particularly from the party that is out of power—are constantly monitoring public opinion for shifts in position on existing issues, or for signs of new issues emerging.[5] As they discern shifts and new developments in public opinion, party elites respond by reiterating, altering, or clarifying their own stances relating to the issue or issues in question. These elite responses are based on what the elites believe will best serve their interests and the interests of their party, as well as on their existing beliefs and issue positions. In the final analysis, the elites are responding to public opinion, or at least their perception of it.[6]

But the party elites still play a key role in political change. Their responses to the initial stirrings of public opinion will be crucial in further shaping public opinion as an issue unfolds. Most Americans get exposed to political issues through the words and actions of elites.[7] Therefore elites are critical in shaping mass opinion.[8] The decisions of elites ultimately dictate the policy options presented to voters on Election Day. The point here is that just because we start with elites does not mean that we see them as the only, or even the dominant players, in the political process. The mass clearly matters as well. The relationship between elites and masses is a dynamic relationship that resembles a feedback loop, where the general public initiates change with shifts in public opinion, but where elite response structures and further influences public opinion and ultimately produces meaningful political change.[9]

PARTY PLATFORMS

Have the partisan elites in fact responded to the cultural developments within society? To answer this we examine the Democratic and Republican platforms. Every four years, in the lead-up to the national party conventions, both the Democrats and the Republicans undertake the task of crafting their party's platform. First appearing on the American political scene in the mid-nineteenth century, platforms are detailed statements of what the party stands for, what its positions are on a variety of issues, and what it will do (or at least attempt to do) if it attains government power. While parties and candidates produce many other documents and make a seemingly infinite number of statements, the platform is the *only* official declaration of what the party as a whole stands for and believes in. Indeed, in issuing their platforms the Democrats and the Republicans tell the American people in clear and simple terms what they are all about.

What are the parties telling Americans about cultural issues? First, there are some things we will likely never see in the platforms—statements in favor of easily available pornography, high amounts of sexual content in the media, lots of divorces, rampant teen-age sex, or increasing out-of-wedlock births. So we do not expect to see partisan differences on these issues. But there are a number of cultural issues on which we can reasonably expect the parties to potentially differ— religion in schools, abortion, questions surrounding women and the family, and homosexual rights. Because many of the social changes and political developments that created cultural concerns in society first appeared in the 1960s (or later), our examination begins with the 1960 platforms, and then moves to the platforms for 1972, 1980, 1992, and 2004.[10]

Tables 6-1 through 6-5 present the cultural material contained within the Democratic and Republican platforms for the years under examination here. In 1960, as Table 6-1 shows, cultural issues were barely mentioned by either party. Both parties called for equal pay for equal work for men and women, and the Democrats pledged to end job discrimination

| TABLE 6-1 | Cultural Material in the Party Platforms, 1960 |

DEMOCRATIC PLATFORM	REPUBLICAN PLATFORM
• pledge to end job discrimination based on sex	• call for guarantee of equal pay for equal work
• plank stating "we support legislation which will guarantee to women equality of rights under the law, including equal pay for equal work"	

Note: The platforms of all parties whose presidential candidate received at least one electoral vote can be found at www.presidency.ucsb.edu/platforms.php.

based on sex and to support equal rights for women. But that was it. This dearth of attention would seem to indicate that cultural issues simply did not concern either party at this time. Such inattention makes sense when we recall from Chapter 5 that most cultural issues had yet to arise in 1960—they did not yet concern citizens, so they certainly did not concern the parties. And on the one issue that was somewhat on the agenda in 1960—women's rights—the parties were essentially the same in their positions. Both took "liberal" stands.

In 1972 we can see the first signs of change in regard to the parties and cultural issues as Table 6-2 shows. The Republicans were still pretty much silent, and what they did offer provided little hint of growing concern with or changing stances on cultural issues. A plank—first added in 1964—supported the return of prayer to public schools, but all other cultural material presented by the GOP in 1972 dealt with the role of women in society, and it was all liberal in nature. The platform contained two separate endorsements of the Equal Rights Amendment (ERA), a plank supporting equal pay for equal work, and a pledge to assist women in higher education and government programs. The Democrats too were adamant in their support for women, matching the Republican's positions and then adding support for universal maternity benefits and a pledge to appoint more women to prominent positions in the federal government. But the 1972 Democratic party platform hinted at coming

TABLE 6-2	Cultural Material in the Party Platforms, 1972

DEMOCRATIC PLATFORM	REPUBLICAN PLATFORM
• pledge to remove barriers that limit women	• pledge to increase access of women to higher education
• pledge to increase efforts to open education to women	• statement that "voluntary prayer should be freely permitted in public places," especially public schools
• two pledges to end government discrimination based on sex	• lengthy section on "equal rights for women," which includes two separate pledges of support for the ERA, support for equal pay for equal work, and an end to all discrimination against women by the federal government
• pledge to support "the right to be different, to maintain a cultural or ethnic heritage or lifestyle, without being forced into a compelled homogeneity"	
• statement that "Americans should be free to make their own choice of lifestyles and private habits without being subject to discrimination or prosecution"	
• lengthy section devoted to the "rights of women," which includes explicit support for ratification of the ERA, provision of maternity benefits to all women, and "equal pay for comparable work"	
• statement that family planning services should be available to all citizens	
• a second statement of support for the ERA	
• pledge to appoint more women to prominent positions in government, with the aim of creating an "equitable ratio of women and men"	

cultural divides. In two somewhat vague statements, the party pledged its support for the right of Americans to engage in different "lifestyles" or "private habits" without threats of discrimination or prosecution. These could certainly be perceived as supporting homosexual rights. The platform also called for the universal availability of "family planning services," which while undefined could certainly be seen as a culturally liberal stand. There were no big differences in 1972, but the Democrats were beginning to think about cultural issues and grapple with how to respond.

By 1980 the grappling was over. In their respective platforms for this year, each party made it very clear that it was concerned with cultural issues, and also announced in no uncertain terms where it stood on these issues, as Table 6-3 shows. For the first time, the Democratic Party firmly embraced cultural liberalism, even with a Southern born-again Christian as its presidential nominee. The party's commitment to women's rights remained, with continued support for the ERA; equal pay for equal work; pledges to end discrimination based on sex in employment, government programs, higher education, and the military; and a concern with domestic violence. But for the Democrats in 1980, the big move concerned the biggest issue on the cultural battlefield—abortion. *Roe v. Wade* was decided in 1973, so the 1976 platforms represented the first chance for both parties to officially declare their positions on abortion. While the parties did respond in 1976, both were somewhat vague in what they offered. Both parties recognized the difficulty of the issue, and both admitted that there were conflicting positions within their own party. The Democratic position in 1976 was pro-choice, but weakly stated. The Republicans were somewhat more strongly pro-life in 1976, but here too the statement was cautious.[11] By 1980 caution was thrown to the wind and ambiguity was dismissed. The Democrats came out strongly in support of a woman's "right to choose," in support of the Court's decision in *Roe*, and fundamentally opposed to any constitutional amendment that would ban abortion. The party also stated that it recognized "reproductive freedom as a fundamental human right."

The Republicans in 1980 were equally clear on abortion. They strongly indicated their disagreement with *Roe*, and called for a constitutional amendment to ban abortion. The party also supported preventing federal funds from being used in any way that related to abortion. But abortion was not the only cultural issue addressed by the Republicans in 1980. The party closed the preamble to its platform with the following statement: "And so, in this 1980 Republican Platform, we call out to the American people: With God's help, let us now, together, make America

TABLE 6-3	Cultural Material in the Party Platforms, 1980

DEMOCRATIC PLATFORM	REPUBLICAN PLATFORM
• pledge to continue efforts to assist women in the field of business • lengthy section on "women and the economy," which includes specific commitments to equal pay for comparable work, increasing child care availability, and full enforcement of anti-discrimination laws • strong statement of support for women's "right to choose," support for the decision in *Roe v. Wade*, and opposition to a constitutional amendment to ban abortion • commitment to ensure equal participation in the military "regardless of sex" • pledge to eliminate discrimination based on sex in education, and fully enforce Title IX of the 1972 education amendments • pledges support "to make federal programs more sensitive to the needs of the family, in all its diverse forms" • pledge of support for ratification of the ERA • statement of recognition of "reproductive freedom as a fundamental human right" • pledge to continue to appoint more women to federal government positions • pledge to address domestic violence	• numerous statements about restoring "the family, the neighborhood, the community, and the workplace" • lengthy section on "women's rights," which repeatedly states the party's support for equal rights but explicitly avoids a statement of support for the ERA • statements that "we reaffirm our belief in the traditional role and values of the family in our society" and that "the importance of support for the mother and homemaker in maintaining the values of this country cannot be over-emphasized" • statement of opposition to quotas as a remedy for discrimination • statement of support for a constitutional amendment to ban abortion • statement of support for preventing the use of federal funds for abortion • statement that "the family is the foundation of our social order" • statement of support for voluntary prayer in public schools • pledge of support for school choice • statement that expresses the party's "support for legislation protecting and defending the traditional American family against the ongoing erosion of its base in our society" • statement that the political and legal institutions of the U.S. are "steeped in the Judeo-Christian ethic" • pledge to "work for the appointment of judges at all levels of the judiciary who respect traditional family values and the sanctity of innocent human life"

great again; let us now, together, make a new beginning." What followed this call to arms can be accurately described as a conservative manifesto on cultural issues. The party withdrew its explicit endorsement of the ERA, while acknowledging "the legitimate efforts of those who support or oppose ratification of the Equal Rights Amendment," thus reversing almost sixty years of strong support for legislation ensuring equal rights for women.[12] The platform repeatedly stated its support of the "traditional" American family and the importance of family values in American society, including the crucial role played by the "mother and homemaker." Republicans also renewed their support of school prayer, and added support of school choice to the mix. The platform also stated that the legal and political institutions of the United States are "steeped in the Judeo-Christian ethic," and promised to "work for the appointment of judges at all levels of the judiciary who respect traditional family values and the sanctity of innocent human life." By 1980, the gloves were off when it came to cultural issues, and as Geoffrey Layman notes, it was clear on which side of the fight each party stood.[13]

The platforms in the years since 1980 have only served to more starkly demonstrate the differences between the Democrats and the Republicans on cultural issues. In 1992, as Table 6-4 shows, the Democrats maintained their support of equal rights for women and their pro-choice position on abortion. They added an explicit call to extend civil rights protections on the basis of sexual orientation, condemned homophobia, and supported federal patronage of art that some might consider offensive or obscene. The Republicans in 1992 once again called for the return of prayer to school; supported school choice; repeatedly noted the importance of family values, including a statement about the importance of having a married father and mother in the home; called for an amendment banning abortion; and again pledged to appoint "judges who respect traditional family values and the sanctity of human life." But the GOP also added to its 1992 cultural message a statement that the laws of the United States should reflect "faith in God," support for abstinence programs in public schools, opposition to civil rights protections based on sexual preference, opposition to gay marriage and gay adoption, a promise to mount a "national crusade against pornography," and a condemnation of using tax dollars "to subsidize obscenity and

TABLE 6-4	Cultural Material in the Party Platforms, 1992

DEMOCRATIC PLATFORM	REPUBLICAN PLATFORM
• pledge to continue efforts to assist women in the field of business	• statement that "the traditional family is under assault"
• pledge to work to restore the "basic American values" of "tolerance, faith, [and] family"	• statement that the laws of the nation should reflect "faith in God"
• pledge to "act against sexual harassment in the workplace"	• lengthy section on the family includes a statement on the importance of family values, a call for state legislatures to find ways to "promote marital stability," and a statement that "recognize[s] the importance of having fathers and mothers in the home"
• pledge to work to end discrimination based on sexual orientation	
• pledge to "provide civil rights protection for gay men and lesbians and an end to Defense Department discrimination"	• statement of support for school choice
• strong statement of support for "the right of every woman to choose, consistent with *Roe v. Wade*"	• statement of opposition to the provision of birth control or abortion services in public schools and support for promoting abstinence
• condemnation of homophobia	• pledge of support for voluntary prayer in public schools
• pledge of support for national support of the arts that is consistent with the "First Amendment's freedom of expression guarantee"	• statement of opposition of civil rights protections based on sexual preference
• statement of belief in "traditional family values and in the Judeo-Christian heritage that informs our culture"	• statement of opposition to same-sex marriage
	• statement of opposition to allowing same-sex couples to adopt children or provide foster care
	• pledge to mount a "national crusade against pornography"
	• condemnation of the "use of public funds to subsidize obscenity and blasphemy masquerading as art"
	• statement of support for "the rights of women"
	• statement of support for constitutional amendment banning abortion
	• pledge to appoint "judges who respect traditional family values and the sanctity of human life"

blasphemy masquerading as art." The culture wars were clearly expanding, at least among the partisan elites responsible for the platforms.

What did the 2004 party platforms say about cultural issues? Table 6-5 shows that the Democrats produced a noticeably shorter platform than in recent years, and thus there was less material, including less cultural material. But the positions were strong, unmistakable, and liberal. The party once again strongly supported *Roe* and a pro-choice stance, as well as equal rights for women and equal pay for equal work. They added support for federal funding of embryonic stem cell research and opposition to a constitutional amendment banning gay marriage, stating that the issue should be left to individual states. Finally, the Democrats offered perhaps their strongest statement on homosexual rights to date, stating "we support full inclusion of gay and lesbian families in the life of our nation and seek equal responsibilities, benefits, and protections for these families."

The 2004 Republican platform was somewhat longer than those produced by the party in years past, and some of that added length was devoted to cultural issues. In fact, a reader can pick any cultural issue and most likely find it addressed—in a conservative fashion—in the 2004 GOP platform. In addition to the by-now-expected statements against abortion, for school prayer, against judicial activism, and recognizing the vital importance of families and family values, the Republicans added much new cultural material in 2004—opposition to using federal money for embryonic stem cell research, a condemnation of "unwarranted and unconstitutional restrictions on the free exercise of religion in the public square," support for a constitutional amendment banning gay marriage, opposition to physician-assisted suicide and other forms of euthanasia, and a call for a "reasonable approach" to Title IX of the Education Amendments of 1972 to the Civil Rights Act of 1964 which deals with discrimination based on sex. In all instances, the GOP adopted a culturally conservative stance. The Republicans' stance on cultural issues was crystal clear, as was that of the Democrats. The 2004 offerings of the parties differed from each other as much as night differs from day.[14]

Those who study party activists would not be surprised by this dramatic increase in differences between the party platforms on cultural issues. Party activists, after all, craft and approve the parties' platforms,

TABLE 6-5	Cultural Material in the Party Platforms, 2004

DEMOCRATIC PLATFORM	REPUBLICAN PLATFORM
• pledge to continue efforts to assist women in the field of business • pledge to increase tax credits for childcare • statement that "strong families… guided by faith… are the heart of America" • statement of support for embryonic stem cell research • statement of equal pay for equal work for women • statement of support for a "woman's right to choose, consistent with *Roe v. Wade*" • statement that "we support full inclusion of gay and lesbian families in the life of our nation and seek equal responsibilities, benefits, and protections for these families" • statement of opposition to constitutional amendment banning gay marriage • statement of support for involvement of faith-based organizations in social service provision so long as involvement is consistent with "First Amendment protections"	• statement that "we respect the family's role as a touchstone of stability and strength" • statement of support for school choice, including home schooling • statement of support for using federal funds to "encourage the future destruction of human embryos" • strong statement of support for involvement of faith-based organizations in social service provision • statement of support for a "reasonable approach" to Title IX • statement of opposition to quotas as a remedy for discrimination • strong attack on "activist judges," which includes "we condemn judicial activists and their unwarranted and unconstitutional restrictions on the free exercise of religion in the public square" • lengthy section on "protecting our families," which includes statement "we…believe that while families exist in many different forms, there are ideals to strive for. evidence shows us that children have the best chance for success when raised by a mother and a father who love and respect each other as well as their children" and statement "we recognize the importance of having in the home a father and a mother who are married" • statement of support for adoption • statement of opposition to the provision of birth control or abortion services in public schools and support for promoting abstinence • statement of support for voluntary prayer in public schools • statement of strong support for constitutional amendment banning gay marriage • lengthy section on "promoting a culture of life," which includes support for a constitutional amendment banning abortion, preventing federal money from being used for abortion, "appointment of judges who respect traditional family values and the sanctity of innocent human life," and opposition to physician-assisted suicide and other forms of euthanasia

and studies of these activists over the past thirty years have shown ever increasing differences between Democratic activists and GOP activists in terms of religious and cultural matters. In their study of contributors to partisan, ideological, and interest group political action committees conducted from 1982–1983, John Green and James Guth found that dramatic differences of opinion existed between Democratic/liberal donors and Republican/conservative donors on the issue of school prayer and other cultural issues such as abortion, gay rights, and the ERA.[15] In a more recent study of delegates to both the Republican and Democratic national conventions, Geoffrey Layman demonstrates the truly massive differences that now exist between the activists for the respective parties. Over the past thirty years, church attendance has risen for Republican delegates, while it has declined for Democratic delegates. The portion of GOP delegates who are evangelical Protestants has gone up, while among Democrats the percentage of secular delegates has risen. Finally, Layman finds that differences between the delegates of each party in their view on cultural issues such as abortion, gay rights, and women's issues have grown substantially over time. Based on Layman's findings, it would not be an overstatement to claim that the two parties appear to draw their respective delegates from entirely different segments of the American public.[16] As such, the growing chasm between the party platforms on cultural issues makes perfect sense.

CONGRESSIONAL ACTION

At least since 1980 the platforms have presented clear differences between the parties for all the public to see.[17] But did the public actually see these differences? As L. Sandy Maisel points out, very few Americans have even a faint idea of what the platforms contain, and hardly anyone actually reads them.[18] In fact, we know of some fellow political scientists who have never even once read a party platform. The media provide little help here, as they give platform contents scant coverage.

Fortunately for citizens—and supporters of representative democracy—platforms are not the only way to learn about partisan differences. Politicians are certainly aware of any differences that exist between the parties; indeed these party elites are primary factors in creating divergent stands. Through their rhetoric and actions, politicians can inform and educate the mass public about partisan differences on issues, including cultural issues.

Members of Congress are prime candidates to perform these amplifying functions for everyday people. A large part of each day in Congress is devoted to talking and voting publicly on a variety of issues. Now it is true that most citizens do not closely monitor what Congress is doing— very few Americans set aside time each day for C-Span or C-Span 2, let alone reading the *Congressional Record*. However, this does not mean that people are unaware of what Congress as a whole or what certain individual members, such as their own representatives or other high profile members, are doing. While many of the routine activities of passing budget bills receive limited media coverage and little public attention, high profile issues such as abortion and gay marriage do receive considerable attention. We also know that members work hard to make their positions known to their constituents on certain issues through intense cultivation of local media outlets and extensive travels throughout their districts.[19] Members, and their opponents, also clearly state their issue stands during election campaigns, and incumbents constantly consider how any vote they cast or comment they make might be used by a future opponent.[20]

So while the average American is not a devoted Congress watcher, she or he has multiple opportunities to pick up issue positions and partisan cues from members. In fact, as Samuel Popkin notes of political information in general,[21] such cues from members of Congress would be hard to avoid for most people. We will look briefly here at the actions of Congress on four cultural issues—the ERA, school prayer, abortion, and homosexual rights—to see what partisan messages have been transmitted to the public.

The Equal Rights Amendment

First introduced in 1923, for years the ERA was prevented from receiving a floor vote by recalcitrant committee chairs, particularly Southern Democratic ones. One of the first recorded votes came in 1946, in the Senate only. As a constitutional amendment, the ERA needed to secure two-thirds of those members present and voting in order to pass, Table 6-6 shows that it failed to meet that threshold. However, the patterns of

TABLE 6-6	Congressional Votes on the Equal Rights Amendment (ERA), Selected Years

	HOUSE		SENATE	
	Pro-Era	Anti-Era	Pro-Era	Anti-Era
S J Res 61: Equal Rights Amendment, 1946				
Democrats			15 (38%)	24 (62%)
Republicans			23 (70%)	10 (30%)
H J Res 208 Equal Rights Amendment (Final Passage), 1971 (House) and 1972 (Senate)				
Democrats	217 (95%)	12 (5%)	47 (96%)	2 (4%)
Republicans	137 (92%)	12 (8%)	37 (86%)	6 (14%)
H J Res 638: Proposal to extend the ERA ratification deadline by 39 months, 1978				
Democrats	186 (69%)	85 (31%)	44 (75%)	15 (25%)
Republicans	41 (28%)	103 (72%)	16 (43%)	21 (57%)
H J Res 1: Equal Rights Amendment (Reintroduction), 1983				
Democrats	225 (86%)	38 (14%)		
Republicans	53 (33%)	109 (67%)		

Sources: 1946 vote taken from *Congressional Quarterly.* All other votes from *CQ Almanac,* appropriate years. Individual votes can be found on the following pages: 1946, 568; 1971, 68-H–69-H; 1972, 18-S; 1978, 176-H–177-H and 66-S; 1983, 138-H–139-H.

partisan support are quite interesting. In 1946, 70 percent of Republicans in the Senate voted in favor of the ERA, while only 38 percent of Democratic senators did so.

Fast forward to 1971 and 1972, when the ERA actually passed in the House and Senate respectively. The GOP remained strong in its support for the ERA, with 92 percent of House Republicans and 86 percent of those in the Senate approving the amendment. But look at the dramatic change within the Democratic Party. Democratic members now supported the ERA at rates even higher than the Republicans, with 95 percent in the House and 96 percent in the Senate. While the most adamant critic of the ERA was Democratic Senator Sam Ervin of North Carolina—he denounced the amendment saying that it would crucify women "upon the cross of dubious equality and specious uniformity"— the party as a whole was now clearly and strongly supportive.[22]

Look finally at the last two votes in Table 6-6—a successful proposal to extend the ratification deadline by thirty-nine months in 1978 and an unsuccessful last-ditch effort in 1983 to reintroduce the ERA after it had failed to be ratified. In both cases, Democrats in Congress supported the ERA by large margins. But this was not true for their Republican counterparts. The party that had historically been the strongest in its support for equal rights for women now had a majority of its members in Congress opposed to the ERA. Over the course of about thirty years, the parties switched positions on the ERA. The Democrats moved from opposition to support, while the Republicans moved in the opposite direction.[23] Previous research has found that the parties switched and polarized on a number of other women's issues as well in the past few decades.[24] The congressional voting record on the ERA indicates that the Democratic Party is more liberal on women's issues, while the GOP is the conservative choice.

School Prayer

How does Congress divide on the matter of prayer in public schools? As noted in Chapter 5, the Supreme Court decisions in *Engel* (1962) and *Abington* (1963) were very unpopular, and Congress was inundated with letters and phone calls from unhappy Americans as soon as the decisions were announced.[25] Reacting to *Engel*, Rep. George Andrews, a Democrat from Alabama, thundered, "They put the Negroes in the schools and now they've driven God out."[26] After *Abington* removed Bible reading from public schools, members of Congress reacted again. Richard Roudebush, a Republican House member from Indiana, declared that "Congress must act if our Christian heritage is to be preserved for future generations." His Republican Senate colleague, Jacob Javits from New York, was more circumspect, stating that an attempt by Congress to reverse the Court's decision would be "so serious in its implications to religious freedom that I do not feel we should jump into it."[27]

So there was some variety in how individual members responded to the matter of prayer. But how did the parties overall in Congress react to the question? Table 6-7 presents five votes on this matter.[28] In 1966 a constitutional amendment to allow voluntary prayer in public schools received its first congressional roll call, in the Senate only. As the table

| TABLE 6-7 | **Congressional Votes on Prayer in Public Schools, Selected Years** | | | |

| | HOUSE | | SENATE | |
	Pro-Prayer	Anti-Prayer	Pro-Prayer	Anti-Prayer
S J Res 144: Proposed constitutional amendment to allow voluntary prayer in public schools, 1966				
Democrats			22 (39%)	34 (61%)
Republicans			27 (90%)	3 (10%)
H J Res 191: Proposed constitutional amendment to allow persons in public buildings to participate in voluntary prayer, 1971				
Democrats	102 (43%)	137 (57%)		
Republicans	138 (84%)	26 (16%)		
S 210: Proposal to remove state laws relating to prayer in public schools from jurisdiction of federal courts, 1979				
Democrats			25 (48%)	27 (52%)
Republicans			22 (69%)	10 (31%)
S J Res 73: Proposed constitutional amendment to permit organized, recited prayer in public schools and other public buildings, 1984				
Democrats			19 (42%)	26 (58%)
Republicans			37 (67%)	18 (33%)
HR 6 and S 1513: Proposal to withhold federal funds from schools that prohibit constitutionally protected, voluntary prayer, 1994				
Democrats	178 (74%)	64 (26%)	12 (21%)	44 (79%)
Republicans	166 (100%)	0 (0%)	35 (80%)	9 (20%)

Note: HR 6 and S 1513 in 1994 contained different language and somewhat different elements.

Sources: All votes from *CQ Almanac*, appropriate years. Individual votes can be found on the following pages: 1966, 978; 1971, 82-H-83–H; 1979, 9-S; 1984, 9-S; 1994, 24-H–25-H and 40-S.

shows, Republicans were strongly in favor (90 percent), a fact that is true in all the prayer votes shown here. For Democrats, on the other hand, a majority of senators (61 percent) opposed the amendment. This pattern held true for the votes in 1971, 1979, and 1984 as well, although the margins by which Democrats were opposed to prayer shrank a bit from the

1966 level. The final prayer vote presented here, from 1994, requires a bit more explanation. The Republicans remained strongly supportive of prayer, in fact unanimously so in the House. The Democrats were a bit more divided. In the Senate, where the proposal contained much stronger language on denying funds to schools, Democrats took a strong "anti-prayer" position. In the House, where the funding language was weaker, Democrats were much more supportive of the "pro-prayer" position. But even here, they were much less supportive than the Republican members. Anyone looking to Congress since the 1960s for the positions of the parties on school prayer could easily discern that the Republicans are staunch supporters of prayer, while the Democrats tend to be opposed, although they are not as united as their GOP counterparts on this cultural issue.[29]

Abortion

Of all the issues present in the American culture wars, none is more incendiary than abortion. No other issue generates the passion, the antagonism, the heat that abortion does. For many involved in the issue, it literally is a matter of life and death. Opponents see abortion as murder, and regularly use words such as "holocaust," "slaughter," and "infanticide" to describe it. Defenders of the option of abortion see the issue as a matter of individual rights and liberties, specifically the right of women to control their own bodies and the right of privacy. For pro-choice individuals, government has no business interfering in the private reproductive decisions of women other than to ensure that the option of a safe abortion is legally available.

These two divergent positions are reflected in some of the congressional rhetoric over the years. Consider the following statements from members of both parties on the pro-choice side of the issue. Defending his pro-choice position, Rep. David Obey, D-Wisc., stated: "I will be damned if I, a male legislator, will vote to prohibit a woman from having a therapeutic abortion to save her life."[30] Sen. Jacob Javits, R-N.Y., also saw abortion as a women's rights issue, arguing, "This is what is at stake: the enfranchisement of women. Are we going to relapse to the Dark Ages?"[31] Similar sentiments were offered by Sen. Robert Packwood, R-Ore., when he stated simply, "A woman's right to make a child-bearing decision is part of her right of bodily integrity."[32] The rhetoric is even more heated on the pro-life side of the aisle. In the eyes of Dewey Bartlett, a Republican senator from Oklahoma, "It is only a matter of degree to shift from the extermination of the fetus to the extermination of children with birth defects, to the extermination of the elderly, the sick, the crippled."[33] Sen. Jeremiah Denton, R-Ala., took a similar view: America's abortion policy "begins the slippery slope to infanticide.... We are emulating the Chinese in deciding that girl babies are undesirable. They are not wanted. We will destroy them."[34] Finally, consider this description of the procedure known as "partial birth abortion" from Rep. Henry Hyde, R-Ill., who has been centrally involved in abortion debates in Congress for the past thirty years: "It's an extermination of a defenseless little life whose little arms and legs are wiggling until that scissors gets shoved into its neck and they stiffen."[35]

An attentive citizen could certainly pick up partisan cues by hearing or reading the above statements, but again, partisan stances are more likely to be transmitted by the voting patterns of all party members in Congress. How have the parties actually behaved on abortion? Table 6-8 presents nine abortion votes from the first vote on barring federal funds for abortion in 1974 through the 2003 vote to ban late-term abortion. Because of its prominence, abortion has been the subject of more congressional roll call votes than any other cultural issue, thus there are a number of votes that could be shown here. But the choice of specific votes matters little. The pattern over the last thirty years is strong and consistent—Democrats have become increasingly pro-choice and Republicans have voted increasingly pro-life.[36]

Democrats in Congress have always been more supportive of abortion than Republicans, but the gap between the parties was not that large in the 1970s, as can be seen in the first three votes in Table 6-8. There are even two instances shown where Republicans were more pro-choice than pro-life, and two more where the splits between Democrats are relatively small. Illustrative of the congressional parties in the 1970s are the sentiments of then Democratic Speaker of the House Thomas P. "Tip" O'Neill. Discussing a vote from 1977 that is not shown here, O'Neill admitted that his strong personal opposition to abortion prevented him from pressuring his fellow Democrats to vote in a pro-choice fashion.[37] During the

TABLE 6-8	Congressional Votes on Abortion, Selected Years			

	HOUSE		SENATE	
	Pro-Choice	Pro-Life	Pro-Choice	Pro-Life

HR 15580: Proposal to prevent federal money from being used for abortion in all cases (House) and except to save life of mother (Senate), 1974

	Pro-Choice	Pro-Life	Pro-Choice	Pro-Life
Democrats	149 (74%)	53 (26%)	20 (42%)	28 (58%)
Republicans	98 (58%)	70 (42%)	14 (39%)	22 (61%)

S J Res 178: Proposed constitutional amendment to outlaw abortion under any circumstances, 1976a

	Pro-Choice	Pro-Life	Pro-Choice	Pro-Life
Democrats			32 (62%)	20 (38%)
Republicans			15 (43%)	20 (57%)

HR 14232: Proposal to prohibit the use of federal funds to pay for or promote abortion, 1976b

	Pro-Choice	Pro-Life	Pro-Choice	Pro-Life
Democrats	133 (54%)	113 (46%)	37 (73%)	14 (27%)
Republicans	34 (27%)	94 (73%)	20 (59%)	14 (41%)

H J Res 520: Proposed constitutional amendment to ban abortion, 1982

	Pro-Choice	Pro-Life	Pro-Choice	Pro-Life
Democrats			29 (69%)	13 (31%)
Republicans			18 (35%)	33 (65%)

HR 4783: Proposal to prohibit use of federal funds for abortion except when life of the mother is endangered, 1988

	Pro-Choice	Pro-Life	Pro-Choice	Pro-Life
Democrats	136 (60%)	90 (40%)	30 (60%)	20 (40%)
Republicans	30 (19%)	126 (81%)	13 (32%)	27 (68%)

HR 2518: Proposal to prohibit use of federal funds for abortion except in cases of rape, incest, or to save the life of the mother, 1993

	Pro-Choice	Pro-Life	Pro-Choice	Pro-Life
Democrats	161 (62%)	98 (38%)	34 (62%)	21 (38%)
Republicans	16 (9%)	157 (91%)	6 (14%)	38 (86%)

HR 1833: Proposal to ban late-term abortion, 1996

	Pro-Choice	Pro-Life	Pro-Choice	Pro-Life
Democrats	121 (63%)	70 (37%)	35 (74%)	12 (26%)
Republicans	15 (10%)	215 (90%)	6 (12%)	45 (88%)

HR 4691: Proposal to allow hospitals to refuse to perform abortions without losing federal funds, 2002

	Pro-Choice	Pro-Life	Pro-Choice	Pro-Life
Democrats	164 (82%)	37 (18%)		
Republicans	24 (11%)	192 (89%)		

S 3: Proposal to ban late-term abortion, 2003

	Pro-Choice	Pro-Life	Pro-Choice	Pro-Life
Democrats	137 (68%)	63 (32%)	30 (64%)	17 (36%)
Republicans	4 (2%)	218 (98%)	3 (6%)	47 (94%)

Note: the 1974 vote on abortion funding in the Senate is actually a vote to table the amendment. The 1976 vote on the proposed constitutional ban on abortion is a vote to table the amendment. The 1982 vote on the proposed constitutional ban on abortion is a vote to table the amendment. The 1988 vote in the Senate on abortion funding is a vote on a motion for the Senate to reconsider its previous vote. Both votes on the late-term abortion ban in 1996 are attempts to override a presidential veto.

Sources: All votes from *CQ Almanac*, appropriate years. Individual votes can be found on the following pages: 1974, 76-H–77-H and 59-S; 1976a, 22-S; 1976b, 98-H–99-H and 49-S; 1982, 58-S; 1988, 96-H–97-H and 53-S; 1993, 74-H–75-H and 38-S; 1996, H-138–H-139 and S-53; 2002, H-130–H-131;

1970s partisanship was not always a good indicator of how a member of Congress would vote on abortion.

This began to change in the 1980s. During this decade the gap between the parties on abortion widened, as is shown in the two votes from this decade presented in Table 6-8. The Democrats remained pro-choice, although there was still significant pro-life sentiment within the party's congressional membership. The Republicans changed more in the 1980s, becoming more consistently and more strongly pro-life in their voting behavior. By the 1990s, the divide between the parties was large and clear—the Democrats were the pro-choice party in Congress, while the GOP stood for pro-life. If anything, this division has become even stronger in the first decade of the twenty-first century, as the final two votes in Table 6-8 show. Today it would be unthinkable for a congressional leader from either party to announce that their personal position on abortion differed from the party line, as O'Neill did in 1977.

Homosexual Rights

This analysis of congressional behavior on cultural issues closes with a brief look at votes involving homosexuality. Homosexual rights have only recently gotten on the congressional agenda, and thus there are relatively few roll call votes to examine, and those that are available represent a short time frame. But what we have is illustrative. Table 6-9 presents six votes on various matters involving homosexual rights.

Once again, the overall picture depicts an increasingly large divide between the Democrats and the Republicans. For the GOP, the analysis is short and easy. Republicans in Congress have always been strongly opposed to gay rights, beginning with the 1977 proposal to prohibit the Legal Services Corporation from becoming involved in gay rights cases and continuing through to the 2004 vote on a constitutional amendment to ban marriage between gays. For Democrats the story is a bit more complicated, but the outcome is the same. In the 1977 vote, the party is almost evenly split between the pro-homosexual and anti-homosexual rights positions. By the 1993 vote on President Clinton's ill-fated proposal to end the ban on homosexuals in the U.S. military, a majority of congressional Democrats are supportive of gay rights, but it is not a large majority in either House. In 1996, the Democrats seem to have taken a

TABLE 6-9	**Congressional Votes on Homosexual Rights, Selected Years**

	HOUSE		SENATE	
	Pro Gay Rights	Anti Gay Rights	Pro Gay Rights	Anti Gay Rights

HR 6666: Proposal to prohibit the Legal Services Corporation from involvement in cases relating to homosexuality or gay rights, 1977

Democrats	116 (49%)	120 (51%)		
Republicans	17 (13%)	110 (87%)		

HR 2401 and S 1298: Proposal to allow president to determine policy on homosexuals in the military, 1993

Democrats	157 (59%)	101 (41%)	30 (55%)	25 (45%)
Republicans	11 (6%)	163 (94%)	3 (7%)	38 (93%)

HR 3396: Defense of Marriage Act, 1996a

Democrats	65 (36%)	118 (64.0%)	14 (30%)	32 (70%)
Republicans	1 (.4%)	224 (99.6%)	0 (0%)	53 (100%)

S 2056: Proposal to prohibit job discrimination based on sexual orientation, 1996b

Democrats			41 (89%)	5 (11%)
Republicans			8 (15%)	45 (85%)

HR 4205 and S 2549: Proposal to extend hate crime categories to include crimes related to sexual orientation, 2000

Democrats	190 (92%)	17 (8%)	44 (98%)	1 (2%)
Republicans	41 (19%)	174 (81%)	13 (24%)	41 (76%)

H J Res 106 and S J Res 40: Proposed constitutional amendment to ban gay marriage, 2004

Democrats	158 (81%)	36 (19%)	43 (93%)	3 (7%)
Republicans	27 (12%)	191 (88%)	6 (12%)	45 (88%)

Note: The 2000 hate crime vote in the House was on a non-binding motion to instruct conference committee members to support the inclusion of hate crime status for crimes related to sexual orientation in the final legislation. The 2004 vote on marriage between gays in the Senate was actually a cloture vote to end debate on the proposal.

Sources: All votes except 2004 from *CQ Almanac*, appropriate years. Votes from 2004 taken from *CQ Weekly*. Individual votes can be found on the following pages: 1977, 106-H–107-H; 1993, 112-H–113-H and 33-S; 1996a, H-104–H-105 and S-50; 1996b, S-50; 2000, H-146–H-147 and S-26; 2004, 2964 and 2961.

step back in their support of homosexual rights, as large majorities in both the House and Senate voted to approve the Defense of Marriage Act, which was widely seen as being anti-homosexual. But in the last three votes shown in Table 6-9, Democratic members of Congress leave no doubt about their position—they are strongly supportive of homosexual rights. In fact, the gaps between the parties are now the largest of any of the cultural issues presented in this chapter.[38] The parties in Congress now leave no doubt about where they stand on cultural issues, and they very clearly are not standing anywhere near each other.

PRESIDENTIAL POLITICS

The platforms clearly show that the Democrats and the Republicans have come to differ dramatically on cultural issues since 1960. So do the words and actions of the parties' respective members of Congress. But perhaps readers remain unconvinced that these differences are actually penetrating the consciousness of the American public. Platforms are irrelevant, one could argue, because nobody reads them, and only a select few—such as interest group lobbyists—actually pay attention to what Congress does. While we disagree with these claims, we do recognize the validity of the concerns, and so we look next at the actions of presidential candidates and presidents in regard to cultural issues.

Presidential Cues to a Culture Divide

If the parties differ on cultural issues, and we have already presented a strong case that they do, then the candidates that the respective parties put forward for the top political office in the nation should reflect these differences. And if the public is to ever become cognizant of partisan differences on any issues, the words and actions of presidents and presidential candidates provide the best chance for such awareness to develop. The president of the United States is by far the most high profile political office in the United States, and perhaps in the entire world. The media follow him 24 hours a day, 7 days a week, 365 days a year. We are told what he reads, what he eats, what he does for fun, even his blood pressure readings at his last physical examination. We are certainly informed of where he stands on the issues; if an issue makes it on to the political agenda, we will eventually—likely sooner rather than later—know where the president stands on that issue. So the president's behavior certainly has the potential to deliver partisan cues on issues, including of course cultural issues.

The same is true—perhaps even more so—for presidential candidates, at least for the two candidates that in the end receive the nominations of the Democratic and Republican Parties. As David Leege and his colleagues note, presidential elections stand at the very center of American politics.[39] If ever an American is going to pay attention to politics, the presidential election every four years is when it will happen. In fact, it would be almost impossible to avoid. The candidates and their surrogates appear all across the nation trying to garner support. They run advertisements on radio, television, and now even on the Internet. The candidates appear before their respective conventions to accept their parties' nominations, and in recent times they meet face-to-face late in the election to answer questions and debate the issues. And the media reports on all of these things, to a degree that some—if not many—would find excessive. In each of these venues the candidates are attempting to deliver a message to the American people, and in so doing they tell Americans where they stand on the issues, and what they will do if they are elected to office. By paying even an absolute minimum amount of attention during a presidential election campaign, a voter will be exposed to a good deal of substantive information about the parties' positions.[40]

So what do the presidential candidates and eventual presidents tell us about the parties and cultural issues? The short answer is the same thing that the platforms and members of Congress did—that Democrats and Republicans differ on cultural issues, and the differences have grown so much over time that the divide between the parties can now be described as a chasm.

Acceptance Speeches and Other Cues

To highlight these growing differences as presented by presidential candidates and presidents, we examine the nominees' acceptance speeches for the same years considered in the discussion of party platforms, as well as candidate words and actions outside the convention context. While far from the only public statements the candidates make during the campaign, the acceptance speeches have multiple advantages for analysis.

First, all candidates make them. Second, the speeches can be seen by any American with a television—or now a computer and Internet connection—or heard by anyone with a radio, and large audiences do tune in. Third, the acceptance speeches provide an opportunity for the candidates to speak directly to the American public, with their remarks uninterrupted and also not interpreted by anyone else. Finally, the acceptance speech is perhaps a candidate's best chance to try and convince citizens to vote for him, and indications are that the candidates recognize this. As James Stimson points out, far from being events of only pure spectacle, the national party conventions are still important opportunities for political learning on the part of the American public, and the acceptance speeches of the two presidential candidates are the pinnacles of the conventions.[41]

Table 6-10 presents the cultural references contained in the acceptance speeches of the Democratic and Republican presidential nominees in 1960, 1972, 1980, 1992, and 2004.[42] The first thing that jumps out from this table is how little cultural issues were addressed in 1960. Richard Nixon called for a "renewed faith in the eternal ideals of freedom and justice under God," while John F. Kennedy only offered his endorsement of a "complete separation of church and state," which was primarily included to reassure Americans concerned that his Roman Catholicism might cause divided loyalties on his part. This lack of attention should not surprise us, however. We know by now that cultural issues simply were not on the agenda yet in 1960.

The first major party presidential candidate of the last fifty years to attempt to inject cultural issues into the campaign was Republican Barry Goldwater in 1964. While his acceptance speech (not included in Table 6-10) did not contain any statements on specific cultural issues on the policy agenda, it did make a number of references to God and divine will, and Goldwater certainly accorded cultural themes an important place in his campaign.[43] In a critique of the Democratic Party, Goldwater stated, "You will search in vain for any reference to God or religion in the Democratic platform. This is a matter of... regret when we realize that this platform, with its utter disregard of God, was written to the exact specifications of Lyndon Johnson."[44] But Goldwater's rhetoric aside, the parties still did not differ much on cultural issues in 1964, and they mattered little in that year's campaign.

TABLE 6-10	Cultural Material in the Presidential Nominees' Acceptance Speeches, Selected Years

1960

John F. Kennedy (Democrat)	Richard M. Nixon (Republican)
• Supports "complete separation of church and state"	• Statement that in the decade of the 1960s we will see "the continual revitalization of America's moral and spiritual strength, with a renewed faith in the eternal ideals of freedom and justice under God which are our priceless heritage as a people"

1972

George McGovern (Democrat)	Richard M. Nixon (Republican)
• Calls for an end to "prejudice based on ... sex"	• Opposes "quotas" as a way to end discrimination

1980

Jimmy Carter (Democrat)	Ronald Reagan (Republican)
• Supports the ERA • Wants "women free to pursue without limit the full life of what they want for themselves"	• Pledges to work with all fifty governors and also monitor federal law "to eliminate, where it exists, discrimination against women" • Ends his remarks by asking that "we begin our crusade joined together in a moment of silent prayer"

1992

William J. Clinton (Democrat)	George H. W. Bush (Republican)
• Pledges to "fight to make sure women in this country receive respect and dignity" • Expresses his support for the American family, including "every two-parent family, every single-parent family, and every foster family" • States he will force fathers to fulfill their child support responsibilities • Supports parental leave upon the birth of a child • Strongly declares his support for "women's right to choose" • States that gays are a legitimate and valuable part of an unified America	• When discussing his four-year record, states that "we took a stand for family values by saying that when it comes to raising children, government doesn't know best; parents know best" • States his opposition to quotas as a remedy for discrimination • Supports the option of prayer in public schools • States his opposition to "liberal judges" • On the importance of family, he states "I believe in families that stick together, fathers who stick around" • States that he "believe[s] very deeply in the worth of each individual human being, born or unborn"

(continued)

TABLE 6-10	Cultural Material in the Presidential Nominees' Acceptance Speeches, Selected Years

2004

John F. Kerry (Democrat)	George W. Bush (Republican)
• On faith, states "I don't wear my own faith on my sleeve. But faith has given me values and hope to live by"	• States that "our society rests on a foundation of responsibility and character and family commitment"
• Pledges support for stem cell research	• Pledges support for "welfare reform that strengthens families and requires work"
	• States that American society "must make a place for the unborn child"
	• Emphasizes the importance of religious charities and states that "government must never discriminate against them"
	• On marriage, states "because the union of a man and a woman deserves an honored place in our society, I support the protection of marriages against activist judges"
	• Pledges to "continue to appoint federal judges who know the difference between personal opinion and the strict interpretation of the law"
	• Discussing Senator Kerry, states that "if you voted against the bipartisan Defense of Marriage Act, which President Clinton signed, you are not the candidate of conservative values"

Note: The texts of all Democratic and Republican presidential candidates' nomination acceptance speeches since 1960 are available at www.4president.org.

In somewhat of a surprise, neither Democratic nominee George McGovern nor Republican nominee Richard Nixon had much to say about cultural issues in their 1972 acceptance speeches. While McGovern is today widely regarded as an extremely liberal candidate, and we know from Kevin Phillips that Nixon used cultural issues as part of his strategy in 1968,[45] it is important to remember that the platforms of both parties in 1972 were somewhat muted on cultural issues, and what was there—mostly in the Democratic platform—was quite vague. Nixon and McGovern were both more concerned with Vietnam, race, law and order, and youth behavior than the cultural issues under examination here,[46] and on the one cultural issue prominent in 1972—women's rights and the ERA—both men were highly supportive and differed little.[47] In fact, in a letter to the Republican minority leader in the Senate in 1972, Nixon stated his position thusly: "Throughout twenty-one years I have not altered my belief that equal rights for women warrant a constitutional guarantee—and I therefore continue to favor the enactment of the constitutional amendment to achieve this goal."[48]

The acceptance speeches of both candidates in 1980 do not contain much cultural material, which might lead us to conclude that the parties remained relatively undifferentiated on those issues. Such a conclusion would be wrong. We know from the 1980 platforms that cultural issues concerned both parties, and the lack of attention in the acceptance speeches belies the important role that cultural matters played in the 1980 campaign. During his tenure as president and during the 1980 campaign, Jimmy Carter took the liberal position on abortion, school prayer, and the ERA, but he did not seem particularly enthusiastic about any of those stands, except perhaps on the ERA. But despite his own seeming personal misgivings, he did clearly support the culturally liberal options.[49] Ronald Reagan, on the other hand, was not conflicted on cultural issues. He perhaps provided an indication of what was to come when he ended his 1980 acceptance speech by asking his audience to "begin our crusade joined together in a moment of silent prayer." For Reagan his nomination in 1980 represented the continuation of the crusade that he had been leading since the 1960s—to make the Republican Party the conservative party across the board, not only on economic issues but on cultural issues as well.[50] Cultural issues played a central role in the eight-year presidency of Ronald Reagan. By the time he left office in January 1989, Reagan had succeeded beyond what even he could have hoped for. No one has played a larger role in the contemporary cultural divide that exists between the Republicans and the Democrats than Ronald Reagan.

Throughout his political career, Reagan consistently and frequently invoked the importance of family values for the health of American society. He made no secret of his opposition to the ERA and his insistence, along with the efforts of activists like Phyllis Schlafly and Beverly LaHaye, was crucial in removing support for the ERA from the GOP platform in 1980.[51] Reagan was a strong proponent of returning prayer to public schools, saying in his 1983 State of the Union address that "God should never have been expelled from America's classrooms in the first place."[52] He promised the American people that he would try to amend the Constitution to allow the return of prayer, and he did use his influence to force an unsuccessful vote on such an amendment in 1984.[53] But the cultural issue that mattered most to Reagan was abortion. On this issue there could be no compromise; abortion was murder on an unprecedented scale and every effort had to be made in order to stop abortion from occurring.[54] In 1988 Reagan promised to veto a bill if it contained a provision allowing federal funds to be used for abortion in cases of rape and/or incest, stating in a letter to then Senate Minority Leader Bob Dole, "The Senate language would permit the use of federal funds for the slaughter of unborn children, depriving the innocent of the most basic of civil rights, the right to life."[55] There was no mistaking the cultural conservatism of Ronald Reagan.

Subsequent presidential nominees and eventual presidents have followed Reagan's example by clearly and forcefully presenting their stands on cultural issues. In fact, they have even expanded the field of conflict on these matters. As Table 6–10 shows, neither Bill Clinton nor George H. W. Bush was shy about including cultural positions in their respective 1992 acceptances speeches. Clinton strongly defended a woman's right to choose on abortion, indicated his acceptance of the family in a variety of forms, and in an acceptance speech first, stated his support for the legitimacy of homosexuality. As J. David Woodard notes, no presidential candidate before or since has been as supportive of gays as was Clinton.[56] George H. W. Bush countered with his belief that unborn human beings need to be protected, strong support for returning prayer to schools, and condemnation of "liberal judges." Both George H. W. Bush and Bill Clinton also indicated their positions on abortion through their messages on abortion legislation that they vetoed, with George H. W. Bush decrying "the tragedy in America of abortion on demand"[57] and Bill

Clinton stating that "I have always believed that the decision to have an abortion generally should be between a woman, her doctor, her conscience, and her God. I support the decision in *Roe v. Wade.*"[58]

But perhaps no presidential candidate or president has been more clear and adamant on cultural issues than current president George W. Bush. He is, after all, the man who when asked about his favorite political philosopher in a 1999 debate among candidates for the Republican presidential nomination responded, "Christ, because he changed my heart." In his 2004 acceptance speech, George W. Bush touted the importance of religious charities, repeatedly noted the importance of families, stated that marriage is between a man and a woman, and pledged his support for the unborn. He has emphasized his opposition to abortion, euthanasia, same-sex marriage, and many restrictions on the mixing of church and state again and again through his words and actions as president. Adding his support to an additional issue in the culture wars that no previous president or presidential candidate has addressed—although who can forget William Jennings Bryan—George W. Bush told reporters that he believed "intelligent design" should be taught in public schools alongside evolution as a competing explanation of human origins.[59] George W. Bush regularly cites Ronald Reagan as his political hero, and indeed the similarities between the two men as cultural warriors are hard to miss.

CONCLUSION

This discussion of presidential politics and cultural issues makes it quite clear—the Republican and Democratic Parties of the early twenty-first century present very different options on cultural issues. These differences are not mere matters of degree, but rather represent diametrically opposed stands on the cultural issues prominent in contemporary America. Thus far we have shown that society changed in such ways as to produce cultural concerns, and that the parties responded to these cultural concerns by placing them on the political agenda and offering Americans clear and different options for how to deal with the issues. The final element to be demonstrated is whether cultural issues affect the political beliefs and choices of individual citizens—whether Americans recognize the differences on cultural issues that exist between the two parties, and if so, whether these differences influence individual party identification and vote choice.

We also need to directly address a topic that thus far has entered our analysis only tangentially—religion. Religion has been like the proverbial elephant in the room—we all know about the elephant in the room and its influences on all else that is going on, but no one talks about it. Of course religion is important to the rise of cultural issues in American politics—in fact nothing else is more important. Religious beliefs and traditions are crucial for understanding why many Americans are troubled by the cultural trends we have presented here, and also for explaining the parties' responses.[60] The next chapter, focusing on the general public, will directly address the elephant that is religion. After all, in the story of cultural issues and American politics, it is the religious identities, beliefs, and behaviors of average Americans that matter most.

CULTURAL DIVIDES IN THE AMERICAN PUBLIC

Our examination of cultural issues and American politics has finally reached the mass public—the voters. Chapter 5 documented the social changes and political events that led to the rise of cultural concerns in American society, laying the groundwork for political conflict to potentially develop over these issues. Chapter 6 showed that over time the Republican and Democratic Parties have taken highly divergent positions across the entire range of cultural issues, providing citizens very clear and very different options on these matters. Therefore the stage is set for cultural issues to dramatically affect American politics. But social conditions and elite reactions to those conditions alone are not enough for political change. The masses must respond as well, and respond in such a way that the social changes and elite reactions in question come to structure individual partisan identification and vote choice. Has the American public responded in such a way when it comes to cultural issues?

MASS RECOGNITION OF ELITE CHANGES

Before voters can respond to party positions on a particular set of issues, they must first be cognizant of the parties' stands. We know the parties have sharply diverged on cultural issues—but has the general public perceived this development? The short answer here is "yes." As Figure 4-2 showed, Americans have increasingly seen important differences between the parties since the early 1970s.[1] And as Figure 7-1 shows, white

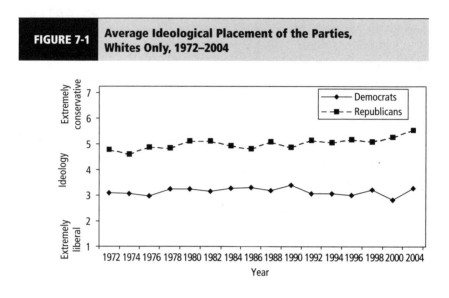

FIGURE 7-1   **Average Ideological Placement of the Parties, Whites Only, 1972–2004**

Note: Respondents are asked to place the parties on a 7-point scale that runs from 1 (extremely liberal) to 7 (extremely conservative).

Sources: NES Cumulative Datafile, 1972–2002, vcf0503 and vcf0504; NES 2004, v043090 and v043091.

Americans (for the same reasons explained in Chapter 4, all analyses in this chapter are for whites only) have clearly perceived the Republican Party as more conservative than the Democrats since the early 1970s.

So Americans see important differences between the parties, and they are also aware that the GOP is the more conservative option in general. But the key issue for this chapter is whether the general public perceives the parties as different on cultural issues. While the evidence here is not as direct as for party differences in general, it is still clear that the mass has received the party elites' signals on cultural issues. As a follow-up to the party difference question reported in Figure 7-1, the NES asks about the substance behind any differences the respondents see between the parties.[2] Also, since 1952 the NES has asked respondents if there is anything they like and anything they dislike about both the Democrats and the Republicans. Those who answer "yes" to these questions are then given the opportunity to state specifically what they like and/or dislike about each party. Figure 7-2[3] presents the percentages of party likes and dislikes and substantive differences accounted for by cultural issues since

| FIGURE 7-2 | Percentage of Party Likes/Dislikes and Differences between the Parties Comprised of Cultural Issues, Whites Only, 1952–2004 |

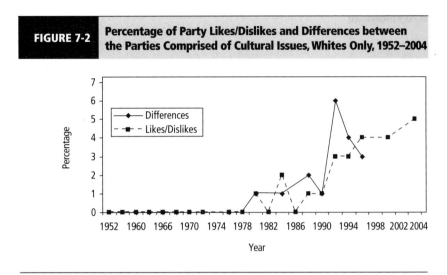

Note: Only first responses considered for both party likes/dislikes and party differences.

Source: NES Individual Year Studies.

1952 and 1960, respectively.[4] As the figure indicates, cultural issues went virtually unmentioned until the early 1980s. From that point forward, cultural issues have become a slowly increasing component of both individuals' perceived differences between the parties and their affect toward the parties.[5] Although some might see figures of 5 percent and 6 percent as low, it is important to keep in mind that roughly 50 percent of respondents per study offer no likes/dislikes or differences between the parties. So the growth from zero to levels of 5–6 percent is relatively impressive.

As further evidence of public awareness of partisan differences on cultural issues, the 2004 NES asked respondents to place the Democratic and Republican Parties based on their perceptions on where the parties stood on two of the cultural issues under discussion here—abortion and the proper role of women in society. On a four-point scale where 1 stood for the position that abortion should never be allowed and 4 represented the position that women should always have the option of abortion as a matter of personal choice, the mean for the Democrats was 3.32, while for the GOP it was 1.93.[6] For positions on the role of women, on a seven-point scale in which 1 represented the position that women should have an equal role and 7 represented the position that women's place should

FIGURE 7-3	**Percentage of Respondents Identifying a Cultural Issue as the Most Important National Problem, Whites Only, 1960–2004**

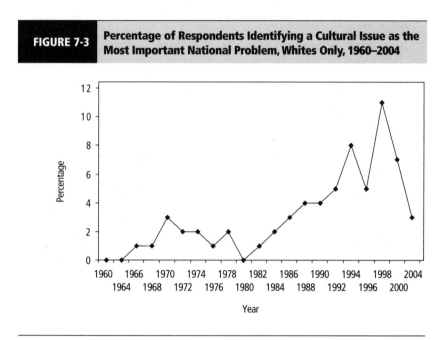

Note: There are two possible reasons besides real opinion change for the decrease in cultural issue mentions in 2004. The first is a change in question wording. Prior to 2004, the question asked respondents to identify the most important problem facing the country. In 2004, the question asked respondents to identify the most important issue facing the nation over the past 4 years. Not surprisingly, mentions of 9/11, al Qaida, terrorism, and the war in Iraq dominated in 2004, accounting for 57 percent of the total mentions. The coding for cultural issues is available from the authors upon request.

Source: NES Cumulative Datafile, 1948–2004; NES 2004.

be in the home, the Republican mean was 3.71, and the Democratic mean was 2.61. Americans are clearly aware that the Democrats and Republicans differ on cultural issues. When this awareness is combined with the growing percentage of Americans who believe that a cultural issue is the most important problem facing the nation, as shown in Figure 7-3, the environment is ripe for cultural issues to affect electoral behavior.[7]

CULTURAL ISSUES AND ELECTORAL BEHAVIOR

There are plenty of reasons to believe that the impact of cultural issues on individual electoral behavior has increased in recent years. Cultural issues are almost perfect examples of what Edward Carmines and James Stimson term "easy" issues. Easy issues are issues that people respond to on a fundamental or "gut" level. No particular expertise is required, nor is any vast amount of political knowledge. On an easy issue, a person can and does form an opinion almost immediately, and just about every citizen does in fact adopt a position.[8] This is not to say that the issue in question is not complicated, but only that it is not perceived as such by most individuals. Citizens are confronted with the issue and they form an opinion based on emotional reactions and basic values, without the messy uncertainty brought about by consideration of nuance or complicated analysis. The cultural issues we have considered in this book thus far—such as homosexual rights and abortion—certainly fit this bill, and previous research supports such a view. A number of scholars report that the vast majority of Americans have a position on abortion,[9] and Benjamin Page and Robert Shapiro show the same is true for a wide variety of social issues, including all those under consideration here.[10]

Besides being easy issues, cultural issues are also highly emotional issues for many, if not most Americans. They play on deeply held beliefs and prejudices, and can incite powerful passions. Powerful passions, of course, can affect political behavior. Ted Jelen and Clyde Wilcox note that this is most certainly true of the abortion issue, and other scholars make similar cases for women's rights, school prayer, and homosexual rights.[11] Going even further, Nicol Rae argues that except for periods of extreme national economic distress it is these passionate cultural issues that determine the outcomes of American elections.[12] Finally, Ronald Inglehart argues that cultural issues have become even more important in the politics of western democracies—including the United States—over the past thirty to forty years as relative prosperity has become more widespread and citizens worry less about questions of material well-being and more about quality of life concerns.[13] When these arguments are combined with the social developments that created contemporary cultural issues in the first place (as described in Chapter 5), we should not be surprised to find cultural issues affecting electoral behavior in the United States. Rather, we should be surprised to find that they do not.

So, what do the data tell us? Do cultural issues affect Americans' electoral behavior, and how has this influence, if there is any, changed over time? While theoretically these questions may seem easily answered, the reality is a bit more difficult. The NES has been quite light on questions

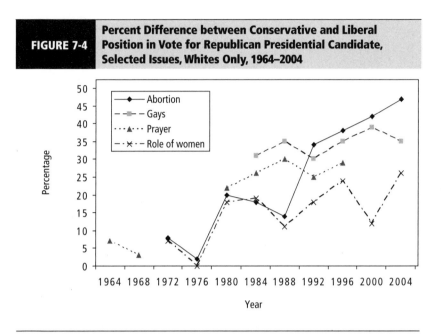

FIGURE 7-4 **Percent Difference between Conservative and Liberal Position in Vote for Republican Presidential Candidate, Selected Issues, Whites Only, 1964–2004**

Note: For abortion, the conservative position is that abortion should never be allowed and the liberal position is that abortion should never be restricted as an option. To measure views toward gays and lesbians, a 0–100 degree thermometer measuring degree of feeling is used—the conservative position is a rating from 0–49 degrees, and the liberal position is a rating from 51–100 degrees. For school prayer, the conservative position is that schools should schedule a time for students to say a non-denominational or a Christian prayer (1986–1998) and schools should be allowed to start the day with prayer (1964–1984), and the liberal position is that prayer should not be allowed in public schools. For the role of women, the conservative position is a response of 5–7 on a seven-point scale where point 1 is "women and men should have an equal role" and point 7 is "women's place is in the home," and the liberal position is a response of 1–3 on this same scale.

Source: NES Cumulative Datafile, 1948–2004.

regarding cultural issues. While this is not terribly surprising during the 1950s and 1960s, when cultural issues were either not yet present or just coming on the scene, the relative dearth of questions from the 1970s on is somewhat surprising and most definitely problematic for researchers. However, there are a few appropriate questions on social issues that have been asked repeatedly over time, and fortunately four of them correspond with the cultural issues examined in the last chapter—school prayer (first asked in 1964), abortion (first asked in 1972), the proper role of women in society (first asked in 1972), and a question asking respondents if they feel warmly or coolly toward gays and lesbians (first asked in 1984). Figures 7-4, 7-5, and 7-6 present the difference between respondents having a conservative view on these four issues and respondents

| FIGURE 7-5 | Percent Difference between Conservative and Liberal Position in Vote for Republican Party House Candidate, Selected Issues, Whites Only, 1964–2004 |

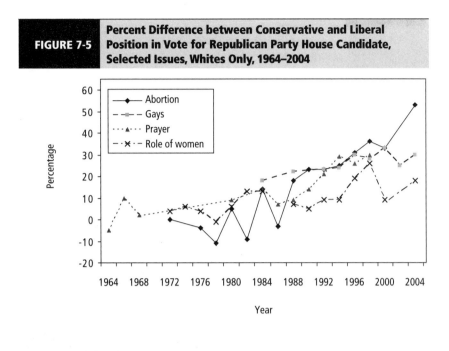

Note: The same classification of conservative and liberal positions in Figure 7-4 is used here.

Source: NES Cumulative Datafile, 1948–2004.

with a liberal view in their vote for Republican presidential candidates, Republican House candidates, and identification with the Republican Party, respectively.[14] A positive figure indicates that more conservatives than liberals favored the GOP, while a negative figure indicates more liberals favored the GOP.

A quick glance at all three figures indicates two things: first that those respondents with conservative positions on these issues are now much more supportive of the Republican Party than are those with liberal positions, and second that the gaps on these issues between conservatives and liberals have grown over time. A more detailed examination reveals additional information. Beginning first with Figure 7-4, which presents the differences in Republican presidential vote, we can see that the differences between conservatives and liberals in Republican vote choice have increased over time for all four cultural issues, and that the differences are now quite large for all issues except women's role in society. Those

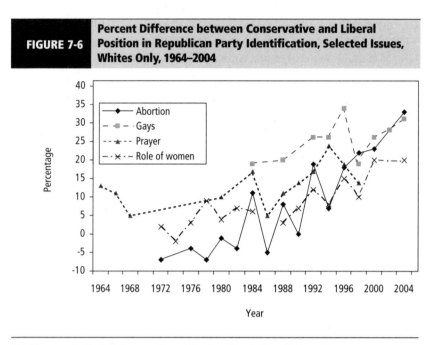

| FIGURE 7-6 | Percent Difference between Conservative and Liberal Position in Republican Party Identification, Selected Issues, Whites Only, 1964–2004 |

Note: The same classification of conservative and liberal positions in Figure 7-4 is used here.

Source: NES Cumulative Datafile, 1948–2004.

who were conservative on school prayer were only 7 percentage points more likely than prayer liberals to vote Republican for president in 1964; this difference increased to 29 points in 1996. For the abortion issue, a difference of 8 points in 1972 rose to 47 points in 2004. Differences on the role of women in society started out relatively small at 7 points in 1972, but increased to 26 points in 2004. Finally, the differences in Republican support on feeling toward gays and lesbians started out large in 1984 at 31 points and stayed large, increasing to 35 in 2004. Although these figures are only simple cross-tabulations, they are relatively impressive differences, nonetheless. It certainly appears that cultural issue positions—at least the four shown here—now have a large impact on presidential vote, and also that these effects have grown at least somewhat over time.

Examinations of Figures 7-5 and 7-6 show largely the same picture presented by the results for presidential vote, although with a few differences in magnitude—but none in direction. In all instances conservatives are now more likely to support the GOP, and in all cases the differences grew. The differences in Republican support between conservatives and liberals are consistently the largest on the abortion issue, which is perhaps not surprising given the number of previous studies showing that position on abortion significantly affects electoral behavior.[15] But the differences on feelings toward homosexuals and school prayer are consistently large as well. There is always a gap in GOP support for the view of women's role, although it generally is smaller. The differences on the abortion issue grew the most over time, although the growth for school prayer was impressive as well, except for party identification. The differences on the issue of women's role did not change too much, and the same is true for feeling toward homosexuals, although the differences started out rather large for the issue of feelings towards gays, perhaps leaving less room for expansion.

The bottom line here is that no matter which cultural issue one looks at, or which partisan support indicator one chooses, conservatives are more likely to support the Republican Party than are liberals, and these differences have increased over time.[16] We have pretty strong support for the increasing importance of cultural issues for electoral behavior, at least at the bivariate level (analyzing two variables together to determine a relationship).

RELIGION, CULTURAL ISSUES, AND AMERICAN ELECTORAL BEHAVIOR

While cultural issues have come to play an increasing role in the outcomes of American elections, we need to ask why this development has occurred. To answer this question we examine religion in the United States. To claim that the United States is a religious nation is to state the blatantly obvious. The secularization theory that was so dominant in the 1970s—the belief that the modernization of society would eventually render religion irrelevant or at least much less important in Western democracies—may indeed be useful in understanding changes in Western Europe, but it is most definitely not applicable to the American experience. Whether one focuses on levels of religious belief, behavior, or belonging, Americans are a highly religious people, and the United States, as a whole, is a very religious nation.[17] This was true in the eighteenth century, and it is true today.

Given the religious nature of American society, it is not surprising that religion also has long played an important role in American politics, particularly in American electoral politics.[18] But the manner in which religion affects electoral behavior in the United States has changed somewhat in recent years, and it is these changes that are crucial to understanding the increasing importance of cultural issues for Americans' choices of which party to identify with and which candidates to vote for. Historically, religion exhibited its largest impact on electoral behavior by way of a cleavage based on religious tradition. The most prominent example of this was the steep divide that existed between Protestants and Roman Catholics. In a split that fully manifested itself after the Civil War, Catholics tended to strongly support the Democratic Party, while Protestants—at least those who lived outside of the South—were equally strong backers of the Republicans.[19] This cleavage between Catholics and Protestants was perhaps the most powerful electoral cleavage in the second half of the nineteenth century, and remained vital throughout the New Deal period and into the 1960s.[20] Despite assertions to the contrary by some,[21] the religious tradition cleavage still exists, and is still relevant to American electoral politics. However, it is the case that the contours of the cleavage based on religious tradition have changed, and these changes help us understand the growing importance of cultural issues in American politics.

Religious Traditions and Political Divisions in America

We first briefly discuss religious traditions. We stated above that the primary religious cleavage in nineteenth century America existed between Catholics and Protestants. While there is little concern about treating Roman Catholics as a single group,[22] some might view grouping all Protestants together as problematic. Though this point has some validity when dealing with nineteenth century American Protestantism, it is a much more pressing concern given the evolution of the American religious landscape during the twentieth century.

While it is certainly true that meaningful differences existed between Protestant denominations in nineteenth century America—such as the Pietist/Liturgical distinction discussed by Paul Kleppner and Richard Jensen[23]—it is also true that Protestant groups of this period had much in common. The individual denominations were all spiritual heirs of the Reformation, and as such emphasized one-on-one relationships with God, relatively democratic styles of church governance, and the ability of the individual believer to interpret the meaning of the Bible for himself or herself. There was certainly a shared sense of Protestant identity.[24]

Beginning in the early part of the twentieth century, this unity began to change as tensions arose within American Protestantism. As scientific discoveries and advances increasingly called into question religious doctrines and explanations of the world, elements within Protestantism responded in very different ways. Some chose to embrace science and its theories, while others rejected modernism and held fast to traditional views and explanations. The liberal Social Gospel movement that arose during the Progressive Era at the beginning of the century also divided Protestants, as did, in many cases, geography. By the 1920s it was clear that American Protestantism had split into two largely separate traditions—one that was more amenable to adapting to modernity, referred to today as mainline Protestantism, and another that was more skeptical of science and "progress" and held tightly to tradition, referred to today as evangelical Protestantism.[25] Of course, this division continues to exist within contemporary American religion, and is perhaps stronger now than at any previous point in American history.

The question of religious traditions matters for this analysis because the adherents of the three largest religious traditions among whites in the United States—Roman Catholicism, mainline Protestantism, and evangelical Protestantism—exhibit different patterns of electoral behavior. In addition, secular Americans—those who do not identify with any religion or identify themselves as atheist or agnostic—also behave differently than those Americans who claim a religious identity. Figure 7-7 presents the percentages of white mainline Protestants, evangelical Protestants, Roman Catholics, and seculars identifying with the Republican Party since 1960.[26] Trends in Republican voting by religious tradition for both presidential and House elections are very similar to those for party identification, and thus are not presented here.

Figure 7-7 presents a picture of both stability and change. Mainliners constitute the most stable component of the image. In terms of partisan support, mainline Protestants have been strongly Republican for almost

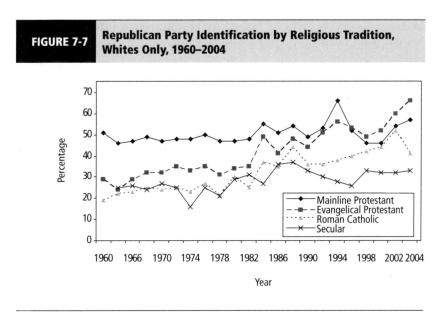

FIGURE 7-7   Republican Party Identification by Religious Tradition, Whites Only, 1960–2004

Note: For a discussion of the classification of religious traditions, see endnote 26 in this chapter. There were too few seculars to report figures for 1960.

Source: NES Cumulative Datafile, 1948–2004.

the entire time period presented here, continuing a history of GOP support that stretches back for well over a century. While there were slight declines in GOP support among mainliners in 1998 and 2000, these declines reversed in the last two election cycles.[27] Seculars, too, have remained for the most part stable in their partisanship, with their levels of Republican identification hovering somewhere between the mid-20s and mid-30s. White seculars' support of the GOP rose in mid-1980s (as did that of most white Americans), but since the late 1980s seculars have consistently exhibited the lowest Republican support of any of the four groups examined here. Roman Catholics contribute more to the changing portion of the picture. After exhibiting incredibly high levels of Democratic support in 1960 as the party selected Catholic John F. Kennedy as its presidential nominee, Catholics have moved slowly but steadily toward increased Republican support. While it is true that Catholics remain more Democratic than Protestants as a whole, it is also true that Catholics have become more Republican over the last thirty years.[28]

The biggest change seen in Figure 7-7 has come from evangelical Protestants. Evangelicals have historically been concentrated in the South.[29] This fact, combined with the one-party Democratic nature of the South from the end of Reconstruction through the 1960s meant that at the beginning of the period being examined here most evangelicals voted for and identified with the Democratic Party.[30] Supporting the GOP was for many evangelicals unthinkable. Beginning in the 1960s this began to change. Republican support began to rise, slowly at first and then at an increasingly rapid clip beginning in the 1980s, a development in which the appeal of Ronald Reagan to evangelicals played a large role.[31] The issue of race was also an important factor here, given the facts that during this period evangelicals were largely concentrated in the South, and that Southerners tended to be more conservative on the question of race.[32] Pushed by both race and culture, evangelical Protestants have undergone a significant political realignment over the past three decades. By 2004 evangelicals were much more Republican than either Catholics or mainline Protestants, and had, by many accounts, become the single most important component of the Republican coalition.[33]

At this point a reader might be thinking, this stuff about religious traditions is a nice story, but why does it matter here? What does all this have to do with the growing importance of cultural issues in American politics generally and elections specifically? The answers to these questions lie in the shifts in partisan support presented in Figure 7-7. Seculars are by definition the least concerned of the four groups with the doctrines and dogmas of a religious tradition. While this of course does not necessarily mean that all seculars will hold liberal positions on cultural issues, it does mean that this segment of the population will not be pushed to the cultural right by their religious beliefs. Next, while it is somewhat dangerous to generalize in this way, most would agree that of the three religious traditions examined here, evangelical Protestantism is clearly the most conservative in terms of theology and doctrine. Mainline Protestantism is certainly more liberal along these lines than evangelicalism, and has moved even further left in recent decades.[34]

In terms of ideology, Roman Catholicism presents an interesting case. On economic and social justice issues, Catholic doctrine and teaching is extremely liberal. But on many issues involving sexuality and morality, the Catholic Church is highly conservative.[35] This matters because the two religious traditions shown here that have become more Republican over the past four decades—Roman Catholics and evangelical Protestants—are those that are more conservative on cultural issues. For Catholics, the move toward the GOP has had much to do with social class, with upper income Catholics being much more likely to support the Republican Party.[36] Cultural issues, however, have also played a role in Catholics' changing electoral patterns, with numerous studies showing that Catholics who are more "traditional" are also more likely to vote for and identify with the Republicans.[37] So while perhaps not the dominant reason, cultural issues are an important factor in Catholics' increasing support of the GOP.

Among evangelicals, the role of cultural issues in producing the growth in Republicanism is much clearer and also much more important. While there is undoubtedly a good deal of diversity among evangelicals in terms of religious thought and beliefs,[38] there are two matters of doctrine at the core of what it means to be an evangelical Protestant that serve to distinguish evangelicals from mainline Protestants, and also from other Christians. The first is the belief that the Bible is the ultimate and only source of religious authority, although not necessarily inerrant. The second is a belief in the necessity of a "born-again" experience—a specific life-altering event in which an individual accepts Jesus as her or his personal savior—in order to achieve personal salvation and guarantee a place in heaven in the afterlife.[39] When carried out into day-to-day life, these tenets result in evangelicals placing a high level of importance on traditional family structure and relations, strongly opposing any relaxation of or alterations to the traditionally accepted norms of sexuality, and vehemently defending traditional ideas and conceptions of morality.[40] The repetitive use of the word "tradition" is of the utmost importance here. After all, contemporary evangelical Protestantism first coalesced in an attempt to defend traditional American Protestantism and religious culture, and this centrality of traditional arrangements remains vitally important today.

The social changes that led to the rise of cultural issues in American society are clearly the antithesis of tradition. In fact, one could argue that the changes in family matters, sexual practices, and morality in general openly flout tradition and attempt to relegate it to irrelevance in American life. The tension between those Americans with more traditional views on these issues and those with more progressive views has pushed cultural issues to the fore in American politics.[41] Many of the Americans holding the views often referred to as traditional and pushing their views of appropriate behavior are evangelical Protestants. While it would be a mistake to claim that all evangelicals are cultural conservatives, or that all cultural conservatives are evangelicals,[42] there is little doubt that evangelicals are at the core of cultural issues' rise to prominence in the American public dialogue. Evangelicals' reentry into American politics and the changes in their electoral behavior have significantly increased the importance of cultural issues in American politics. More so than any other group, evangelical Protestants are critical to understanding the cultural divide that now exists in the United States.

After American Protestantism split into mainline and evangelical camps during the early decades of the twentieth century, evangelical Protestantism in many ways withdrew from the public arena. For roughly the next forty years, evangelicals remained somewhat aloof from the political sphere, content to mind their own affairs and build their own religious institutions and networks.[43] This concentration on their own affairs proved quite fruitful for evangelicals. They were able to construct impressive communication networks and organizational structures, and at first maintain and then eventually increase their membership numbers.[44] This meant that evangelicals were well positioned to have an impact in the political arena, if they chose to get involved. Spurred by the social changes discussed in Chapter 5, an increasing number of evangelicals began making such a choice. The *Engel* decision in 1962 to ban prayer in public schools was a wake-up call for many evangelicals. The removal of prayer from schools was a first notice that society might be headed in a direction that they did not agree with. The sexual revolution and emergence of a reenergized women's movement that soon followed the prayer decision confirmed for many evangelicals that culture was decaying all around them. Traditional values and morals were being threatened and, in some cases, disregarded altogether. When the Supreme Court legalized abortion nationwide with the *Roe* decision in 1973, many evangelicals decided the time had come to act politically.[45]

For many evangelical Protestants, this decision to act meant at least in part increasing support for the Republican Party. This realignment of evangelicals to the GOP, combined with a similar movement on the part of at least some Catholics, altered the religious tradition cleavage in American electoral politics in such a way as to make cultural issues more important. It was after all cultural issues that pushed at least some evangelicals and conservative Catholics into the Republican coalition. But the changing behavior of evangelicals and more traditional Catholics also points to the development of a new cleavage in the electoral landscape, one that is far more important to understanding the increasing role of cultural issues in American politics. Although this new cleavage has been called many different things, it is most often referred to as "the culture war."

As we discussed in Chapter 5, the growing importance of cultural issues in American society did not end with the decision in *Roe*. Abortions rose dramatically (at least legal abortions did) immediately after the Court removed most of the restrictions on the practice. The number of divorces continued to increase as well, and more and more children were being born outside of marriage. The sexual revolution continued unabated, and increasingly included efforts aimed at securing recognized legitimacy and protection for homosexuality in American society. Obscenity and pornography received greater protection from the courts, and such material became more widespread and easier to obtain. Even the content of mainstream entertainment became ever more salacious and titillating. The presence of sex education and the absence of prayer in public schools continued to receive the attention of parents' groups and school boards across the country. The so-called values controversies were clearly not going away; if anything they were intensifying.

Cultural Issues and a New Religious Cleavage

By the mid-1980s, some were beginning to take notice of the increasingly important place of cultural issues in American public life. Sociologists Robert Wuthnow and the already heavily discussed James Davison Hunter were prominent here. According to both men, the emergence of issues such as school prayer, abortion, pornography, and homosexuality was increasingly dividing Americans into two camps. On one side were the religiously liberal or progressive (which included the irreligious), who tended to support the removal of prayer from public schools and also be more tolerant of protections for abortion rights, homosexuals, and the allowing of sexual content in a variety of forms even if they themselves did not approve of the particular matter in question.

On the other side were the religiously conservative or orthodox, who wanted prayer back in schools where it belonged, and had little tolerance for abortion, homosexuality, or sexual content in the media. While evangelical Protestants were—and are—important to the rise of cultural issues, the religiously motivated divide described here is not one based on denomination or religious tradition. It is rather based on religious ideology, and therefore an entirely new and different development. Individuals from all denominations and traditions occupied spots on both sides of the cleavage. In fact, the differences between Catholics and Protestants (both mainline and evangelical) and, to a lesser extent, Jews that had traditionally been important in American society and politics were now decreasing in importance. The important divide now was between religious groups with dramatically different views of moral authority, and different views on what the "good" community should look like. According to this view, the cultural issues that first appeared on the radar screen in the early 1960s were dominating American politics by the early 1990s. The bottom line was that Americans were increasingly at odds over cultural issues because they had fundamentally different ideas about the determination of right and wrong.[46]

The earliest efforts at empirical assessment claimed to not find much support for the existence of a culture war. These first studies found little evidence of a public divided over cultural issues, or of a cultural cleavage affecting vote choice or party identification.[47] However, arguments could be made against the interpretations of some of these researchers, as their studies did contain findings showing significant differences between the religiously orthodox and the religiously progressive on issues such as abortion and other reproductive rights, the proper relationship between women and men in society, and certain issues in public education.[48] These issues are of course all central to claims of a cultural divide in the United States, and at least hinted that there might yet be some empirical backing for the culture wars claims.

The empirical evidence for the existence of a division in American politics based on cultural issues has increased dramatically over the past few years. It is now clear that substantial differences of opinion on cultural issues exist between those Americans on the orthodox and those on the progressive side of the social spectrum. Perhaps the strongest empirical evidence for division in the American public over moral issues is provided by John Evans. Among the population as a whole, opinions on issues of sexuality joined abortion as examples of areas where attitudes were growing increasingly polarized. Evidence for moral issue polarization between liberals and conservatives also grew, as the issues of sex education and school prayer joined abortion as examples of polarized topics. Finally, Evans presented strong support for cultural issue polarization between partisans with the electorate on the cultural issues of abortion, women's roles, family gender roles, sexual morality, and school prayer.[49] Looking more directly at electoral politics, a number of recent empirical analyses present results showing that attitudes on cultural issues are increasingly affecting electoral behavior, most notably in presidential voting, but also to a lesser extent for House voting and party identification.[50] These findings support the bivariate results presented earlier in this chapter, and certainly lend credence to those voices announcing the presence of cultural conflict within the United States.

One final piece of evidence supports the view that cultural battles now drive American politics. Religious salience simply means how important religion is to an individual.[51] For many years, religious salience seems to have had little impact on Americans' electoral behavior. When it came to religion, it was religious tradition that affected partisan support, not salience. This is no longer true. Numerous studies over the past few years have found that religious salience is now significantly affecting individuals' electoral behavior. Those individuals for whom religion is highly salient are increasingly likely to support the Republican Party, while those with low levels of religious salience are now more Democratic in the vote choice and partisanship.[52]

While there is some disagreement on the best way to measure religious salience, most agree that at the very least the measure used needs to have both cognitive and behavioral components.[53] In other words, the indicator needs to incorporate both thought and action. While the

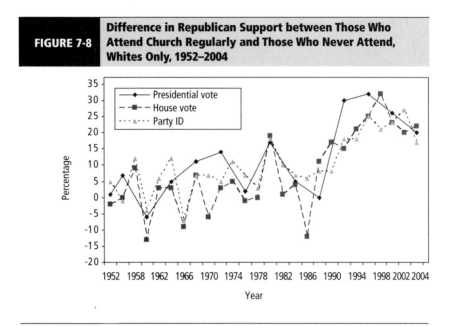

| FIGURE 7-8 | Difference in Republican Support between Those Who Attend Church Regularly and Those Who Never Attend, Whites Only, 1952–2004 |

Note: From 1952–1968, regularly denotes a response of "regularly." From 1970–2004, regularly denotes a response of "every week."

Source: NES Cumulative Datafile, 1948–2004.

NES has historically been limited in the religious questions that it asks,[54] it does ask two questions that allow us to create a sound measure of religious salience. The first of these questions asks respondents about their frequency of attendance at worship services, and data have been available since 1952. This will serve as our behavioral component. The second question queries respondents as to the amount of guidance they receive from religion in their daily lives, and was introduced in 1980. The guidance question will act as our cognitive dimension.

Figure 7-8 presents for the period 1952–2004 the differences in Republican support for presidential vote, House vote, and party identification between those who regularly attend worship services and those who never attend services. Similarly, Figure 7-9 presents these same differences for 1980–2004 between those who exhibit high levels of religious salience and those who exhibit low levels, based on an index of salience created from the church attendance and religious guidance questions.[55]

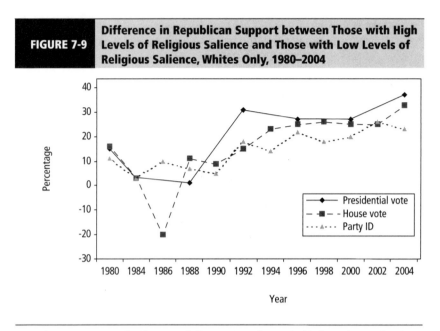

FIGURE 7-9 Difference in Republican Support between Those with High Levels of Religious Salience and Those with Low Levels of Religious Salience, Whites Only, 1980–2004

Note: Religious importance and guidance not asked in 1982. See endnote 55 in this chapter for an explanation on the creation of the religious salience index.

Source: NES Cumulative Datafile, 1948–2004.

What is clear from both figures is that since the late 1980s, the more salient religion is to an individual, the more likely that individual is to vote for or identify with the Republican Party. The differences for all three partisan support indicators, for both salience measures, are consistently over 20 percentage points in recent years. The growing talk of a "church attendance gap" in American electoral politics is supported by these results.[56] In today's America, if religion is very important to you, you likely support the GOP. If religion matters little or not at all to you, then the odds are pretty good that you support the Democratic Party.

Taken as a whole, the case for a cultural cleavage in American electoral politics is quite strong. While it would clearly be a mistake to claim that a high level of religious salience automatically translates to correspondingly high degrees of religious conservatism or orthodoxy, there is a correlation between these phenomena. The growing importance of religious salience, combined with rising levels of attitude polarization on cultural issues within American society and the growing impact of moral issue

FIGURE 7-10	Difference in Republican Support between Biblical Literalists and Biblical Minimalists, Whites Only, 1964–2004, Selected Years

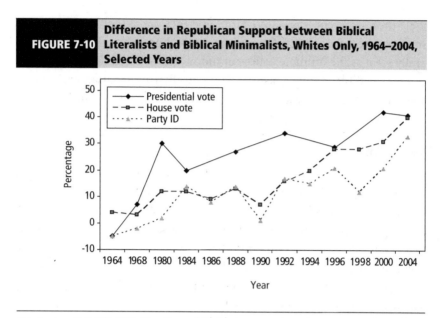

Note: For years 1964–1990, Biblical literalists are defined as those respondents who selected "The Bible is God's word and all it says is true" when asked their view of the Bible, and Biblical minimalists were those respondents who chose either "The Bible is a good book because it was written by wise men, but God had nothing to do with it" or "The Bible was written by men who lived so long ago that it is worth very little today" as best representative of their view of the Bible. For years 1992–2004, Biblical literalists are defined as those who selected "The Bible is the actual Word of God and is to be taken literally, word for word" and Biblical minimalists are those respondents who chose "The Bible is a book written by men and is not the Word of God."

Source: NES Cumulative Datafile, 1948–2004.

opinions on electoral behavior certainly point to a significant divide over cultural issues in contemporary American politics. The cultural divide among the mass public closely mirrors the one that exists between partisan elites, with liberals aligning with the Democratic Party and conservatives choosing the Republicans.

Some continue to be skeptical of the culture war's existence.[57] Morris Fiorina and his colleagues are prominent among these skeptics, flatly stating: "The simple truth is that there is no culture war in the United States—no battle for the soul of America rages."[58] The evidence to the contrary, however, is increasingly too strong to ignore. Recalling Hunter's claims about the differing sources of moral authority between the two sides in the culture war, examine Figure 7-10, which presents the differences in Republican support between Biblical literalists and Biblical minimalists from 1964 to 2004. In 1964, the differences were minimal. By

2004 these differences are quite large, and they are at their highest points in the entire time series. Of course, many of those who take the Bible literally see it as the ultimate source of moral authority, while those who do not see the Bible in such a fashion would likely strongly disagree. In many ways this is the strongest piece of evidence in support of Hunter's argument about the existence of a culture war.[59]

CONCLUSION

Culture matters in current electoral politics. The growing importance of religious salience, combined with rising levels of attitude polarization on cultural issues within American society and the growing impact of moral issue opinions on electoral behavior certainly point to a significant divide over cultural issues in contemporary American politics. The cultural divide among the mass public closely mirrors the one that exists between partisan elites, with liberals aligning with the Democratic Party and conservatives choosing the Republicans.

By now there can be little doubt that cultural issues are affecting American politics. It might not be a war, but it's not simply a friendly dispute either. The argument over cultural issues in the United States has grown increasingly heated over the past thirty years, and this rising intensity has undoubtedly spilled over into American politics. In our final chapter we ask whether or not cultural issues have displaced class concerns in American politics, as many claim.

CHAPTER 8

THE DUAL DIVISIONS OF CLASS AND CULTURE

Inequality is increasing and class political divisions are now greater than thirty years ago. The parties differ in their economic concerns, and Democrats receive more support from the less affluent than Republicans do. At the same time, cultural issues are now more prominent, and there is a growing division between the parties in their respective positions on these issues. Voters are more responsive to these differing party stands, and in recent years a significant cultural cleavage has developed in American electoral politics at the mass level. Both class and culture affect partisanship and elections in the United States.

The intriguing matter is the relationship between these two sources of political division. As discussed earlier, it is widely assumed that cultural issues are displacing class issues, and questions of morality and proper behavior are drowning out concerns about inequality when Americans turn out on Election Day. Many see this trend continuing indefinitely, meaning that the central concerns in future political debates are likely to be about morality issues and not economic ones. Culture trumps class, or so the story goes.

The essence of the displacement-of-class argument is as follows.[1] The argument begins with the claim that the country is becoming more conservative on social issues, or at the very least that cultural issues have become political issues and activated a social conservatism that has long existed, but was previously latent. As cultural issues become more salient to voters and support for conservative positions on cultural issues rises, so the argument goes, support for the Republican Party rises while voters increasingly turn their backs on the Democrats.

Central to this argument is the presumption that lower income voters are more conservative on cultural issues. Many academics and other political analysts see the working class as more conservative or authoritarian. That is, the working class is often seen as more inclined to accept set and defined sources of authority (especially religious authority), see the virtue in rules about proper conduct, and believe in traditional patterns of behavior, such as prayer in public schools or heterosexual marriage. If the working class is more authoritarian and less tolerant, and cultural issues are becoming more important, then this combination may be pulling the working class away from voting on the basis of economic issues. Working class individuals who might have voted Democratic out of concern with economic issues will now vote Republican because of their concern with declining morality. So not only is culture trumping class overall, but the dominance of cultural issues is particularly prominent among less affluent Americans.

Our goal here is to examine such claims to assess the relative roles of class and cultural divisions in American politics. Have both dimensions emerged as important electoral cleavages, or is one displacing the other? Are debates about both sets of issues likely to continue, or is one likely to dominate the American political agenda? We first examine whether the country has become more conservative. Then we assess whether the working class is more concerned with cultural issues and whether these citizens in particular have become more conservative. We then examine how each set of concerns affects voters' partisan support.

Finally, we noted at the beginning of this book that there are competing explanations of what shapes American politics. Our findings differ from those who argue that there really is no "culture war" going on, and the only divisions over culture that exist are among elites. We assess that argument and explain why our conclusions differ.

A MORE CONSERVATIVE NATION?

Has America become more conservative on cultural issues? Is there an increase in the overall percentage of people opposed to abortion, reacting negatively to gays and lesbians, and defining themselves as conservative?

Has America become more religious? This last question is especially important because within many religious traditions increased religiosity—attendance at services and faith in religious guidance—is associated with increased conservatism on cultural issues.

Figure 8-1 presents trends for the last thirty years on these questions, showing the percentages of Americans who hold conservative positions on abortion, hold less positive reactions to homosexuals, identify overall with conservative ideology, and who attend church regularly. It is difficult to see a conservative trend here. The percentage of Americans holding negative reactions to gays and lesbians has declined. The percentage wishing to prohibit abortion has declined. The percentage attending church regularly has remained essentially flat. Only the percentage identifying themselves as conservative has increased over time, rising from 26 to 32 percent over thirty-two years.[2] Given this evidence, it is difficult to see much merit in claims that the public is becoming more conservative, especially on cultural issues.[3]

While there is little evidence of a general drift toward conservative positions on cultural issues, perhaps the more important matter is whether those with lower incomes—and generally less education—are more conservative than those with higher incomes. Has this segment of society become more conservative, troubled by the trends reviewed in the last several chapters? After all, low income levels are strongly associated with low education levels, and the link between increased education and increased tolerance and acceptance of differing views is well known.[4] Figures 8-2 through 8-4 shed some light on this possibility, presenting trends on church attendance, opinions on abortion, and feelings towards homosexuals for both low- and high-income Americans. If the less affluent are becoming more conservative, this trend should show up in the graphs.

There are two important questions relating to all three trends. Is the lower class more attached to religion or conservative cultural positions than the more affluent and has the lower class become more conservative over time? Figure 8-2 summarizes two forms of religious attachment by income groups. The top two lines, starting at about 40 percent, indicate the percentage of low- and high-income individuals who attend religious services weekly or more. There is very little difference between lower and

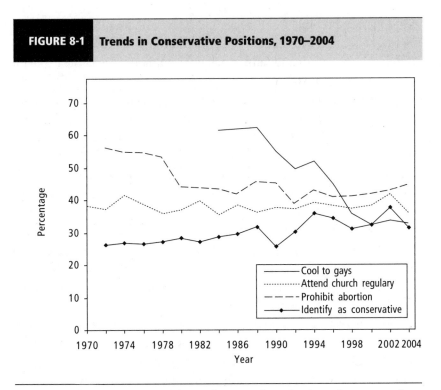

FIGURE 8-1 Trends in Conservative Positions, 1970–2004

Note: The questions asked and the responses designated as conservative are: how frequently a person attends church (the person attends church weekly or more—see Figure 8-2); reactions to gays (the question uses a 0 to 100-scale thermometer to rate degrees of feeling and all responses below 50 are classified as "cool to gays"—see Figure 8-4); position on abortion (respondent believes abortion should be prohibited—see Figure 8-3); and ideological position (when a respondent is asked to self-identify as a liberal, moderate or conservative, and respondent identifies as a conservative—see Figure 8-6).

Source: NES Cumulative Datafile, 1948–2004.

higher income individuals, and for most years lower income individuals actually have lower rates of attendance. Another way to assess religious attachment is the percentage that never attends services, which is shown in the two lines that start at a lower level. This trend rises abruptly in 1990 because the question was changed,[5] but the important finding is the degree of difference between income groups and trends since 1990. Again, there is little difference between income groups and no trend over the last decade or so of lower income groups becoming more attached to religion, at least based on attendance at worship services. Indeed, beginning in the 1990s, those with lower incomes are more likely to never attend.

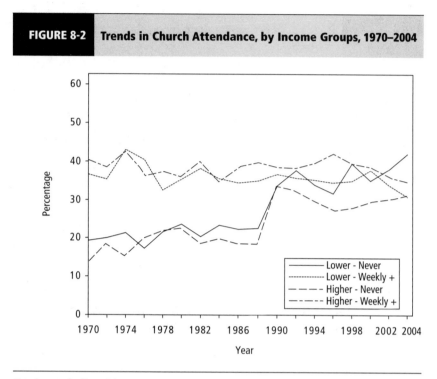

FIGURE 8-2 Trends in Church Attendance, by Income Groups, 1970–2004

Note: See note for Figure 8-1.

Source: NES Cumulative Datafile, 1948–2004.

As discussed earlier, views on abortion are central to the cultural wars. Perhaps no issue is more important. To conservatives abortion is murder, and permissive abortion practices are the ultimate indicator of the decline of morality in American society, while to liberals the essential principle is a woman's right to make such decisions without government interference. For liberals, restricting abortion is restricting liberty.

Figure 8-3 presents the percentage of the public that says abortion should always be allowed by law and the percentage that says it should never be allowed. The evidence here is mixed and complicated. As shown in the bottom two lines—those who support banning abortion—there has been no increase in support for this position for either income group over the last three decades. The major change has been the increase in support—shown in the top two lines—for providing the legal right of women to choose whether to have an abortion. Compared to the 1970s,

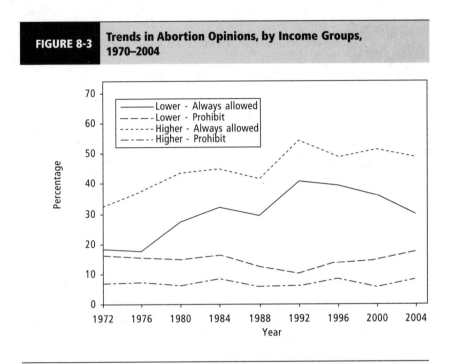

FIGURE 8-3 Trends in Abortion Opinions, by Income Groups, 1970–2004

Note: See note for Figure 8-1.

Source: NES Cumulative Datafile, 1948–2004.

both lower and higher income groups have become more supportive of this right over time. There has been a recent decline among both income groups since 1992, with the greatest drop among the less affluent, but overall levels are still higher than thirty years ago. The difficult matter in discerning trends is whether to focus on the overall difference over time or on the declines of the last decade.

While support for a woman's right to choose has increased, those in the bottom third of the income distribution are consistently *less support-ive* of this right. The evidence here is mixed, then. Lower income indi-viduals support abortion rights less than higher income individuals do, but the net change is toward more support for this right, even taking into account the recent declines. Overall, the trends do not indicate that the lower class is becoming more agitated by abortion issues, although they are clearly less supportive than the more affluent.

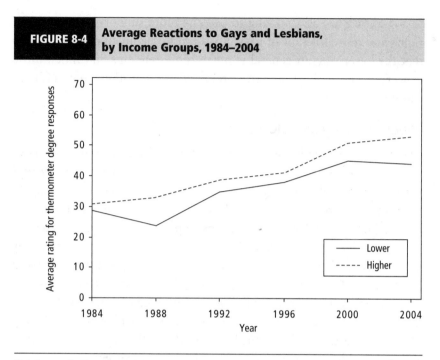

FIGURE 8-4 **Average Reactions to Gays and Lesbians, by Income Groups, 1984–2004**

Note: See note for Figure 8-1.

Source: NES Cumulative Datafile, 1948–2004.

Finally, there is the issue of the public's views of gays and lesbians. The NES surveys began to ask people to give their reaction to homosexuals in 1984. Respondents were asked to give their general reaction on a "thermometer" scale of 0 to 100, with 0 being cold, 50 neutral, and 100 being warm. Figure 8-4 presents the trends in these reactions over the last twenty years, once again for both low- and high-income thirds. Overall, the trend has been a shift from a largely cool reaction to a more neutral position. As with abortion views, the less affluent are somewhat less accepting than the more affluent, but the differences are small, and both groups have moved to much more positive positions over time. There is no sign of increased conservatism here either.

In summary, there is no general trend toward more conservative views on cultural issues in the electorate. Lower income individuals in particular are slightly more conservative on abortion rights and reactions to gays, but they are also moving to become more supportive of abortion rights and more tolerant of gays. It is hard to see much merit in claims that the lower class in general is much more religious and much more concerned about abortion and homosexuality than their more affluent counterparts.

CONCERN WITH ECONOMIC ISSUES

While there is no evidence of a conservative drift on cultural issues, have lower income individuals become less concerned about economic issues? Perhaps a general rise in affluence, even if more income is going to upper-income groups, has diminished concerns about jobs and economic security.[6] The evidence, however, does not indicate this has happened.

To take just one example, Figure 8-5 presents the percentage by income group that thinks the government should help ensure a job and good standard of living for everyone. Only whites are included because the commonly heard argument about the growing cultural divide is that the white working class has become less concerned with economic issues. The data show that whites in the bottom third of the income distribution are consistently more supportive of government involvement than those with higher family incomes. Other analyses, which have examined multiple economic issues over the last thirty years, also find no evidence that lower income voters have become less concerned about economic issues. In fact, the evidence points in the opposite direction, finding that the less affluent have become more concerned about economic matters over time.[7]

ADDING NEW ISSUES TO EXISTING ONES

So if cultural issues do not trump class concerns, but both seem to affect electoral behavior, where do we find ourselves? The answer is relatively simple. Both class and cultural issues have risen in prominence. Both are now a greater source of partisan support and political division than they were twenty to thirty years ago. One division has been added to another. It is not class *or* culture, but rather class *and* culture.

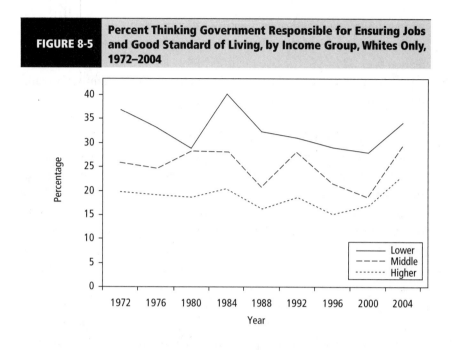

FIGURE 8-5 **Percent Thinking Government Responsible for Ensuring Jobs and Good Standard of Living, by Income Group, Whites Only, 1972–2004**

Note: NES survey respondents were asked: "Some people feel that the government in Washington should see to it that every person has a job and a good standard of living. Suppose these people are at one end of a scale, at point 1. Others think the government should just let each person get ahead on his/their own. Suppose these people are at the other end, at point 7. And, of course, some other people have opinions somewhere in between, at points 2, 3, 4, 5, or 6. Where would you place yourself on this scale, or haven't you thought much about this?" Those with opinions at 1–3 were coded as supporting government involvement in this issue.

Source: NES Cumulative Datafile, 1948–2004.

Building Party Coalitions

E. J. Dionne, a *Washington Post* columnist, wrote several years ago that Republicans were seeking to create a coalition of anti-government "free-marketers" who saw less need for government and cultural conservatives who were troubled about the decline in morality in American society.[8] To many this coalition seemed an unlikely concoction because of the contradiction between those who wanted to reduce the role of government in our lives and those who wanted to use government to structure individual morality. To Republicans, this combination is not at all contradictory. The party's goal is to create a society in which capitalism and free markets are allowed to flourish without government intervention and a society where traditional values are honored and supported with government action. They see the two goals as highly compatible. Individualism should be allowed to flourish in markets but virtue—defined in traditional terms—should also be encouraged, and in some cases enforced, if need be.

Republicans thought that making inroads into the South was crucial to building this coalition.[9] The South was, and still is, a region where Republicans thought that a carefully crafted anti-government[10] message could attract voters. From the last half of the 1880s through the 1960s the South sought to ward off federal government intrusion to keep the national government from interfering with segregation. This desire to restrain federal efforts to institute desegregation in the 1950s and 1960s expanded to include a more general anti-government sentiment after the 1970s as the South began to experience tremendous economic growth. Markets were developing rapidly and business interests sought to minimize regulations, labor unions, and taxes so job growth and wealth could increase.[11] Most of the many Southern conservatives who supported policies to restrain the role of government were Democrats up through the 1960s and 1970s. The GOP sought to bring these voters into the Republican Party. There were also many in the West who resented government ownership and regulation of lands, and Republican leaders believed that they, too, could be appealed to and brought into the party's changing coalition.[12]

The Republican efforts to attract conservatives are producing steady success, [13] as the two indicators in Figure 8-6 show. First Figure 8-6 indicates the percentage of those identifying themselves as conservative who also identify with the Republican Party. In 2004, for instance, 61 percent of conservatives identified with the Republican Party (39 percent of conservatives did not). It also presents the percentage of the party that is comprised of conservatives. In 2004, nearly 80 percent of Republicans identified themselves as being conservative. Over the last thirty years, more conservatives have come to identify with the Republican Party, and they also constitute a larger percentage of the party.[14] There are, to be sure, moments when the party struggles to hold together libertarians who oppose government and moralists who wish to legislate behavior,

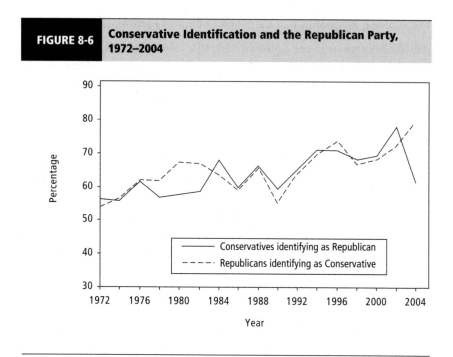

FIGURE 8-6 | Conservative Identification and the Republican Party, 1972–2004

Source: NES Cumulative Datafile, 1948–2004.

but the efforts to attract conservatives with somewhat different goals has largely worked. No one has to wonder which party is more conservative in contemporary America.

As the Republicans attracted more cultural conservatives, they have also consistently maintained a concern with representing the views of those who want less government taxation and regulation. Over the last decade, Republicans have consistently cut taxes and sought to direct most of the cuts at successful entrepreneurs, who they see as generating more investment and jobs for the economy. They have also supported significant cuts in regulations affecting businesses.[15] As Republicans have sought to appeal to conservatives of all stripes, Democrats have sought to appeal to liberals. The party has consistently supported programs for the less affluent and opposed tax cuts.[16] They have also consistently defended a woman's right to choose whether to have an abortion and they have, with less enthusiasm, sought to protect the rights of gays. Both class and cultural issues have come to separate the parties.

The Evolving Relationship of Class and Culture to Partisan Choice

As we have shown in previous chapters, the divisions between the parties and within the electorate on these two sets of issues have been growing, but does one set of issues dominate the other? To answer this, we have conducted a statistical analysis in which we assess the impact of variations in opinions or income, controlling for other opinions. That is, we take people with similar incomes and ask how their party support varies as their opinions on abortion vary. We also take people with the same opinions on abortion and ask how their party support varies as their income varies. The effect is known as a regression coefficient, which is an estimation of changes in party support as income or abortion views vary.[17] A regression analysis allows us to assess whether variations in income and abortion views have *separate* and distinct effects on party support. If we do such estimations over time, then we also can assess the relative role of class and cultural issues as a source of partisan divisions over time.[18] Only whites are examined because the common presumption is that class divisions have declined within this part of the electorate.

Figures 8-7 and 8-8 present the results of such analyses. The figures present the effects of variations in income, abortion views, and religious attendance on Republican presidential voting and then on party identification. In each case, the analysis is set up so the relationship expresses the extent to which support for the Republicans increases as individuals move from liberal to conservative positions. For income the issue is how increases in income affect Republican support. For cultural cleavages the issue is how movement toward opposing abortion and attending religious services affects party support. In each case, if these variations affect party support, the relationship should be positive. The larger the regression coefficient, the greater the support for the Republicans among those individuals holding more conservative views. A person who makes more money should be more supportive of the Republicans. A person who opposes abortion should be more supportive of the Republicans than a person who thinks abortion should always be allowed by law.

If there is a positive impact for any of these variables—which also means a declining inclination to support the Democratic Party—then does this relationship become stronger over time? Do variations in income create greater differences in partisan support now than they did

FIGURE 8-7	Voter Traits and Support for Republican Presidential Candidates, Whites Only, 1972–2004

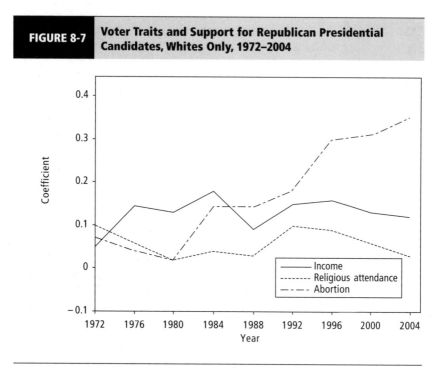

Source: NES Cumulative Datafile, 1948–2004.

in previous years? Do differences in opinion about abortion separate people more now than they did twenty to thirty years ago and are both growing stronger in impact?

Figure 8-7 presents these relationships over time for presidential voting. Religious attendance, despite all the attention it receives, does not have much of an association with voting Republican. It has been positive but close to zero for most of the last thirty years. The interesting changes are for income and abortion views. Compared to thirty years ago the impact of income is now greater and has a consistently strong impact on partisan voting. Those who make more money are consistently more supportive of the Republican Party. Variations in abortion views have become an even more significant source of partisan divisions. Variations in these views had little impact in 1972 but now have a greater impact than the other voter traits considered. The important finding is that over thirty years partisan divisions within the electorate have grown for both

FIGURE 8-8	Voter Traits and Inclination to Identify as a Republican, Whites Only, 1972–2004

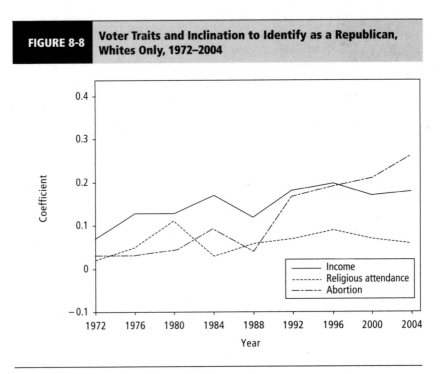

Source: NES Cumulative Datafile, 1948–2004.

income and abortion opinion differences. An increase in the significance of one has not resulted in the displacement of suppression of another.

Essentially the same pattern occurs when party identification, a much broader measure of partisanship, is considered (see Figure 8-8). Variations in religious attendance have experienced no systematic change as a source of divisions. Income has steadily grown in impact, and now has an impact considerably greater than it did during the 1970s. As with presidential voting, the impact of abortion views has increased over time and is now a significant source of division between the parties. Both class and cultural views—captured here by position on abortion—now structure partisanship at the mass level.

CLASS, VIEWS ON ABORTION, AND VOTING PATTERN DYNAMICS

Both class and cultural issues have emerged to have an impact in American politics. Their joint effect can be seen by comparing the effects of income and abortion views on the inclination to vote Republican in presidential and House elections over the last thirty years. Table 8-1 presents the percentage voting Republican by income and whether someone thinks abortion should be allowed (always or with few restrictions) or largely restricted (always or only allowed to protect the health of the mother or cases of rape). Elections are grouped to reduce the volume of numbers presented and to average election results so the focus is on broad changes over time more than specific elections.

In the 1976 and 1980 elections those with greater percentages of higher incomes voted for Republican presidential and House candidates. This phenomenon of those with higher incomes voting Republican at higher percentages was true for all respondents and within the groups of those who wanted to allow or restrict abortions. These higher levels of Republican voting can be assessed by examining whether the percentage voting Republican increases as income increases from lower to higher. In all the abortion view groups—all, allow, and restrict—support for Republicans increases with income. The difference between lower and higher income voters (shown in the far right column) was 17.7 percentage points in the presidential race and 20.0 in the House elections.

Is there a difference in Republican support between those who wish to allow or restrict abortion within each income category? Did people with similar incomes but differing views about abortion vote differently? In 1976–1980 there is almost no difference between those with different abortion views within each income category for both presidential and House elections. Abortion views were having little impact at that time. For example, in presidential elections, for those with higher incomes, 61.9 percent of those supporting abortion rights (allow) voted Republican and 60.1 percent of those opposing abortion (restrict) voted Republican. In House elections the differences were equally small. Class mattered and abortion views were not very important.

In 1984–1988 the differences by income remained, but there were now greater differences in support for Republicans between those wishing to allow and those wishing to restrict abortion. In 1992–1996 differences by

| TABLE 8-1 | Percentage Voting Republican in Presidential and House Elections by Income and Abortion Views, Whites Only, 1976–2004 |

ABORTION VIEWS	President			House			Low–High Income Difference	
	Lower	Middle	Higher	Lower	Middle	Higher	Pres	House
1976–1980								
All	49.5	54.1	60.9	41.8	48.3	53.6	11.4	12.2
Allow	45.2	46.3	61.9	38.9	46.4	54.0	16.7	15.1
Restrict	51.0	60.4	60.1	44.6	49.2	54.3	9.1	9.7
A–R Difference	5.8	14.1	-1.8	5.7	2.8	.3		
1984–1988								
All	55.4	60.3	69.3	42.4	48.7	52.7	13.9	10.3
Allow	45.6	54.0	64.8	37.4	43.6	48.4	19.2	11.0
Restrict	63.6	68.3	78.3	47.0	54.3	60.7	14.7	13.7
A-R Difference	18.0	14.3	13.5	9.6	10.7	12.4		
1992–1996								
All	32.4	39.4	46.7	38.8	50.8	58.4	14.3	19.6
Allow	23.3	25.8	37.1	33.4	40.0	52.6	13.8	19.2
Restrict	43.8	59.2	66.2	47.9	66.6	69.4	22.4	21.5
A–R Difference	20.5	33.4	29.1	14.5	26.6	16.8		
2000–2004								
All	48.8	55.3	58.5	47.3	54.7	57.3	9.7	10.0
Allow	40.0	42.3	44.9	39.1	41.0	45.0	4.9	5.9
Restrict	57.9	74.7	82.5	62.7	73.8	77.1	24.6	14.4
A–R Difference	17.9	32.4	37.6	23.6	32.8	32.1		

Notes: Results for each pair of years are the average of the percentages for the noted years. Results are for white respondents only. A–R difference refers to the difference in voting support between those who wish to allow abortion and those who wish to restrict it. The allow percentage is subtracted from the restrict percentage to express how much more opponents to abortion rights support the Republican Party.

Source: NES Cumulative Datafile, 1948–2004.

income persisted, but differences by abortion views increased even more. In the 1992–1996 presidential elections, among those with higher incomes, 37.1 percent of those wanting to allow abortion voted Republican, while 66.2 percent of those wanting to restrict it voted Republican.

Then, in the 2000–2004 elections, an important and interesting change emerged. The impact of abortion views was even greater, providing support for the argument that cultural issues have come to play a major role as a source of political divisions. The overall differences by income declined somewhat, but the interesting change is how voting by income varied among those supporting or opposing abortion. It appears that cultural issues had an impact on class voting, but not in the way that many are presuming. Among those wanting to restrict abortion rights, the differences by income were as large as in prior elections. But among those supporting abortion rights, income differences were a very modest 4.9 for presidential and 5.9 for House elections.

Several things are important about this pattern in 2000–2004. For those opposing abortion rights, the combination of higher income and agreement with the party's position on abortion results in high levels of support for Republicans. The two conditions—income and opposition to abortion— reinforced each other and produced high Republican support. Those who were what we call cross-pressured—one condition increases their support and another lowers it—were much less supportive of the Republican Party. While there has been a great deal written about how Republicans are able to move white, lower-income, anti-abortion individuals to vote Republican, it is still the case that just 57.9 percent of this group voted for George W. Bush in 2000 and 2004. Receiving this percentage of this group's votes may be seen as a significant achievement in and of itself, but since most of those in the lower income group wish to allow abortion, the accomplishment also involves a limitation on building political support. Even among those supporting the party's cultural position on this issue, a significant class division persists.

Equally interesting is what is occurring among those supporting abortion rights. While the primary discussion has been about the ability of Republicans to reduce class divisions by appealing to lower income voters on cultural issues, it appears that any reduction—not elimination— of class divisions has come from the effect of the party's position on high-income voters who support abortion rights. Almost two-thirds of high-income voters support abortion rights. In 2000–2004 only 45 percent of this group voted for George W. Bush and Republican House candidates. Despite repeated cuts in the taxes of the more affluent, the party's position on abortion alienated the more affluent who support abortion rights. If any group is being "suppressed" in terms of possible class voting, it is among high income voters who are troubled by the Republican Party's stance on this issue. The party's position attracts some voters and alienates others. Even while this complicated division over a cultural issue has emerged, differences by income persist.

CLASS, VIEWS ON GAYS, AND VOTING PATTERN DYNAMICS

The addition of cultural divisions to class divisions can also be seen with regard to gay issues. Our data on this issue start later, with 1984 the first year questions measuring reactions to gays were asked in the NES surveys. Table 8-2 presents an analysis for reactions to gays similar to that for abortion. Respondents are asked to place their reaction to gays and lesbians on a hypothetical thermometer from 0 to 100, with 100 being very positive, and are then grouped into whether their reaction is cool or warm. The concern is again whether class differences exist and whether a division also emerges around a cultural issue.

By the 1984–1988 elections, reactions to gays were already creating a partisan division. For both presidential and House elections, those who were cool to gays, for similar income levels, were voting Republican by 11.9 to 36.8 more percentage points. This partisan impact of reactions to gays has grown over time. By the 2000–2004 elections, those cool to gays were voting more Republican more frequently by 23.6 to 42.2 more percentage points. Yet class divisions persisted even as reactions to gays were playing a greater role.

OPPOSING INTERPRETATIONS

At the beginning of this book, we noted that there are diverse interpretations of trends in American politics. There are those who argue that there really is no cultural war occurring in America. The quote from *Culture War?* presented in Chapter 1, bears repeating:

> *The simple truth is that there is no culture war in the United States—no battle for the soul of America rages, at least none that most Americans are aware of. Many of the activists in the political parties and the various cause groups do, in fact, hate each*

| TABLE 8-2 | Percentage Voting Republican in Presidential and House Elections by Income and Reactions to Gays, Whites Only, 1984–2004 |

REACTIONS TO GAYS	President Lower	President Middle	President Higher	House Lower	House Middle	House Higher	Low-High Income Difference Pres	Low-High Income Difference House
1984–1988								
All	55.4	60.3	69.3	42.4	48.7	52.7	13.9	10.3
Warm	38.7	31.8	44.9	31.4	27.1	36.8	6.2	5.4
Cool	62.0	68.6	77.9	43.3	54.2	57.8	15.9	14.5
W–C Difference	23.3	36.8	33.0	11.9	27.1	21.0		
1992–1996								
All	32.4	39.4	46.7	38.8	50.8	58.4	14.3	19.6
Warm	18.4	17.7	22.0	22.9	35.2	39.0	4.6	16.1
Cool	43.1	55.9	63.0	47.2	61.1	70.1	19.9	22.9
W–C Difference	24.7	38.2	41.0	24.3	25.9	31.1		
2000–2004								
All	48.8	55.3	58.5	47.3	54.7	57.3	9.7	10.0
Warm	28.4	41.2	41.3	24.8	40.3	43.7	12.9	18.9
Cool	70.6	75.9	83.1	60.6	63.9	72.3	12.5	11.7
W–C Difference	42.2	34.7	41.8	35.8	23.6	28.6		

Note: Results for each pair of years are the average of the percentages for the noted year. Results are for white respondents only. Respondents were presented with this question: "We'd also like to get your feelings about some groups in American society. When I read the name of a group, we'd like you to rate it with what we call a feeling thermometer. Ratings between 50 degrees–100 degrees mean that you feel favorably and warm toward the group; ratings between 0 and 50 degrees mean that you don't feel favorably towards the group and that you don't care too much for that group. If you don't feel particularly warm or cold toward a group you would rate them at 50 degrees. [then]: gays and lesbians?" All responses below 50 are classified as cool and all those above 50 are classified as warm. Responses for those in the neutral category are not shown here. W–C difference refers to the difference in voting support between those who are warm towards gays and those cool to gays. The warm percentage is subtracted from cool to express how much more those using a cool rating support the Republican Party.

Source: NES Cumulative Datafile, 1948–2004.

other and regard themselves as combatants in a war. But their hatreds and battles are not shared by the great mass of the American people.

There is little evidence that Americans' ideological or policy positions are more polarized today than they were two or three decades ago, although their choices often seem to be. The explanation is that the political figures Americans evaluate are more polarized. A polarized political class makes the citizenry appear polarized, but it is only that—an appearance.[19]

How could social scientists reviewing the same evidence produce such different conclusions? Some of the difference is semantic. The use of the word "war" to describe conflicts between cultural conservatives and those willing to tolerate diverse patterns of living is very charged and implies a level of physical conflict that is unlikely to be found. Under such a view, the conflict between Catholics and Protestants in Northern Ireland represents a true culture war, and nothing even remotely resembling that situation exists in the United States. This point reminds us to take care with matters of language. But there are clear trends of growing political divisions between those with differing views. That divide is real and is becoming more significant.

Still, how can interpretations differ so much? Whether one sees conflict developing depends on how one defines conflict. Fiorina et al. largely define division or polarization by whether aggregate public opinion has become more divided. Their primary focus is on overall opinion over time.[20] That is, have the percentages that support and oppose abortion rights changed and diverged in ways that would create more conflict within our society? If 20 percent were within each camp twenty-five years ago (and 60 percent had no opinion) and now the percentages are 40 percent within each group (and only 20 percent with no opinion) then presumably Fiorina and his colleagues would conclude that there is a greater basis for conflict within our society. They do not find such changes and argue that the public is more moderate than the stories about conflict acknowledge. They argue that political elites may be disagreeing more vehemently now than thirty years ago, but the public has remained mostly moderate.

While Fiorina and his colleagues focus largely on these aggregate trends, they neglect the notion of political conflict that we focus on— changes in the degree to which people with differing policy views divide in which party they support. We argue that the focus should be on both aggregate shifts and political divisions by the views people hold. To take aggregate views first, opinions might at one time be 20 percent in favor of allowing abortion, 20 percent wanting to prohibit abortion, and 60 percent undecided or in-between. If overall opinion shifted to 40 percent allow, 40 percent prohibit, and 20 percent in-between, but opinions did not divide people—those for and against abortion rights support Republicans at the same rate—the overall shift in opinions might not become a political issue and a source of partisan conflict.

On the other hand, if overall opinions do not shift over time, as Fiorina et al. find in some situations, but there is an increase in the impact of differing views on which party the respondents support, then there would be a basis for greater division. Over the last twenty to thirty years, voter situations and opinions now have a greater impact on political choices than they previously did. Income had a very limited impact on party support through the 1970s, but now its impact is greater. Abortion views once had limited impact on party support, but that impact is steadily growing. Tracking aggregate or overall responses of the electorate does not capture the division by opinion.

The differences between the two approaches are evident in a recent analysis of differences in how the parties are seen by voters.[21] Voters are regularly asked to offer their reactions to both parties. They are again presented with a hypothetical thermometer and asked to place each party somewhere between 0 and 100, with 100 being very positive. Each party then gets an average rating and we can also calculate the difference in the average rating between the two parties. The average differences are shown in Figure 8-9. Over thirty-two years there is little change in the average difference in how the two parties are seen.

Figure 8-10 presents the same results in a very different way. The focus here is on the individual level association between the two rankings. Rather than just compile all responses and see if their averages differ, the focus is on the association between the rankings a person gives each party. If a reaction to one party is not associated with a reaction to the other then the correlation is 0. If respondents give a positive reaction to one and a negative reaction to the other, the association will be negative. Over the last thirty years, this association has changed from 0 to −0.48. Those who like one party increasingly dislike the other. While the aggregate analysis suggests there is no change, the individual analysis indicates considerable polarization is occurring. Thirty years ago those who liked

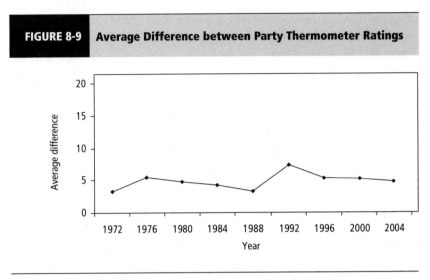

FIGURE 8-9   **Average Difference between Party Thermometer Ratings**

Source: NES Cumulative Datafile, 1948–2004.

the Democratic Party did not systematically dislike Republicans. Now those who like the Democrats do not like the Republicans, and vice versa.

In focusing on aggregate opinions, Fiorina and his colleagues miss the growing body of evidence that indicates the trend is toward greater polarization at the elite *and* mass level. Recent studies have shown that the percentage of people defining themselves as liberal or conservative is increasing, that self-defined ideology (liberal or conservative) is increasingly associated with favoring one party over the other, that religious attachment (without the controls we just utilized) is increasingly a good indicator of partisan preferences, and that views about abortion, homosexuals, and the obligation of government to do something about jobs and health insurance increasingly affect partisan preferences.[22] Increasingly, when a voter gives one party or its presidential candidate a positive rating, she or he gives the other a negative rating. Differences between Republicans and Democrats in presidential job approval ratings have risen steadily since the 1950s and are now greater than ever recorded.[23] Those who vote for one party's candidate in a House race also vote for the same party's candidate for president and the Senate.[24]

The electorate may not be at war, but the trends indicate that voters are steadily moving to a situation of greater partisan division and that

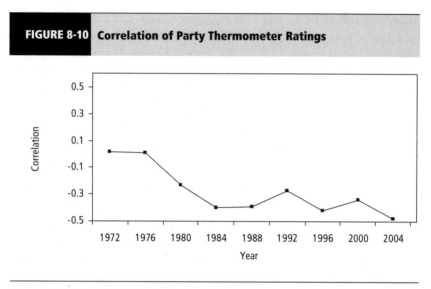

FIGURE 8-10 **Correlation of Party Thermometer Ratings**

Source: NES Cumulative Datafile, 1948–2004.

division is driven by differences in class and culture. As anyone who tried to have a conversation about George W. Bush in 2004 realized, people are developing very strong opinions about him and the parties.

American politics has changed in the last several decades. Republicans set out to bring conservatives to their party, and they are steadily succeeding in this goal. They have managed to pull conservatives out of the Democratic Party, using both class and cultural issues to attract them. The party has aggressively pursued tax cuts that deliver significant benefits to the more affluent. It has opposed abortion and gay marriages and advocated support for traditional families and a greater role for religion in public life. Democrats have supported maintaining government programs that help the less affluent, they have opposed tax cuts, advocated for the right of women to make abortion choices with a doctor, and decried the efforts to make homosexuality a political issue. They have also defended the separation of church and state. Attentive voters have gradually been able to discern differences between the parties. In fact, the partisan differences are now so stark that even some inattentive voters know what is going on.

As these party differences have emerged, voters have been and continue to gradually choose sides based on their own situations and preferences.

Class differences in partisan voting, which were minimal in the 1950s and 1960s, have reemerged and have persisted. Cultural issues, which were not central to political discussions prior to the 1980s, have emerged and become a steadily more significant source of political divisions. An electorate that was once not divided by these two sets of issues is now quite divided. The behavior of the parties and the reactions of the electorate do not suggest that these divisions will soon disappear. Those who argue against the existence of a "culture war" may have a valid point, especially if one uses Northern Ireland or the Balkans as the measuring sticks of cultural conflict.[25] But at the very least we have aroused passions and increasingly heated disagreements about cultural issues in the United States, and these passions and disagreements clearly impact our politics at both the mass and elite levels. Along similar lines, recent trends toward growing inequality seem unlikely to reverse in the short term, and the battles over taxes will likely only heat up even further.[26] Questions of both class and culture will affect American politics for some time to come.

ENDNOTES

CHAPTER ONE

1. Senator John Edwards (D-N.C.), accepting the Democratic nomination for vice president of the United States at the Democratic National Convention in Boston, Massachusetts, July 29, 2004. A transcript of Edwards' speech is available at www.washingtonpost.com/wp-dyn/articles/A22230-2004Jul28.html.

2. For a discussion of the limits of those approaches, relative to income, see Jeffrey M. Stonecash, *Class and Party in American Politics* (Boulder, CO: Westview Press, 2000), chapter 7.

3. Patrick J. Buchanan, endorsing George H.W. Bush as the Republican nominee for president of the United States at the Republican National Convention in Houston, TX, August 17, 1992. A transcript of Buchanan's speech is available at www.buchanan.org/pa-92-0817-rnc.html

4. Morris P. Fiorina, with Samuel J. Abrams and Jeremy C. Pope, *Culture War? The Myth of a Polarized America* (New York: Pearson/Longman, 2005).

5. E. E. Schattschneider, *The Semi-Sovereign People* (New York: Holt, Rinehart, and Winston, 1960).

6. This of course ignores the role of courts in the policy-making process, although one could certainly argue that partisanship has become increasingly important in judicial matters, particularly in the area of appointment and confirmation.

7. Jennifer L. Hochschild, *Facing Up to the American Dream: Race, Class, and the Soul of the Nation* (Princeton, NJ: Princeton University Press, 1995), xvii.

8. For an overview of economic conditions during the Great Depression, see James T. Patterson, *America's Struggle against Poverty in the Twentieth Century* (Cambridge: Harvard University Press, 2000), 37–54.

9. William E. Leuchtenburg, *The Perils of Prosperity 1914–1932* (Chicago: University of Chicago Press, 1958); and Arthur M. Schlesinger, Jr., *The Crisis of the Old Order* (Boston: Houghton Mifflin, 1957).

10. Carl N. Degler, "American Political Parties and the Rise of the City: An Interpretation," *Journal of American History* 51 (June 1964): 41–59; Samuel J. Endersveld, "The Influence of Metropolitan Party Pluralities in Presidential Elections Since 1920: A Study of Twelve Key Cities," *American Political Science Review* 43 (December 1949): 1189–1206; Everett Carll Ladd, Jr., with Charles D. Hadley, *Transformations of the American Party System* (New York: Norton, 1975); Samuel Lubell, *The Future of American Politics*, 2d ed., rev. ed. (Garden City, NY: Doubleday, 1956); James L. Sundquist, *Dynamics of the Party System*, rev. ed. (Washington, DC: The Brookings Institution, 1983); and Julius Turner and Edward V. Schneier, *Party and Constituency: Pressures on Congress*, rev. ed. (Baltimore: Johns Hopkins Press, 1970).

11. John Braeman, Robert H. Bremner, and David Brody, eds., *The New Deal: The National Level* (Columbus: Ohio State University Press, 1975); William E. Leuchtenburg, *Franklin D. Roosevelt and the New Deal, 1932–1940* (New York: Harper & Row, 1963); Arthur M. Schlesinger, Jr., *The Coming of the New Deal* (Boston: Houghton Mifflin, 1959); and Arthur M. Schlesinger, Jr., *The Politics of Upheaval* (Boston: Houghton Mifflin, 1960).

12. Sar A. Levitan and Robert Taggart, "The Great Society Did Succeed," *Political Science Quarterly* 91 (Winter 1976–1977): 601–618; and James L. Sundquist, *Politics and Policy: The Eisenhower, Kennedy, and Johnson Years* (Washington, DC: The Brookings Institution, 1968).

13. Sheldon Danziger and Peter Gottschalk, *America Unequal* (Cambridge, MA: Harvard University Press, 1995), 53.

14. Ronald Inglehart, "The Silent Revolution in Europe," *American Political Science Review* 65 (December 1971): 991–1017; Ladd with Hadley, *Transformations of the American Party System*, 195–200.

15. Paul R. Abramson, "Generational Change in American Electoral Behavior," *American Political Science Review* 68 (March 1974): 93–105; Ladd with Hadley, *Transformations of the American Political System*, 73 and 233–239; Everett Carll Ladd, Jr., "The Shifting Party Coalitions- 1932–1976," in *Emerging Coalitions in American Politics,* ed. Seymour Martin Lipset (San Francisco: Institute for Contemporary Studies, 1978), 81–121; Everett Carll Ladd Jr., "Like Waiting for Godot," in *The End of Realignment,* ed. Byron E. Shafer (Madison, WI: University of Wisconsin, 1991), 24–36; William J. Keefe, *Parties, Politics and Public Policy in America* (Washington, DC: CQ Press, 1994), 214; and Paul R. Abramson, John H. Aldrich, and David W. Rohde, *Change and Continuity in the 1992 Elections* (Washington, DC: CQ Press, 1995), 146 and 152–153.

16. Edward G. Carmines and James A. Stimson, *Issue Evolution: Race and the Transformation of American Politics* (Princeton, NJ: Princeton University Press, 1989), 14.

17. Harold W. Stanley, *Voter Mobilization and the Politics of Race: The South and Universal Suffrage* (New York: Praeger, 1987); and Richard J. Timpone, "Mass Mobilization or Government Intervention? The Growth of Black Registration in the South," *Journal of Politics* 57 (May 1995): 425–442.

18. John Micklethwait and Adrian Wooldridge, *The Right Nation: Conservative Power in America* (New York: Penguin, 2004).

19. Martin Gilens, "Racial Attitudes and Opposition Welfare," *Journal of Politics* 57 (November 1995): 994–1014; and Martin Gilens, "Race Coding and White Opposition to Welfare," *Journal of Politics* 90 (September 1996): 593–604.

20. For an excellent discussion of the overall dynamics surrounding the racial issues, the parties, and voting behavior, see Carmines and Stimson, *Issue Evolution: Race and the Transformation of American Politics.*

21. Editorial, *New York Times,* "Does Race Doom the Democrats?" November 20, 1988, A25; Michael Oreskes, "In Racial Politics, Democrats Losing More than Elections," *New York Times,* November 20, 1988, sec. 4, 1; Wilson C. McWilliams, "The Meaning of the Election," in *The Election of 1996: Reports and Interpretations,* ed. Gerald M. Pomper, et al. (Chatham, NJ: Chatham House, 1991), 241–272; and Michael Goldfeld, *The Color of Politics: Race and the Mainsprings of American Politics* (New York: The New Press, 1997).

22. Ladd with Hadley, *Transformations of the American Party System,* 27.

23. Thomas Byrne Edsall and Mary D. Edsall, "Race," *Atlantic Monthly* (May 1991): 53–86.

24. Elizabeth Kohlbert and Adam Clymer. "The Politics of Layoffs: In Search of a Message," *New York Times,* March 6, 1996, A23.

25. Janny Scott and David Leonhardt, "Class in America: Shadowy Lines That Still Divide," *New York Times,* May 15, 2005, A27.

26. Many would disagree with these views, and argue that views on racial issues still play a very important role in American politics. For some recent examples of such an argument, see Vincent L. Hutchings and Nicholas A. Valentino, "The Centrality of Race in American Politics," *Annual Review of Political Science* 7 (2004): 383–408; David C. Leege, Kenneth D. Wald, Brian S. Krueger, and Paul D. Mueller, *The Politics of Cultural Differences* (Princeton, NJ: Princeton University Press, 2002); Christopher Tarman and David O. Sears, "The Conceptualization and Measurement of Symbolic Racism," *Journal of Politics* 67 (August 2005): 731–761; and Nicholas A. Valentino and David O. Sears, "Old Times Are Not Forgotten: Race and Partisan Realignment in the Contemporary South," *American Journal of Political Science* 49 (July 2005): 672–688.

27. Edsall and Edsall, "Race"; and Nicol C. Rae, "Class and Culture: American Political Cleavages in the Twentieth Century," *Western Political Quarterly* 45 (September 1992): 629–650.

28. James Davison Hunter, *Culture Wars: The Struggle to Define America* (New York: Basic Books, 1991), 34. See also James Davison Hunter, *Before the Shooting Begins: Searching for Democracy in America's Culture War* (New York: The Free Press, 1994).

29. Hunter defines "orthodox" in the following manner: "The commitment on the part of adherents to an external, definable, and transcendent authority. Such objective and transcendent authority defines, at least in the abstract, a consistent, unchangeable measure of value, purpose, goodness, and identity, both personal and collective. It tells us what is good, what is true, how we should live, and who we are" (Hunter, *Culture Wars,* 44). In contrast, for progressivism, "moral authority tends to be defined by the spirit of the modern age, a spirit of rationalism and subjectivism." Progressivism is marked by "the tendency to resymbolize historic faiths according to the prevailing assumptions of contemporary life.... Binding moral authority tends to reside in personal experience or scientific

rationality, or either of these in conversation with particular religious or cultural traditions," (Hunter, *Culture Wars*, 44–45).

30. Hunter, *Culture Wars*, 42.
31. This comment comes from a truck driver in Missouri during the 2004 presidential election campaign. Diane Cardwell, "For Many in Missouri, Values Outweigh Policy," *New York Times*, September 19, 2004, A25.
32. Scott and Leonhardt, "Class in America: Shadowy Lines That Still Divide."
33. John Micklethwait and Adrian Wooldridge, *The Right Nation: Conservative Power in America* (New York: Penguin, 2004), 236.
34. For an interesting discussion of this development, see E. J. Dionne, Jr., "What Kind of Hater Are You?" *Washington Post*, March 15, 2006, A19.
35. Thomas Frank, *What's the Matter with Kansas? How Conservatives Won the Heart of America* (New York: Metropolitan Books, 2004), 5.
36. As Frank puts it: "[T]hose parts of Johnson City [Kansas] with the lowest per capita income and lowest median housing values consistently generated the strongest support for the conservative faction. The more working class an area is, the more likely it is to be conservative." Frank, *What's the Matter with Kansas*, 105.
37. Paul Krugman, "Bush's Class-War Budget," *New York Times*, February 11, 2005, A25
38. Fiorina, with Abrams and Pope, *Culture War*, 5.
39. Donald C. Baumer and Howard J. Gold, "Party Images and the American Electorate," *American Politics Quarterly* 23 (January 1995): 33–61; Donald C. Baumer and Howard J. Gold, "Party Images after the Clinton Years," paper presented at the annual meeting of the New England Political Science Association, Portland, ME, 2002; Mark D. Brewer, "A Divided Public? Party Images and Polarization in the United States," paper presented at the annual meeting of the American Political Science Association, Boston, MA, 2002; John G. Geer, "The Electorate's Partisan Evaluations: Evidence of a Continuing Democratic Edge," *Public Opinion Quarterly* 55 (Summer 1991): 218–231; Donald Green, Bradley Palmquist, and Eric Schickler, *Partisan Hearts and Minds: Political Parties and the Social Identities of Voters* (New Haven: Yale University Press, 2002); and Arthur Sanders, "The Meaning of Party Images," *Western Political Quarterly* 41 (September 1988): 583–599.
40. Stonecash, *Class and Party in American Politics*.
41. Sheldon Ganzinger and Peter Gottschalk, *America Unequal* (Cambridge, MA: Harvard University Press, 1995); and Isaac Shapiro, Robert Greenstein, and Wendell Primus, "Pathbreaking CBO Study Shows Dramatic Increases in Income Disparities in 1980s and 1990s" (Center on Budget and Politics Priorities, May 31, 2001).
42. For a recent analysis of racial differences in income and wealth, see Jared Bernstein, "Minority Wealth Gap: Net Worth Gap Twice That of Income," Economic Policy Institute, March 15, 2006. Available at www.epi.org/content.cfm/webfeatures_snapshots_20060315.
43. Theodor W. Adorno, *The Authoritarian Personality* (New York: Harper & Row, 1950); and Daniel Bell, ed., *The Radical Right*, rev. ed. (Garden City, NY: Doubleday, 1964).

CHAPTER TWO

1. Jeffrey M. Stonecash, *Class and Party in American Politics* (Boulder, CO: Westview Press, 2000). Chapter 7 discusses the emergence of this consensus.
2. Lisa A. Keister, *Wealth in America: Trends in Wealth Inequality* (New York: Cambridge University Press, 2000), 64.
3. For a review of what we know about the distribution of wealth in recent years, see Keister, *Wealth in America;* and Edward N. Wolff, *Top Heavy: The Increasing Inequality of Wealth in America and What Can Be Done About It* (New York: The New Press, 2005). For graphical presentations of the U.S. situation compared to other countries, see www.inequality.org/facts.cfm.
4. Edward N. Wolff, "Changes in Household Wealth in the 1980s and 1990s in the U.S.," The Levy Economics Institute of Bard College, Working Paper No. 407, May, 2004, available at www.levy.org/default.asp?view=publications_view&pubID=fca3a440ee.
5. The classic book on this subject is Jonathan Kozol, *Savage Inequalities* (New York: Crown, 1991). For more recent books on this subject, see Jennifer Hochschild and Nathan Scovronick, *The American Dream and the Public Schools* (New York: Oxford, 2003); and Jonathan Kozol, *The Shame of the Nation: The Restoration of Apartheid Schooling in America* (New York: Crown, 2005).

6. Kenneth T. Jackson, *Crabgrass Frontier: The Suburbanization of the United States* (New York: Oxford University Press, 1985), 231–271; and Dennis R. Judd and Todd Swanstrom *City Politics: Private Power and Public Policy,* 2d ed. (New York: Longman, 1998), 194–205.

7. Michael N. Danielson, *The Politics of Exclusion* (New York: Columbia University Press, 1976), 27–106.

8. Peter Dreier, John Mollenkopf, and Todd Swanstrom, *Place Matters: Metropolitics for the Twenty-first Century,* 2d ed. (Lawrence: University Press of Kansas, 2004); Douglas S. Massey and Nancy Denton, *American Apartheid: Segregation and the Making of the Underclass* (Cambridge: Harvard University Press, 1993), 24–88; and Paul A. Jargowsky, "Take the Money and Run: Economic Segregation in U.S. Metropolitan Areas," *American Sociological Review* 61 (December 1996): 984–998. In the last two decades the effort to separate populations has increased even further with the emergence of "gated" communities, or communities with walls around them and gates used to screen those without proper identification. By 1997 it was estimated that 20,000 such communities existed, encompassing over 3 million housing units. Edward J. Blakely and Mary Gail Snyder, *Fortress America: Gated Communities in the United States* (Washington, DC: Brookings Institution Press, 1997), 7.

9. David Rusk, *Cities Without Suburbs,* 2d ed. (Washington, DC: The Woodrow Wilson Center Press, 1995), 27–37.

10. Tony Schwartz, "The Test under Stress," *New York Times Magazine* (January 1999), 30–35 and passim.

11. Sandy Baum and Kathleen Payea, *Education Pays 2004: The Benefits of Higher Education for Individuals and Society* The College Board, www.collegeboard.com, 11.

12. Ibid., 13–17.

13. Commission on National Investment in Higher Education, *Breaking the Social Contract: The Fiscal Crisis in Higher Education* (New York: Council for Aid to Education, 1996), 6–8.

14. Baum and Payea, *Education Pays 2004,* 10.

15. Ibid.

16. Thomas G. Mortenson, "Educational Attainment by Family Income 1970 to 1994," *Postsecondary Education Opportunity* 41 (November 1995): 1–8.

17. Laurence E. Gladieux, "Federal Student Aid Policy: A History and an Assessment," paper delivered at the Conference on Financial Postsecondary Education: The Federal Role, Charleston, S.C., October 1995, 2–3.

18. The College Board, *Trends in Student Aid 2005,* 12. Data are available at: www.collegeboard.com/prod_downloads/press/cost05/trends_aid_05.pdf.

19. The College Board, *Trends in Student Aid,* (Washington, DC, 1998), 12–13.

20. Mortenson, "Educational Attainment by Family Income."

21. Richard Fossey, "The Dizzying Growth of the Federal Student Loan Program," in *Condemning Students to Debt: College Loans and Public Policy,* eds. Richard Fossey and Mark Bateman (New York: Simon and Schuster, 1998), 7–18.

22. Jacquelin King, "Student Aid: Who Benefits Now?" *Educational Record* (Winter 1996), 25.

23. *Trends in Student Aid 2005,* 17.

24. The enrollment rate is defined as the percentage of high school graduates who enrolled in college. From 1970 to 1986 the college participation rate is among those who are unmarried 18 to 24 year olds. From 1987 to 2003 it is for dependent 18 to 24 year old family members. The data are provided by Tom Mortenson, who we thank a great deal for providing the information. He used data from Table 14 in the Census Bureau's annual report on school enrollments at www.census.gov/population/www/socdemo/school/cps2003.html.

25. Mortenson, "Educational Attainment by Family Income," 1.

26. For a broad overview of how change in the private sector has evolved in recent years, see Jacob S. Hacker, "The Politics of Risk Privatization in U.S. Social Policy," in Marc Landy, Martin Levin, and Martin Shapiro eds., *Creating Competitive Markets* (Washington, DC: Brookings, 2006).

27. U.S. Bureau of the Census, *Statistical Abstract of the United States* (U.S. Government Printing Office, Washington, DC, 1956), 571.

28. U.S. Bureau of the Census, *Statistical Abstract of the United States* (U.S. Government Printing Office, Washington, DC, 1965), 571.

29. U.S. Bureau of the Census, *Statistical Abstract of the United States* (U.S. Government Printing Office, Washington, DC, 1975), 295.

30. DeNavas-Walt, Carmen, Bernadette D. Proctor, Robert J. Mills, U.S. Census Bureau, Current Population Reports, P60–226, *Income, Poverty, and Health Insurance Coverage in the United States, 2003* (United

States Government Printing Office, Washington, DC, 2004), 15. www.census.gov/prod/2004pubs/p60-226.pdf.

31. Robert Pear, "Government Lags in Steps to Widen Health Coverage," *New York Times*, August 9, 1998, A1.

32. Eric Eckholm, "Double Sword for President," *New York Times*, August 23, 1993, A9.

33. Lawrence Mishel, Jared Bernstein, and John Schmitt, *The State of Working America, 1996–97* (Armonk, NY: M. E. Sharpe, 1997), 267–270.

34. Marc Miringoff and Marque-Luisa Miringoff, *The Social Health of the Nation: How America is Really Doing* (New York: Oxford University Press, 1999), 93; and The Kaiser Commission, "The Uninsured and Their Access to Health Care," December 2003, 1, www.kff.org.

35. John A. Turner and Daniel J. Beller, eds., *Trends in Pensions 1992* (Washington, DC: U.S. Department of Labor, Pension and Welfare Benefits Administration, 1992), 75.

36. Steven A. Sass, *The Promise of Private Pensions: The First Hundred Years* (Cambridge, MA: Harvard University Press, 1997), 113–144.

37. Turner and Beller, *Trends in Pensions 1992*, 75.

38. Roger Lowenstein, "The End of Pensions?," *New York Times Magazine*, October 30, 2005, 56–63, 70, 82, 90.

39. Alicia H. Munnell, Annika Sunden, and Elizabeth Lidstone, *How Important are Private Pensions?* Issue in Brief, Center for Retirement Research at Boston College, February 2002, Number 8, 4.

40. Edward N. Wolff, *Retirement Insecurity: The Income Shortfalls Awaiting the Soon-to-Retire*, Economic Policy Institute, 2002 available at www.epinet.org.

41. Employee Benefits Research Institute, *The 1997 Retirement Confidence Survey Summary of Findings*, October 16, 1997, www.ebri.org/rcs/1997/97rcs_es.htm.

42. This evidence is presented in a series done in the *Los Angeles Times*. See the stories by Peter G. Gosselin, "If America Is Richer, Why Are Families So Much Less Secure?" October 10, 2004; "The Poor Have More Things Today—Including Wild Income Swings," December 12, 2004; and, "The Source of the Statistics and How They Were Analyzed." The series can be found at www.latimes.com/business/la-fi-riskshift3oct10,1,4792299.story?coll=la-home-headlines&ctrack=1&cset=true. For an interesting set of graphics summarizing the patterns, see www.latimes.com/business/la-100804risk-g,1,2388975.graphic?coll=la-home-headlines.

43. For recent figures, see www.bls.gov/opub/working/data/chart3.txt.

44. For a good overview of the mobility issue, see *CQ Researcher*, "Upward Mobility: Does Income Inequality Threaten the American Dream?" 15 (April 19, 2005): 369–392. The *New York Times* also has a general overview of the role of class in America www.nytimes.com/pages/national/class/index.html.

45. For defenses of inequality based on the argument that they reflect mobility, see Joint Economic Committee Study, United States Congress, "Income Mobility and Economic Opportunity," June 1992; John Hinderaker and Scott Johnson, "Income, Inequality, and Work," The American Enterprise Online (Originally published July/August 1996 in *Economic Anxiety?*), www.taemag.com/print Version/print_article.asp?articleID=16313; and D. Mark Wilson, "Income Mobility and the Fallacy of Class-Warfare Arguments Against Tax Relief," The Heritage Foundation, Policy Research and Analysis, March 8, 2001, www.heritage.org/Research/Taxes/BG1418.cfm.

46. Quoted in Jennifer L. Hochschild, *Facing Up to the American Dream: Race, Class, and the Soul of the Nation* (Princeton, NJ: Princeton University Press, 1995), 18.

47. George Will, "Healthy Inequality," *Newsweek*, October 28, 1996, 92.

48. For arguments about the importance of rewarding effort and the benefits from this, see Milton Friedman, *Capitalism and Freedom* (Chicago: University of Chicago Press, 1962); and Michael Barone, *Hard America Soft America: Competition vs. Coddling and the Battle for the Nation's Future* (New York: Three Rivers Press, 2004).

49. A shorter article on the income mobility data is Katharine Bradbury and Jane Katz, "Are Lifetime Incomes Growing More Unequal?" *Regional Review* Quarter 4 2002 September 2002, available at www.bos.frb.org/economic/nerr/rr2002/q4/issues.pdf. For a graphical presentation of these data, see the *New York Times*' series on "How Class Matters," www.nytimes.com/packages/html/national/20050515_CLASS_GRAPHIC/index_03.htm.

50. Dennis L. Gilbert, *The American Class Structure in an Age of Growing Inequality* (Belmont, CA: Wadsworth Press, 1998); Daniel P. McMurrer, Mark Condon, and Isabel V. Sawhill, "Intergenerational

Mobility in the United States," www.urban.org/urlprint.cfm?ID=6177; and Samuel Bowles, *Unequal Chances: Family Background and Economic Success* (Princeton: Princeton University Press, 2005).

51. For a discussion of occurrences that alter family fortunes, see Katherine S. Newman, *Falling from Grace: The Experience of Downward Mobility in the American Middle Class* (New York: The Free Press, 1988).

CHAPTER THREE

1. Geoffrey C. Layman and Thomas M. Carsey, "Party Polarization and Party Structuring of Policy Attitudes: A Comparison of Three NES Panel Studies," *Political Behavior* 24 (September 2002): 199–236; Geoffrey C. Layman and Thomas M. Carsey, "Party Polarization and 'Conflict Extension' in the American Electorate," *American Journal of Political Science* 46 (October 2002): 786–802; and John R. Zaller, *The Nature and Origins of Mass Opinion* (New York: Cambridge University Press, 1992).

2. John Aldrich, "Electoral Democracy during Politics as Usual—and Unusual," in *Electoral Democracy,* eds. Michael B. MacKuen and George Rabinowitz (Ann Arbor: University of Michigan Press, 2003), 279–310; Mark D. Brewer, "The Rise of Partisanship and the Expansion of Partisan Conflict within the American Electorate," *Political Research Quarterly* 58 (June 2005): 219–229; and Herbert F. Weisberg, "The Party in the Electorate as a Basis for More Responsible Parties," in *Responsible Partisanship? The Evolution of American Parties Since 1950,* eds. John C. Green and Paul S. Herrnson (Lawrence: University Press of Kansas, 2002), 161–179.

3. Earl Black and Merle Black, *Politics and Society in the South* (Cambridge: Harvard University Press, 1987); Gary C. Jacobson, "Party Polarization in National Politics: The Electoral Connection," in *Polarized Politics: Congress and the President in a Partisan Era,* ed. Jon R. Bond and Richard Fleisher (Washington, DC: CQ Press, 2000), 9–30; Nelson Polsby, *How Congress Evolves: Social Bases of Institutional Change* (New York: Oxford University Press, 2004); Jeffrey M. Stonecash, *Parties Matter: Realignment and the Return of Partisanship* (Boulder, CO: Lynne Rienner, 2005); and Jeffrey M. Stonecash, Mark D. Brewer, and Mack D. Mariani, *Diverging Parties: Social Change, Realignment, and Party Polarization* (Boulder, CO: Westview Press, 2003).

4. John Gerring, *Party Ideologies in America, 1828–1996* (New York: Cambridge University Press, 1998).

5. For an extended discussion of the evolution of these changes, see Stonecash, *Political Parties Matter,* chapters 2–4.

6. The rise of the conservative movement has received considerable attention in the last several years. For good overviews, see Chip Berlet and Matthew N. Lyons, *Right-Wing Populism in America: Too Close for Comfort* (New York: Guilford, 2000); Godfrey Hodgson, *The World Turned Right Side Up: A History of the Conservative Ascendancy in America* (Boston: Houghton-Mifflin, 1996); and John Micklethwait and Adrian Wooldridge, *The Right Nation: Conservative Power in America* (New York: Penguin, 2004).

7. Kevin P. Phillips, *The Politics of Rich and Poor* (New York: Random House, 1990).

8. There are now numerous conservative think tanks, but some examples are the American Enterprise Institute, The Heritage Foundation, The Manhattan Institute, The American Conservative Union, The Hoover Institute, and The Cato Institute. One list of such organizations is at policyexperts.org/organizations/organizations_results.cfm.

9. For a good example of such works, see Charles Murray, *Losing Ground* (New York: Basic Books, 1984).

10. James M. Glaser, *Race, Campaign Politics and the Realignment in the South* (New Haven: Yale University Press, 1996).

11.. Stonecash, Brewer, and Mariani, *Diverging Parties,* chapter 4.

12. These data have been developed by Keith Poole. The data are available at voteview.com/dwnl.htm. The method is explained in Keith T. Poole and Howard Rosenthal, *Congress: A Political-Economic History of Roll Call Voting* (New York: Oxford University Press, 1997).

13. The positions of various conservative groups regarding taxes can be found at numerous Web sites. Several important ones are Americans for Tax Reform, www.atr.org/; The Cato Institute, www.cato.org/fiscal/tax-policy.html; The Club for Growth, www.clubforgrowth.org/; The Heritage Foundation, www.heritage.org/Research/Taxes/index.cfm; and The American Enterprise Institute, www.aei.org/research/filter.all,subjectID.11/projectfilter_detail.asp.

14. See www.whitehouse.gov/infocus/economy/working_families.html.

15. See www.whitehouse.gov/news/usbudget/blueprint/bud02.html.

16. David Kamin and Isaac Shapiro, "Studies Shed New Light on Effects of Administration's Tax Cuts," Center on Budget and Policy Priorities, revised September 13, 2004, 5.

17. David E. Rosenbaum, "Doing the Math on Bush's Tax Cut," *New York Times,* March 4, 2001, 22.

18. Both quotes are from the following story: "Bush Launches Campaign to Sell Tax Relief Plan," *St. Louis Post-Dispatch,* February 6, 2001, A1.

19. "Democratic Candidates Debate," Held September 25, 2003, Posted at www.crocuta.net/Dean/ Democrats_Debate_NYC_25Sept_transcript.html.

20. Debate Transcript: The Cheney-Edwards Vice Presidential Debate, Posted at www.debates.org/ pages/trans2004b_p.html.

21. Comments by Senator Chuck Grassley, R-Iowa, *Congressional Record—Senate,* May 14, 2003, S6161.

22. Comments by Senator Robert Bennett, R-Utah, *Congressional Record—Senate,* May 14, 2003, S6169.

23. Weekly column of Representative Tom Petri, R-Wisc., www.house.gov/Petri/weekly/Jun08col.htm.

24. Jeffrey M. Stonecash, "Parties and Taxes: The Emergence of Distributive Divisions, 1950–2004." Manuscript, Department of Political Science, Maxwell School, Syracuse University, 2005.

25. For an overview of these changes, see Vee Burke, Congressional Research Service "Welfare Reform: An Issue Overview," www.policyalmanac.org/social_welfare/archive/crs_welfare.shtml.

26. For an overview of this program, see www.policyalmanac.org/social_welfare/archive/unemploy-ment_compensation.shtml.

27. Suzanne B. Mettler and Jeffrey M. Stonecash, "How Policy Use Affects Turnout: Results of the Maxwell Poll," presented at the 2006 Midwest Political Science Association meetings, Chicago, Ill., April, 2006.

28. See, for example, Joel Brinkley, "Out of Spotlight, Bush Overhauls U.S. Regulations," *New York Times,* August 14, 2004, A1.

29. "President Signs Class-Action Fairness Act of 2005," White House news release, available at white-house.gov/news/releases/2005/02/print/20050218-11.html.

30. "Bush Signs Bill Putting Limits on Class-Action Suits," *USA Today,* February 18, 2005, www.usato-day.com/news/washington/2005-02-18-bush-lawsuits_x.htm?csp=34.

31. For the debate on this legislation, see the Congressional Record transcript of the House debate on Wednesday, February 16, 2005, at frwebgate4.access.gpo.gov/cgi-bin/waisgate.cgi?WAISdocID= 63921721000+14+0+0&WAISaction=retrieve.

32. For congressional debate on this bill, see frwebgate5.access.gpo.gov/cgi-bin/waisgate.cgi?WAIS docID=641459327825+1+0+0&WAISaction=retrieve.

33. Albert Crenshaw, "Keeping Some Hiding Places," *Washington Post,* March 20, 2005, F 1.

34. Steve Lohr, "Bush's Next Target: Malpractice Lawyers," *New York Times,* February 27, 2005, Section 3, 1.

35. Of course it would also significantly hurt trial lawyers, also an affluent segment of American society.

36. Steven Thomma, "Social Security is Long-Standing Conservative Dream," *Common Dreams News Center,* posted at www.commondreams.org/headlines05/0205-05.htm.

37. For examples of these early writings, see Carolyn L. Weaver, "Social Security: Has the Crisis Passed?" *Cato Policy Report,* January 1979, 1–7; Stuart Butler and Peter Germanis, "Achieving A 'Leninist Strategy," *The Cato Journal,* vol. 3, no. 2 (Fall 1983), 547–556; and Peter J. Ferrara, "The Prospect of Real Reform," *The Cato Journal,* vol. 3, no. 2 (Fall 1983), 609–621.

38. Associated Press, "Disaster Strategy to Push Social Security Reform," *Syracuse Post-Standard,* January 6, 2005, A4.

39. U.S. Government Accounting Office, "Social Security and Minorities," GAO-03-387, April 2003, 10.

40. For an update as of 2005, see www.epinet.org/issuebriefs/206/ib206.pdf.

41. Jason Deparle, "Complexity of a Fiscal Giant: A Primer on Social Security," *New York Times,* February 11, 1993: A29.

CHAPTER FOUR

1. Carroll J. Glynn, Susan Herbst, Garrett J. O'Keefe, Robert Shapiro, and Mark Lindeman, *Public Opinion,* 2d ed. (Boulder, CO: Westview, 2004), 283–354.

2. For an analysis of the misperceptions that many voters have about the distribution of tax cut bene-fits during the early 2000s, see Larry Bartels, "Homer Gets a Tax Cut: Inequality and Public Policy in the American Mind," *Perspectives on Politics* 3 (March 2005): 15–34.

3. For a very interesting study of how the parties have worked to shape how people see the estate or

death tax, see Michael J. Graetz and Ian Shapiro, *Death by a Thousand Cuts: The Fight over Taxing Inherited Wealth* (Princeton, NJ: Princeton University Press, 2005).

4. Leslie McCall and Julian Brash, "What Do Americans Think about Inequality? An Analysis of Polls and Media Coverage of Income Inequality," A Working Paper, May 2004, Demos: A Network for Ideas and Actions, 6, www.demos-usa.org/pubs/What%20Do&20Americans&20Think,&206.3.04.pdf.

5. The data from the 1980s and 2001 are taken from a report by the Pew Research Center for the People & the Press, *Economic Inequality Seen as Rising, Boom Bypasses Poor*, June 21, 2001. The 2005 data are from Jeffrey M. Stonecash, "Inequality and a Conflicted Public," in *The Maxwell Poll: Civic Engagement and Inequality*, The Maxwell School, Syracuse University, April 10, 2005, 3.

6. Stonecash, "Inequality and a Conflicted Public," 3.

7. Ibid.

8. McCall and Brash, "What Do Americans Think about Inequality."

9. Larry M. Bartels, "What's the Matter with *What's the Matter with Kansas?*" paper delivered at the annual meeting of the American Political Science Association, Washington, DC, September 2005, and in *Quarterly Journal of Political Science* 1 (2006): 201–226; and Morris P. Fiorina, with Samuel J. Abrams and Jeremy C. Pope, *Culture War? The Myth of a Polarized America*, 2d ed. (New York: Pearson/Longman, 2006).

10. The best example of this argument is that of Thomas B. Edsall with Mary D. Edsall, *Chain Reaction: The Impact of Race, Rights, and Taxes on American Politics* (New York: Norton, 1991).

11. Stanley B. Greenberg, *Middle Class Dreams: The Politics and Power of the New American Majority* (New York: Times Books, 1995).

12. Katherine Tate, *From Protest to Politics: The New Black Voters in American Elections* (New York: Russell Sage Foundation and Cambridge, MA: Harvard University Press, 1993).

13. Bartels, "What's the Matter with *What's the Matter with Kansas?*" 12.

14. Kenneth D. Wald, *Religion and Politics in the United States*, 4th ed. (Lanham, MD: Rowman & Littlefield, 2003).

15. These results are taken from the 2002 NES survey.

16. Our data prior to that is limited, but it does indicate greater divisions. Sundquist presents data from the late 1930s that indicates that divisions were greater then. James L. Sundquist, *Dynamics of the Party System: Alignment and Realignment of Political Parties in the United States*, rev. ed. (Washington, DC: The Brookings Institution Press, 1983). An analysis using Gallup Poll data from the 1930s and 1940s also indicates divisions were greater at one time. Jeffrey M. Stonecash, "Class Divisions in American Politics, 1932–2004," paper presented at the 2006 Southern Political Science Association meetings, Atlanta, Ga., January 2006.

17. Nolan McCarty, Keith T. Poole, and Howard Rosenthal, *Polarized America: The Dance of Ideology and Unequal Riches* (Cambridge: M.I.T. Press, 2006), find a similar trend, using quintiles (fifths) of the income distribution. They track the ratio of those voting or identifying with the Republican Party in the top and bottom quintiles, using NES data, from 1952 to 2000. In the 1950s that ratio is around 1.0, which means the percentages did not differ much. By the 1990s the ratio was above 2, indicating those in the top quintile supported Republicans twice as much as the bottom quintile did.

18. Stonecash, "Inequality and a Conflicted Public," 3–4.

19. As of now, views about the presence of equality and the sources of success are not polarized. There would be greater conflict if all those who believe everyone has opportunity also believed that hard work is most important *and* those who see opportunity only for some also thought family background was most important. As the following table indicates, those who see opportunity for just some do not see family background as most important. We do not now have a substantial segment of society seeing unfairness *and* believing inequality as just passed from one generation to another by family background.

Opinions about Sources of Success by Views about Existence of Opportunity
(Percentages sum across for each category)

Who has opportunity to succeed?	What affects ability to achieve?		
	Family Background	Both	Abilities and Hard Work
Everyone	4.2	27.7	67.5
Most	7.5	27.7	62.8
Only some	10.9	34.5	50.0

Hard work and perseverance overcome different opportunities?

Who has opportunity to succeed?	Agree	Disagree
Everyone	93.4	5.4
Most	85.1	9.6
Only some	61.4	31.5

Note: "No opinion" responses not reported.

20. See Stonecash, *Class and Party in American Politics* (Boulder, CO: Westview Press, 2000) chapter seven for a discussion of the development of these arguments. This book argues that while evidence from the National Election Study indicates that political divisions by income have increased, the academic community was developing a consensus that political divisions revolving around class were of less relevance.

21. McCall and Brash, "What Do Americans Think about Inequality?" 10.

22. For a recent analysis making that argument, see Thomas Frank, *What's the Matter with Kansas* (New York: Henry Holt, 2005). A contrast is presented in Fiorina, et al., *Culture War.* These commentaries have proliferated after the 2004 elections, in which the CNN exit polls found a substantial percentage cited "moral values" as most important in their decision-making. Oddly enough, most commentators chose to ignore the large divisions by income of respondents.

23. Gary C. Jacobson, "Partisan Polarization in Presidential Support: The Electoral Connection," *Congress and the Presidency* 30 (Spring 2003): 1–36.

24. Jeffrey M. Stonecash, Mark D. Brewer, and Mack D. Mariani, *Diverging Parties: Social Change, Realignment, and Party Polarization* (Boulder, CO: Westview, 2003).

25. For two recent analyses pointing to the importance of terrorism and the war in Iraq in the 2004 elections, see Stanley B. Greenberg, *The Two Americas: Our Current Political Deadlock and How to Break It, Revised Edition* (New York: Thomas Dunne Books, 2005); and Wilson Carey McWilliams, "The Meaning of the Election: Ownership and Citizenship in American Life," in *The Elections of 2004,* ed. Michael Nelson (Washington, DC: CQ Press, 2005), 187–213.

26. Stonecash, *Class and Party in American Politics,* 119–121.

27. These results are presented in Mark D. Brewer and Jeffrey M. Stonecash, "Cultural Politics and Class Political Divisions," presented at the 2005 Midwest Political Science Association meetings, Chicago, Ill. They will be reviewed in Chapter 8.

CHAPTER FIVE

1. James Davison Hunter, *Culture Wars: The Struggle to Define America* (New York: Basic Books, 1991), 42–43.

2. For some discussion of how these changes have been responded to see Clem Brooks, "Religious Influence and the Politics of Family Decline Concern: Trends, Sources, and U.S. Political Behavior," *American Sociological Review* 67 (April 2002): 191–211; Hunter, *Culture Wars;* David C. Leege et al., *The Politics of Cultural Differences: Social Change and Voter Mobilization* (Princeton, NJ: Princeton University Press, 2002); Byron E. Shafer and William J.M. Claggett, *The Two Majorities: The Issue Context of Modern American Politics* (Baltimore, MD: The Johns Hopkins University Press, 1995); John Kenneth White, *The Values Divide: American Politics and Culture in Transition* (New York: Chatham House, 2003); and Robert Wuthnow, *The Restructuring of American Religion: Society and Faith Since World War II* (Princeton, NJ: Princeton University Press, 1988).

3. Hunter, *Culture Wars;* Shafer and Claggett, *The Two Majorities;* and White, *The Values Divide.*

4. For discussion abortion prior to the 1960s, see N.E.H. Hull and Peter Charles Hoffer, *Roe v. Wade: The Abortion Rights Controversy in American History* (Lawrence: University Press of Kansas, 2001), and Kristin Luker, *Abortion and the Politics of Motherhood* (Berkeley: University of California Press, 1984). For good early histories of the movement for sex education in public schools, see Janice M. Irvine, *Talk about Sex: The Battles over Sex Education in the United States* (Berkeley: University of California Press, 2002); and Jeffrey P. Moran, *Teaching Sex: The Shaping of Adolescence in the 20th Century* (Cambridge: Harvard University Press 2000). For discussion of pre-1960s battles over prayer in public schools, see Joan Del Fattore, *The Fourth R: Conflicts over Religion in America's Public Schools* (New Haven: Yale University Press, 2004). For an example of the importance that the moral reform-

ers of the Progressive Era placed on "proper" family and home life, see Josiah Strong, *Our Country* (1891, Reprint, Cambridge, MA: Belknap Press of Harvard University Press, 1963); and Josiah Strong, *The Twentieth Century City* (1898, Reprint, New York: Arno Press, 1970).

5. Ray Allen Billington, *The Protestant Crusade 1800–1860: A Study of the Origins of American Nativism* (New York: Macmillan, 1938).

6. H. Frank Way, Jr., "Survey Research on Judicial Decisions: The Prayer and Bible Reading Cases," *Western Political Quarterly* 21 (June 1968): 189–205. The percentages reported here were calculated by the authors from data presented on pp. 190–191.

7. Kenneth M. Dolbeare and Phillip E. Hammond, *The School Prayer Decisions: From Court Policy to Local Practice* (Chicago: University of Chicago Press, 1971), 26. Capitalization in the original prayer.

8. Del Fattore, *The Fourth R*; and Dolbeare and Hammond, *The School Prayer Decisions.*

9. Kirk W. Elifson and C. Kirk Hadaway, "Prayer in Public Schools: When Church and State Collide," *Public Opinion Quarterly* 49 (Autumn 1985): 317–329; and John C. Green and James L. Guth, "The Missing Link: Political Activists and Support for School Prayer," *Public Opinion Quarterly* 53 (Spring 1989): 41–57. A poll conducted by FOX News in November 2005 found that 82 percent of Americans favored allowing voluntary prayer in public schools. The report on and the results of this survey are available at www.foxnews.com/story/0,2933,177355,00.html.

10. Dolbeare and Hammond, *The School Prayer Decisions*; and Way, "Survey Research on Judicial Decisions."

11. Del Fattore, *The Fourth R.*

12. *Wallace v. Jaffree* (1985). For a discussion of this case, see Del Fattore, *The Fourth R*, chapter 10.

13. Moran, *Teaching Sex*, 105.

14. Ibid.

15. The other founding members of SEICUS were Lester Kirkendall, Professor of Family Life Education at Oregon State College; Wallace C. Fulton, former president of the National Council on Family Relations; William Genné, Director of the Family Life Department at the National Council of Churches; and Clark Vincent, Chief of the Professional Training Division of the National Institute for Mental Health. For discussions of the early years of SEICUS, see Irvine, *Talk about Sex*, and Moran, *Teaching Sex.*

16. Irvine, *Talk about Sex*, 38–39.

17. Ibid.

18. In *Teaching Sex*, Moran reports that Drake claimed the pamphlet sold 90,000 copies within its first three months of publication, while in *Talk about Sex* Irvine quotes Hargis as claiming in 1996 that the pamphlet sold one million copies.

19. Irvine, *Talk about Sex*; and Moran, *Teaching Sex.*

20. Tina Hoff, Liberty Greene, Mary McIntosh, Nicole Rawlings, and Jean D'Amico, *Sex Education in America* (Menlo Park, CA: Henry J. Kaiser Family Foundation, September 2000).

21. Jacqueline E. Darroch, David J. Landry, and Susheela Singh, "Changing Emphases in Sexuality Education in U.S. Public Secondary Schools, 1988–1999," *Family Planning Perspectives* 32 (September/October 2000): 204–211, 265.

22. Both Irvine (*Talk about Sex*) and Moran (*Teaching Sex*) talk about how sex ed opponents began moving away from getting sex ed out entirely out of schools toward replacing comprehensive programs with abstinence-only programs in the mid-1980s.

23. Hoff et al., *Sex Education in America.*

24. Darroch et al., "Changing Emphases in Sexuality Education in U.S. Public Secondary Schools, 1988–1999."

25. Irvine, *Talk about Sex*, 132.

26. For a discussion of the recent moves to enact abstinence-only sex education, see Sandra Vergari, "Morality Politics and the Implementation of Abstinence-Only Sex Education: A Case of Policy Compromise," in *The Public Clash of Private Values: The Politics of Morality Policy*, ed. Christopher Z. Mooney (New York: Chatham House Publishers, 2001), 201–210.

27. Irvine, *Talk about Sex*; and Moran, *Teaching Sex.*

28. Hoff et al., *Sex Education in America.*

29. As reported by Kunkel et al., children age 8–13 average 3 hours, 37 minutes of television per day, while adolescents age 14–18 average 2 hours and 43 minutes of viewing per day. Dale Kunkel, Erica Biely, Keren Eyal, Kirstie Cope-Farrar, Edward Donnerstein, and Rena Fandrich, *Sex on TV, 2003* (Menlo Park, CA: The Henry J. Kaiser Family Foundation, February 2003.)

30. Dale Kunkel, Keren Eyal, Erica Biely, Keli Finnerty, and Edward Donnerstein, *Sex on TV 4, 2005* (Menlo Park, CA: The Henry J. Kaiser Family Foundation, November 2005).

31. Initially we had hoped to present data on the number of indecency complaints filed with the FCC over time. However, the FCC has no data prior to 2000 that it considers reliable. But the increase in the number of complaints from 2000 to 2004 is staggering—111 in 2000 to 1,405,419 in 2004. Even allowing that the vast majority of the increase is likely due to active complaint-generating campaigns by groups such as the Parents Television Council, the magnitude of the rise is still worth noting. FCC complaint data available at www.fcc.gov/eb/broadcast/ichart.pdf.

32. Dale Kunkel, Kirstie M. Cope, and Carolyn Colvin, *Sexual Messages on Family Hour Television: Content and Context* (Menlo Park, CA: Henry J. Kaiser Family Foundation, December 11, 1996). "Sexual Interaction" was defined as "a talk or behavior exchange typically involving two or more characters. Reciprocal talk or behavior from one character to another who initiated the sequence is considered part of the same interaction. An interaction endures so long as it continues within the same scene and maintains the same interactors as primary participants. An interaction ends when no further exchange involving sexuality (either talk or behavior) occurs between the same characters, or when the scene shifts," 6.

33. Susan Linn, *Consuming Kids: The Hostile Takeover of Childhood* (New York: Free Press, 2004).

34. Henry J. Kaiser Family Foundation, "Key Facts: Children and Video Games" (Menlo Park, CA: Henry J. Kaiser Family Foundation, Fall 2002).

35. This controversy erupted in 2005 when it was disclosed that the game contained a hidden feature, accessible by applying a modification available on the Internet, which enabled the player to initiate a sexually explicit feature in which characters in the game engaged in oral sex.

36. Joseph E. Scott and Jack L. Franklin, "The Changing Nature of Sex References in Mass Circulation Magazines," *Public Opinion Quarterly* 36 (Spring 1972): 80–86.

37. For a discussion of the place of pornography in morality politics, see Kevin B. Smith, "Clean Thoughts and Dirty Minds: The Politics of Porn," in *The Public Clash of Private Values: The Politics of Morality Policy*, ed. Christopher Z. Mooney (New York: Chatham House, 2001), 187–200.

38. Irvine, *Talk about Sex*; and Moran, *Teaching Sex.*

39. Senator Debbie Stabenow, D-Mich., put the figure at $12 billion in an interview with Tucker Carlson on his program "The Situation with Tucker Carlson" on July 27, 2005, transcript available at msnbc.msn.com/id/8742696/. Dan Ackman of *Forbes* states that a figure of this magnitude is very much overstated. See Dan Ackman, "How Big is Porn?" Forbes.com, May 25, 2001, available at www.forbes.com/2001/05/25/0524porn.html. The report on pornography on the Internet comes from Third Way, "The Porn Standard: Children and Pornography on the Internet," July 2005, available at www.third-way.com/news/porn_report.htm.

40. Barrie Gunter, *Media Sex: What Are the Issues?* (Mahwah, NJ: Lawrence Erlbaum Associates, 2002).

41. Rebecca L. Collins, Marc N. Elliot, Sandra H. Berry, David E. Kanouse, Dale Kunkel, Sarah B. Hunter, and Angela Mui, "Watching Sex on Television Predicts Adolescent Initiation of Sexual Behavior," *Pediatrics* 114 (September 2004): 280–289.

42. James Davison Hunter, *Before the Shooting Begins: Searching for Democracy in America's Culture War* (New York: Free Press, 1994), 13.

43. Dallas A. Blanchard, *The Anti-Abortion Movement and the Rise of the Religious Right* (New York: Twayne Publishers, 1994); Hull and Hoffer, *Roe v. Wade*; Phillip B. Levine, *Sex and Consequences: Abortion, Public Policy, and the Economics of Fertility* (Princeton: Princeton University Press, 2004), and Luker, *Abortion and the Politics of Motherhood.*

44. Amy Fried, "Abortion Politics as Symbolic Politics: An Investigation into Belief Systems," *Social Science Quarterly* 69 (March 1988): 137–154; and Luker, *Abortion and the Politics of Motherhood.*

45. Blanchard, *The Anti-Abortion Movement and the Rise of the Religious Right*, 30–31.

46. CDC abortion figures are gathered through self-reports on the part of state governments, the District of Columbia, and New York City. In 1998 and 1999, Alaska, California, New Hampshire, and Oklahoma did not report any abortion data to the CDC. In 2000 and 2001, Alaska, California, and New Hampshire did not report any abortion data to the CDC. The other authoritative source for abortion data is the Alan Guttmacher Institute, which compiles its data based on the reports of abortion providers. The Guttmacher Institute figures for abortions are always higher than those produced by the CDC. Many public health researchers who work in the area of abortion believe that the Guttmacher data are more accurate, but we use the CDC data here because they represent the official government figures.

47. Blanchard, *The Anti-Abortion Movement and the Rise of the Religious Right*. In addition to lowering the actual cost of an abortion, Levine argues that legal abortion with few restrictions (as existed in the U.S. post-*Roe* until the late 1980s and early 1990s) acts as a form of insurance, making certain types of sexual activity, such as sex without contraception or sex outside of a committed relationship, less risky, and therefore more likely to occur. The extension of this argument is that the availability of low-cost abortion without restrictions results in more unwanted pregnancies, and therefore more abortions. Levine, *Sex and Consequences*.

48. This statement may no longer apply to women in South Dakota, which in March 2006 enacted a law that would ban abortion in all circumstances except where the life of the pregnant woman is in danger. The text and legislative history of this law is available at legis.state.sd.us/sessions/2006/DisplayBill.aspx.

49. Blanchard, *The Anti-Abortion Movement and the Rise of the Religious Right*; Ted G. Jelen and Clyde Wilcox, "Causes and Consequences of Public Attitudes toward Abortion: A Review and a Research Agenda," *Political Research Quarterly* 56 (December 2003): 489–500; and Darren E. Sherkat and Christopher G. Ellison, "The Cognitive Structure of a Moral Crusade: Conservative Protestantism and Opposition to Pornography," *Social Forces* 75 (March 1997): 957–980.

50. Fried, "Abortion Politics as Symbolic Politics," Michael Hout, "Abortion Politics in the United States, 1972–1994: From Single Issue to Ideology," *Gender Issues* 17 (Spring 1999): 3–34; Luker, *Abortion and the Politics of Motherhood*, Jane J. Mansbridge, *Why We Lost the ERA* (Chicago: University of Chicago Press, 1986); and Christina Wolbrecht, *The Politics of Women's Rights: Parties, Positions, and Change* (Princeton: Princeton University Press, 2000).

51. Kira Sanbonmatsu, *Democrats, Republicans, and the Politics of Women's Place* (Ann Arbor: University of Michigan Press, 2002).

52. Ethel Klein, *Gender Politics: From Consciousness to Mass Politics* (Cambridge: Harvard University Press, 1984).

53. Quote taken from Klein, *Gender Politics*, 45.

54. M. Margaret Conway, David W. Ahern, and Gertrude Steuernagel, *Women and Public Policy: A Revolution in Progress* (Washington, DC: CQ Press, 1995); Klein, *Gender Politics*; Sanbonmatsu, *Democrats, Republicans, and the Politics of Women's Place*; and Wolbrecht, *The Politics of Women's Rights*.

55. Klein, *Gender Politics*; Mansbridge, *Why We Lost the ERA*; Sanbonmatsu, *Democrats, Republicans, and the Politics of Women's Place*; and Wolbrecht, *The Politics of Women's Rights*.

56. Lynne M. Casper and Suzanne M. Bianchi, *Continuity and Change in the American Family* (Thousand Oaks, CA: Sage, 2002).

57. *Murphy Brown* was a situation comedy that aired on CBS from 1988–1998. The title character, played by Candice Bergen, was the star female reporter for a television news magazine. During the show's third and fourth seasons—1991–1992—Murphy Brown became pregnant and decided to have the child on her own, out of wedlock and without the father or any other male partner involved. Such a decision could obviously be problematic for cultural conservatives, a group in which then Vice President Dan Quayle certainly considered himself. In a May 1992 speech to the Commonwealth Club of California, Quayle pointed to *Murphy Brown* as an example of how pop culture was contributing to the "poverty of values" in the United States, stating "it doesn't help matters when primetime TV has Murphy Brown—a character who supposedly epitomizes today's intelligent, highly paid, professional woman—mocking the importance of fathers, by bearing a child alone, and calling it just another 'lifestyle choice.'" Quayle's comment created a media firestorm, and drew considerable criticism from liberal groups and feminists around the nation. For discussions of this controversy, see Sanbonmatsu, *Democrats, Republicans, and the Politics of Women's Place*; and Wolbrecht, *The Politics of Women's Rights*.

58. Sherkat and Ellison, "The Cognitive Structure of a Moral Crusade."

59. Kathleen C. Boone, *The Bible Tells Them So: The Discourse of Protestant Fundamentalism* (Albany: State University of New York Press, 1989). See also Irvine, *Talk about Sex*.

60. Lorraine Fox Harding, "'Family Values' and Conservative Government Policy, 1979–1997," in *Changing Family Values*, ed. Gill Jagger and Caroline Wright (New York: Routledge, 1999), 119–135.

61. Casper and Bianchi, *Continuity and Change in the American Family*, 5.

62. U.S. Census Bureau, Current Population Survey, Selected Years, Reported in Barbara Downs, "Fertility of American Women: June 2002," U.S. Census Bureau, Current Population Reports, P20-548, October 2003.

63. Conway et al., *Women and Public Policy*, 4; and Barbara Downs, "Fertility of American Women: June 2002," U.S. Census Bureau, Current Population Reports, P20-548, October 2003.

64. Federal Interagency Forum on Child and Family Statistics, *America's Children: Key National Indicators of Well-Being, 2005* (Washington, DC: Federal Interagency Forum on Child and Family Statistics, July 2005).

65. Kristin Smith, "Who's Minding the Kids? Child Care Arrangements: Spring 1997," U.S. Census Bureau, Current Population Reports, P70-86 (July 2002), 5.

66. Jason Fields, "America's Families and Living Arrangements: 2003," U.S. Census Bureau, Current Population Reports, P20-553 (November 2004), 12.

67. T. J. Mathews and Brady E. Hamilton, "Mean Age of Mother, 1970–2000," Centers for Disease Control and Prevention, National Vital Statistics Reports, vol. 51, no. 1 (December 11, 2002), 2.

68. This is another example where race becomes entangled with issues of class and culture, in this case culture. In 2003, 29 percent of live births occurred to unmarried women among non-Hispanic whites. For blacks, the corresponding figure was 68 percent, and for Hispanics the figure was 45 percent. Numbers like these often arouse the ire of cultural conservatives. See Figure 5.4 for the source of these data.

69. For a comparative perspective on the percentage of births to unmarried women in the U.S., see Mark Abrahamson, *Out-of-Wedlock Births: The United States in Comparative Perspective* (Westport, CT: Praeger, 1998).

70. Fields, "America's Families and Living Arrangements: 2003," 7-8.

71. U.S. Census Bureau, Current Population Study, all years except 1960, 1970, and 1980. Data for 1960, 1970, and 1980 from decennial census, respective years. Available at www.census.gov/ population/socdemo/hh-fam/ch1.pdf, accessed 22 July, 2005. The following is the Census Bureau's definition of a "Two-Parent Family": "In the Current Population Survey, children live in a two-parent family if they are living with a parent who is married with his or her spouse present. This is not an indicator of the biological relationship between the child and the parents. The parent who is identified could be a biological, step, or adoptive parent. If a second parent is present and not married to the first parent, then the child is identified as living with a single parent."

72. Lynne M. Casper and Philip N. Cohen, "How Does POSSLQ Measure Up? Historical Estimates of Cohabitation," *Demography* 37 (May 2000): 237–245.

73. Ken Bryson and Lynne M. Casper, "Coresident Grandparents and Grandchildren," U.S. Census Bureau, Current Population Reports, Special Studies, P23-198 (May 1999), 1.

74. National Center for Health Statistics, *Health, United States, 2005* (Hyattsville, MD: U.S. Government Printing Office, 2005).

75. Lawrence M. Mead, *Beyond Entitlement: The Social Obligations of Citizenship* (New York: Free Press, 1986); Lawrence M. Mead, *The New Politics of Poverty: The Nonworking Poor in America* (New York: Basic Books, 1992); and Charles Murray, *Losing Ground: American Social Policy 1950–1980* (New York: Basic Books, 1984).

76. Note that California, Colorado, Indiana, and Louisiana did not report divorce numbers since 1998. This may or may not have something to do with why the Census Bureau has not provided more recent figures on divorce.

77. Rose M. Kreider, "Number, Timing, and Duration of Marriages and Divorces: 2001," U.S. Census Bureau, Current Population Reports, (February 2005), 4.

78. For example, see James Q. Wilson, *The Marriage Problem: How Our Culture Has Weakened Families* (New York: Harper-Collins, 2002).

79. J. C. Abma, G.M. Martinez, and B. S. Dawson, *Teenagers in the United States: Sexual Activity, Contraceptive Use, and Childbearing, 2002*, Centers for Disease Control and Prevention, National Center for Health Statistics, Series 23, No. 24, December 2004.

80. Deborah L. Rohde, "Adolescent Pregnancy and Public Policy," *Political Science Quarterly* 108 (Winter 1993–1994): 635–669.

81. Amara Bachu, "Trends in Premarital Childbearing, 1930–1994," U.S. Census Bureau, *Current Population Reports*, Special Studies, P23-197 (October 1999).

82. Karen Wilkinson, "The Broken Family and Juvenile Delinquency: Scientific Explanation or Ideology?," *Social Problems* 21 (June 1974): 726–739.

83. Moran, *Teaching Sex*, 134.

84. The authors thank Melissa Sickmund of the National Center for Juvenile Justice for her assistance with these data.

85. National Center for Education Statistics, "Indicators of School Crime and Safety, 2003," U.S. Department of Education, Institute of Education Sciences, 2004, 54–58.

86. Moran, *Teaching Sex*, 197. See also Barry D. Adam, *The Rise of a Gay and Lesbian Movement*, revised ed., (Boston: Twayne Publishers, 1995).

87. Connie de Boer, "The Polls: Attitudes toward Homosexuality," *Public Opinion Quarterly* 42 (Summer 1978): 265–276; and Alan S. Yang, "Trends: Attitudes toward Homosexuality," *Public Opinion Quarterly* 61 (Autumn 1997): 477–507.

88. Yang, "Trends: Attitudes toward Homosexuality."

89. J. David Woodard, "Same Sex Politics: The Legal Controversy over Homosexuality," in *The American Culture Wars: Current Contests and Future Prospects*, ed. James L. Nolan, Jr., (Charlottesville: University Press of Virginia, 1996), 133–152.

90. Paul R. Brewer, "Values, Political Knowledge, and Public Opinion about Gay Rights: A Framing-Based Account," *Public Opinion Quarterly* 67 (Summer 2003): 173–201.

91. Irvine, *Talk about Sex*; and Woodard, "Same Sex Politics."

CHAPTER SIX

1. E. E. Schattschneider, *Party Government* (New York: Holt, Rinehart, and Winston, 1942).

2. Ralph M. Goldman, *Search for Consensus: The Story of the Democratic Party* (Philadelphia: Temple University Press, 1979); and Robert Allen Rutland, *The Democrats: From Jefferson to Clinton*, rev. ed. (Columbia, MO: University of Missouri Press, 1995).

3. John Gerring, *Party Ideologies in America, 1828–1996* (New York: Cambridge University Press, 1998).

4. For more on this development, see Geoffrey C. Layman, *The Great Divide: Religious and Cultural Conflict in American Party Politics* (New York: Columbia University Press, 2001); David C. Leege et al., *The Politics of Cultural Differences: Social Change and Voter Mobilization Strategies in the Post-New Deal Period* (Princeton: Princeton University Press, 2002); and John Kenneth White, *The Values Divide: American Politics and Culture in Transition* (New York: Chatham House, 2003).

5. Edward G. Carmines and James A. Stimson, *Issue Evolution: Race and the Transformation of American Politics* (Princeton: Princeton University Press, 1989); V. O. Key, Jr., *Public Opinion and American Democracy* (New York: Knopf, 1961); E. E. Schattschneider, *The Semi-Sovereign People* (New York: Holt, Rinehart, and Winston, 1960); and James L. Sundquist, *Dynamics of the Party System*, rev. ed. (Washington, DC: The Brookings Institution, 1983).

6. For more on this relationship, see Robert S. Erikson, Michael B. MacKuen, and James A. Stimson, *The Macro Polity* (New York: Cambridge University Press, 2002); and James A. Stimson, *Public Opinion in America: Moods, Cycles, and Swings*, 2d ed. (Boulder, CO: Westview, 1999).

7. Sharon E. Jarvis, *The Talk of the Party: Political Labels, Symbolic Capital, and American Life* (Lanham, MD: Rowman & Littlefield, 2005).

8. Marc J. Hetherington, "Resurgent Mass Partisanship: The Role of Elite Polarization," *American Political Science Review* 95 (September 2001): 619–631; Geoffrey C. Layman and Thomas M. Carsey, "Party Polarization and Party Structuring of Policy Attitudes: A Comparison of Three NES Panel Studies," *Political Behavior* 24 (September 2002): 199–236; Benjamin Page, *Choices and Echoes in Presidential Elections* (Chicago: University of Chicago Press, 1978); and John R. Zaller, *The Nature and Origins of Mass Opinion* (New York: Cambridge University Press, 1992).

9. For more on this dynamic, see John Aldrich, "Electoral Democracy during Politics as Usual—and Unusual," in *Electoral Democracy*, ed. Michael B. MacKuen and George Rabinowitz (Ann Arbor: University of Michigan Press, 2003), 279–310.

10. The 1972 platforms were selected because this was the first year the parties began to differ on cultural issues. The 2004 platforms were selected because they are the most recent. While there are certainly strong cultural elements in the platforms of both parties in 1980 and 1992, these years were not selected for that purpose. Other years (e.g., 1984, 1988, or 1996) could be substituted with no change in the substance of the material presented here. It is simply unnecessary to examine all the platforms here to show how the parties have evolved on cultural issues.

11. The Democrats' 1976 stand on abortion: "We fully recognize the religious and ethical nature of the concerns which many Americans have on the subject of abortion. We feel, however, that it is undesirable to attempt to amend the U.S. Constitution to overturn the Supreme Court decision in this area." The Republicans' 1976 stand on abortion: "Because of our concern for family values, we affirm

our beliefs, stated elsewhere in this platform, in many elements that will make our country a more hospitable environment for family life... [including] a position on abortion that values human life." And, "The question of abortion is one of the most difficult and controversial of our time. It is undoubtedly a moral and personal issue but it also involves complex questions relating to medical science and criminal justice. There are those in our Party who favor complete support for the Supreme Court decision which permits abortion on demand. There are others who share sincere convictions that the Supreme Court's decision must be changed by a constitutional amendment prohibiting all abortions. Others have yet to take a position, or they have assumed a stance somewhere in between polar positions.... The Republican Party favors a continuance of the public dialogue on abortion and supports the efforts of those who seek enactment of a constitutional amendment to restore protection of the right to life for unborn children."

12. For more on this shift by the GOP, see Anne M. Costain and Steven Majstorovic, "Congress, Social Movements, and Public Opinion: Multiple Origins of Women's Rights Legislation," *Political Research Quarterly* 47 (March 1994): 111–135; Ethel Klein, *Gender Politics: From Consciousness to Mass Politics* (Cambridge: Harvard University Press, 1984); Kira Sanbonmatsu, *Democrats, Republicans, and the Politics of Women's Place* (Ann Arbor: University of Michigan Press, 2002); and Christina Wolbrecht, *The Politics of Women's Rights: Parties, Positions, and Change* (Princeton: Princeton University Press, 2000).

13. Layman, *The Great Divide*, 116–117.

14. The existing platforms of political parties that received at least one electoral vote since 1840 can be found at www.presidency.ucsb.edu/platforms.php.

15. John C. Green and James L. Guth, "The Missing Link: Political Activists and Support for School Prayer," *Public Opinion Quarterly* 53 (Spring 1989): 41–57.

16. Geoffrey C. Layman, "'Culture Wars' in the American Party System: Religious and Cultural Change among Partisan Activists since 1972," *American Politics Quarterly* 27 (January 1999): 89–121; and Layman, *The Great Divide*, chapters 3 and 4.

17. For more discussion of the divergence of the party platforms on cultural issues since 1970, see Jo Freeman, "Sex, Race, Religion, and Partisan Realignment," in *We Get What We Vote For... Or Do We?*, ed. Paul E. Scheele (Westport, CT: Praeger, 1999): 167–190; and Layman, *The Great Divide*, chapter 3.

18. L. Sandy Maisel, "The Platform-Writing Process," *Political Science Quarterly* 108 (Winter 1993–1994): 671–698.

19. Richard F. Fenno, Jr., *Home Style: House Members in Their District* (Boston: Little, Brown, 1978); and David R. Mayhew, *Congress: The Electoral Connection* (New Haven: Yale University Press, 1974).

20. Roger H. Davidson and Walter J. Oleszek, *Congress and Its Members*, 10th ed. (Washington, DC: CQ Press, 2006); and Paul S. Herrnson, *Congressional Elections: Campaigning at Home and in Washington*, 4th ed. (Washington, DC: CQ Press, 2004).

21. Samuel L. Popkin, *The Reasoning Voter: Communication and Persuasion in Presidential Campaigns* (Chicago: University of Chicago Press, 1991).

22. *1972 CQ Almanac* (Washington, DC: Congressional Quarterly, 1972), 199.

23. Jane J. Mansbridge, *Why We Lost the ERA* (Chicago: University of Chicago Press, 1986).

24. For more on the changing partisan positions and polarization on women's issues, see Freeman, "Sex, Race, Religion, and Partisan Realignment"; Klein, *Gender Politics*; and Wolbrecht, *The Politics of Women's Rights*. Sanbonmatsu argues that the parties have not polarized on all women's issues, but only on certain ones such as the ERA, abortion, and family and medical leave. See Sanbonmatsu, *Democrats, Republicans, and the Politics of Women's Place*.

25. *1964 CQ Almanac* (Washington, DC: Congressional Quarterly, 1965), 398.

26. *1962 CQ Almanac* (Washington, DC: Congressional Quarterly, 1962), 240.

27. *1963 CQ Almanac* (Washington, DC: Congressional Quarterly, 1963), 402.

28. While returning prayer to public schools has always been and continues to be popular with the public, the issue has received surprisingly few votes in Congress.

29. For more on school prayer in Congress, see Joan Del Fattore, *The Fourth R: Conflict in Religion in America's Public Schools* (New Haven: Yale University Press, 2004); and Edward Keynes, with Randall K. Miller, *The Court vs. Congress: Prayer, Busing, and Abortion* (Durham, NC: Duke University Press, 1989).

30. *1974 CQ Almanac* (Washington, DC: Congressional Quarterly, 1975), 101.

31. *1976 CQ Almanac* (Washington, DC: Congressional Quarterly, 1976), 566.

32. *1983 CQ Almanac* (Washington, DC: Congressional Quarterly, 1984), 309.

33. *1976 CQ Almanac* (Washington, DC: Congressional Quarterly, 1976), 565.

34. *1983 CQ Almanac*, 309.

35. *1996 CQ Almanac* (Washington, DC: Congressional Quarterly, 1997), 6–43.

36. For more on this, see Greg D. Adams, "Abortion: Evidence of an Issue Evolution," *American Journal of Political Science* 41 (July 1997): 718–737.

37. *1977 CQ Almanac* (Washington, DC: Congressional Quarterly, 1977), 297.

38. For a discussion of how Congress deals with issues involving homosexual rights, see Donald P. Haider-Markel, "Morality in Congress? Legislative Voting on Gay Issues," in *The Public Clash of Private Values: The Politics of Morality Policy*, ed. Christopher Z. Mooney (New York: Chatham House, 2001), 115–129.

39. Leege et al., *The Politics of Cultural Differences*.

40. Popkin, *The Reasoning Voter*.

41. James A. Stimson, *Tides of Consent: How Public Opinion Shapes American Politics* (New York: Cambridge University Press, 2004).

42. The text of the acceptance speeches for all Republican and Democratic presidential nominees since 1960 can be found at www.4president.org/.

43. Janice M. Irvine, *Talk about Sex: The Battles over Sex Education in the United States* (Berkeley: University of California Press, 2002); and Leege et al., *The Politics of Cultural Differences*.

44. *1964 CQ Almanac*, 398.

45. Kevin P. Phillips, *The Emerging Republican Majority* (New Rochelle, NY: Arlington House, 1969).

46. Leege et al., *The Politics of Cultural Differences*.

47. Klein, *Gender Politics*.

48. *1972 CQ Almanac*.

49. For Carter's stands on these issues, see *1977 CQ Almanac* (Washington, DC: Congressional Quarterly, 1977), 297; *1979 CQ Almanac* (Washington, DC: Congressional Quarterly, 1980), 396–397; Klein, *Gender Politics*; Sanbonmatsu, *Democrats, Republicans, and the Politics of Women's Place*; and Wolbrecht, *The Politics of Women's Rights*.

50. White, *The Values Divide*.

51. Anne M. Costain, "After Reagan: New Party Attitudes toward Gender," *Annals of the Academy of Political and Social Science* 515 (May 1991): 114–125; Klein, *Gender Politics*; Mansbridge, *Why We Lost the ERA*; Sanbonmatsu, *Democrats, Republicans, and the Politics of Women's Place*; and Wolbrecht, *The Politics of Women's Rights*.

52. *1984 CQ Almanac* (Washington, DC: Congressional Quarterly, 1985), 246.

53. Ibid, 245–247; and Del Fattore, *The Fourth R*.

54. Costain, "After Reagan: New Party Attitudes toward Gender."

55. *1988 CQ Almanac* (Washington, DC: Congressional Quarterly, 1989), 712.

56. J. David Woodard, "Same Sex Politics: The Legal Struggle over Homosexuality," in *The American Culture Wars: Current Contests and Future Prospects*, ed. James L. Nolan Jr. (Charlottesville, VA: University Press of Virginia), 133–152.

57. *1992 CQ Almanac* (Washington, DC: Congressional Quarterly, 1993), 684.

58. *1996 CQ Almanac*, D-13.

59. Peter Baker and Peter Slevin, "Bush Remarks on 'Intelligent Design' Theory Fuel Debate," *Washington Post*, 3 August, 2005: A01.

60. For discussions of the role religion has played in these developments, see Andrew Kohut et al., *The Diminishing Divide: Religion's Changing Role in American Politics* (Washington, DC: The Brookings Institution, 2000); Geoffrey C. Layman, "'Culture Wars' in the American Party System: Religious and Cultural Change Among Partisan Activists Since 1972," *American Politics Quarterly* 27 (January 1999): 89–121; Layman, *The Great Divide*; Duane Murray Oldfield, *The Right and the Righteous: The Christian Right Confronts the Republican Party* (Lanham, MD: Rowman & Littlefield, 1996); and A. James Reichley, *Faith in Politics* (Washington, DC: The Brookings Institution, 2002).

CHAPTER SEVEN

1. Mark D. Brewer, "The Rise of Partisanship and the Expansion of Partisan Conflict within the American Electorate," *Political Research Quarterly* 58 (June 2005): 219–229; and Marc J. Hetherington, "Resurgent Mass Partisanship: The Role of Elite Polarization," *American Political Science Review* 95 (September 2001): 619–631.
2. The NES used to ask for specifics on the differences between the parties. In 2004, the NES dropped the open-ended component of this question.
3. Full coding schemes for cultural issues available from authors upon request.
4. While the NES offers respondents the opportunity to mention up to three to five likes/dislikes and party differences, only the first mentions are utilized here.
5. See also Geoffrey C. Layman, *The Great Divide: Religious and Cultural Conflict in American Party Politics* (New York: Columbia University Press, 2001), chapter 6.
6. As with the other analyses in this chapter, these figures are for whites only.
7. Brooks presents a similar trend focused specifically on "family decline." He includes responses on child poverty and juvenile delinquency that are excluded here, and also excludes a number of responses (e.g., school prayer, abortion, women's rights, etc.,) that are included here. Clem Brooks, "Religious Influence and the Politics of Family Decline Concern: Trends, Sources, and U.S. Political Behavior," *American Sociological Review* 67 (April 2002): 191–211.
8. Edward G. Carmines and James A. Stimson, "The Two Faces of Issue Voting," *American Political Science Review* 74 (March 1980): 78–91; and Edward G. Carmines and James A. Stimson, *Issue Evolution and the Transformation of American Politics* (Princeton, NJ: Princeton University Press, 1989), 11.
9. Alan Abramowitz, "It's Abortion, Stupid: Policy Voting in the 1992 Presidential Election," *Journal of Politics* 57 (February 1995): 176–186; Ted G. Jelen and Clyde Wilcox, "Causes and Consequences of Public Attitudes toward Abortion: A Review and Research Agenda," *Political Research Quarterly* 56 (December 2003): 489–500; and Christopher B. Wlezien and Malcolm L. Goggin, "The Courts, Interest Groups, and Public Opinion about Abortion," *Political Behavior* 15 (December 1993): 381–405.
10. Benjamin I. Page and Robert Y. Shapiro, *The Rational Public: Fifty Years of Trends in Americans' Policy Preferences* (Chicago: University of Chicago Press, 1992), chapter 3.
11. Jelen and Wilcox, "Causes and Consequences of Public Attitudes toward Abortion"; Ethel Klein, *Gender Politics: From Consciousness to Mass Politics* (Cambridge, MA: Harvard University Press, 1984); Joan Del Fattore, *The Fourth R: Conflicts Over Religion in America's Public Schools* (New Haven: Yale University Press, 2004); Matthew C. Moen, "School Prayer and the Politics of Life-style Concern," *Social Science Quarterly* 65 (December 1984): 1065–1071; and Craig A. Rimmerman, Kenneth D. Wald, and Clyde Wilcox, eds., *The Politics of Gay Rights* (Chicago: University of Chicago Press, 2000).
12. Nicol C. Rae, "Class and Culture: American Political Cleavages in the Twentieth Century," *Western Political Quarterly* 45 (September 1992): 629–650.
13. Ronald Inglehart, *The Silent Revolution: Changing Values and Political Styles among Western Publics* (Princeton: Princeton University Press, 1977); Ronald Inglehart, *Culture Shift in Advanced Industrial Society* (Princeton: Princeton University Press, 1990); and Ronald Inglehart, *Modernization and Postmodernization: Cultural, Economic, and Political Change in 43 Societies* (Princeton: Princeton University Press, 1997).
14. For party identification, "leaners" are considered partisans.
15. Abramowitz, "It's Abortion, Stupid"; Greg D. Adams, "Abortion: Evidence of an Issue Evolution," *American Journal of Political Science* 41 (July 1997): 718–737; and Michael Hout, "Abortion Politics in the United States, 1972–1994: From Single Issue to Ideology," *Gender Issues* 17 (Spring 1999): 3–34.
16. For additional evidence of the growing impact of cultural issues on electoral behavior, see David C. Leege, Kenneth D. Wald, Brian S. Krueger, and Paul D. Mueller, *The Politics of Cultural Differences: Social Change and Voter Mobilization Strategies in the Post–New Deal Period* (Princeton: Princeton University Press, 2002).
17. Seymour Martin Lipset, *American Exceptionalism: A Double-Edged Sword* (New York: Norton, 1996); Pippa Norris and Ronald Inglehart, *Sacred and Secular: Religion and Politics Worldwide* (New York: Cambridge University Press, 2004); and Kenneth D. Wald, *Religion and Politics in the United States*, 4th ed. (Lanham, MD: Rowman & Littlefield Publishers, 2003).

18. Robert Wuthnow, *The Struggle for America's Soul: Evangelicals, Liberals, and Secularism* (Grand Rapids, MI: Eerdmans, 1989).

19. Paul Kleppner, *The Third Electoral System, 1853–1892* (Chapel Hill: University of North Carolina Press, 1979); and A. James Reichley, *Religion in American Public Life* (Washington, DC: The Brookings Institution, 1985).

20. For some discussion of the Catholic/Protestant divide during these years, see Mark D. Brewer, *Relevant No More? The Catholic/Protestant Divide in American Electoral Politics* (Lanham, MD: Lexington Books, 2003); David Burner, *The Politics of Provincialism: The Democratic Party in Transition, 1918–1932* (New York: Knopf, 1968); Kleppner, *The Third Electoral System, 1853–1892*; Paul Kleppner, *Continuity and Change in Electoral Politics, 1893–1928* (New York: Greenwood Press, 1987); Everett Carll Ladd Jr., with Charles D. Hadley, *Transformations of the American Party System* (New York: Norton, 1975); and Paul Lopatto, *Religion and the Presidential Election* (New York: Praeger, 1985).

21. James Davison Hunter presents this view clearly when he states that a new cultural cleavage in American politics "is so deep that it cuts across the old lines of conflict, making the distinctions that long divided Americans—those between Protestants, Catholics, and Jews—virtually irrelevant." Hunter, *Culture Wars: The Struggle to Define America* (New York: Basic Books, 1991).

22. Although some would disagree with this statement, empirical evidence shows that what is perhaps growing diversity of belief and behavior within American Catholicism, American Catholics still largely see themselves as having a shared Catholic identity, and also share adherence to many core doctrines and beliefs. For more on this matter, see William V. D'Antonio, James D. Davidson, Dean R. Hoge, and Katherine Meyer, *American Catholics: Gender, Generation, and Commitment* (Walnut Creek, CA: AltaMira, 2001).

23. Richard J. Jensen, *The Winning of the Midwest: Social and Political Conflict, 1888–1896* (Chicago: University of Chicago Press, 1971); Paul Kleppner, *The Cross of Culture: A Social Analysis of Midwestern Politics, 1850–1900* (New York: Free Press, 1970); and Kleppner, *The Third Electoral System, 1853–1892*.

24. Randall Balmer and Lauren F. Winner, *Protestantism in America* (New York: Columbia University Press, 2002).

25. Ibid. Charles Howard Hopkins, *The Rise of the Social Gospel in American Protestantism, 1865–1915* (New Haven: Yale University Press, 1967); George M. Marsden, *Fundamentalism and American Culture: The Shaping of Twentieth-Century Evangelicalism, 1870–1925* (New York: Oxford University Press, 1980); Wald, *Religion and Politics in the United States* and Clyde Wilcox, *Onward Christian Soldiers?: The Religious Right in American Politics*, 2d ed. (Boulder, CO: Westview, 2000).

26. The NES first separated Protestants into mainline and evangelical traditions in 1960. From 1960–1988 religious tradition is determined using vcf0128a in the NES Cumulative Datafile. This classification scheme is not without problems. The most significant has to do with the classification of Baptists. Prior to 1972 the NES survey instrument did not differentiate among Baptists, meaning that during this period some Baptists are misclassified in the division of Protestants into mainline and evangelical traditions. There is simply no satisfactory way to deal with this problem. Using the NES scheme means utilizing categories that are known to be flawed. Not using them and instead opting to use the more general Catholic/Protestant division means throwing out an important piece of information. In the interests of providing as much precision as possible and in allowing comparability with previous research the original NES classification of Protestants into mainline and evangelical traditions is used here, despite its obvious flaws. From 1990–1996, the revised classification scheme represented by vcf0128b is utilized. Beginning in 1998, NES officials stopped dividing Protestants into "mainline" and "evangelical" categories as they began a review and reevaluation of the construction of the religious tradition variable. This review apparently has yet to be completed, and thus the last three versions of the NES Cumulative File and the 2004 individual year file offer no variable differentiating Protestants by religious tradition. In an attempt to provide at least some differentiation among Protestants for 1998, 2000, 2002, and 2004, white Protestants have been divided into "mainline" and "evangelical" categories by denomination **only**. None of the other characteristics that the NES used to create its categories from 1990–1996, such as charismatic or fundamentalist identification, born-again status, or frequency of church attendance have been included here. The reasons for this decision are as follows. Charismatic or fundamentalist identification was not asked in 2000, 2002, or 2004, born-again status was not asked in 2002 or 2004, and classifying a respondent

as "evangelical" or "mainline" based on frequency of attendance at worship services requires assumptions that are not warranted. View of the authority of the Bible, another possible classification tool, also was not asked in 2002. For a useful discussion of classifying the religious tradition of Protestants based solely on denominational identification, see Steensland et al. (2000). For 1998, 2000, and 2004 denominations were classified as "evangelical" or "mainline" following the guidelines used by the NES from 1990–1996, with two exceptions. Those identifying themselves as members of the American Baptist Churches U.S.A. were moved from the "evangelical" category to the "mainline," and Jehovah's Witnesses were removed from the "evangelical" category and placed into a "Christian other" category that is not utilized here. For 2002, classifications were made following exactly the guidelines used by the NES from 1960–1988 (using the more detailed 1990–1996 scheme was not possible with the 2002 study). Classifying by denomination only obviously results in undifferentiated Protestants and Christians being excluded from theses analyses. This resulted in 53 respondents being removed in 1998, 89 in 2000, 101 in 2002, and 85 in 2004. This is particularly problematic given the recent growth in the number of non-denominational Protestants in the United States. As Steensland et al. (2000) and Woodberry and Smith (1998) point out, this group is one of the fastest growing religious groups in America, and individuals in this group tend to exhibit beliefs that are different from those Protestants who identify themselves as having "no denomination" (as opposed to "non-denominational"). The religious beliefs of non-denominational Protestants resemble those held by evangelicals much more than those possessed by mainliners. However, without information on these beliefs in a dataset it is unwise to classify non-denominational Protestants into either Protestant tradition. Steensland et al. (2000) do classify some non-denominational Protestants into the evangelical tradition solely on the basis of church attendance, with those who attend services once a month or more being classified as evangelicals and those who attend less than once a month being omitted from further analysis. We are reluctant to follow this example because, as noted above, this requires making assumptions that are not clearly warranted or justified. In future versions of the NES survey researchers can hope that sufficient belief and identification questions will be asked so that this important and growing component of the American religious landscape can be more fully analyzed. Finally, seculars are determined in the following manner. From 1960–1996, those respondents who answered "none/no preference," "agnostic," or "atheist" when asked their religious affiliation are coded as secular. From 1998–2004, seculars are those respondents who answered "atheist," "agnostic," "none/no preference," "don't know," or who refused to answer. Coding those who responded "don't know" or who refused to answer as seculars is somewhat problematic, but is unavoidable given how the NES provides its data. Full classification schemes are available from the authors upon request. B. Steensland et al., "The Measure of American Religion: Toward Improving the State of the Art," *Social Forces* 70 (2000): 291–318; and R.D. Woodberry and Christian S. Smith, "Fundamentalism et al.: Conservative Protestantism in America," *Annual Review of Sociology* 24 (1998): 25–56.

27. For additional discussion of the recent electoral behavior of mainline Protestants, see John C. Green, Corwin E. Smidt, James L. Guth, and Lyman A. Kellstedt, "The American Religious Landscape and the 2004 Presidential Vote: Increased Polarization," Report from the Bliss Institute at the University of Akron (Akron, Ohio, 2005); Jeff Manza and Clem Brooks, "The Religious Factor in U.S. Presidential Elections, 1960–1992," *American Journal of Sociology* 103 (July 1997): 38–81; Jeff Manza and Clem Brooks, "The Changing Fortunes of Mainline Protestants," in *The Quiet Hand of God: Faith-Based Activism and the Public Role of Mainline Protestantism*, eds. Robert Wuthnow and John H. Evans (Berkeley: University of California Press, 2002) 159–178; and Pew Research Center, *Trends 2005* (Washington, DC: Pew Research Center, 2005).

28. For more on Catholic electoral behavior, see Brewer, *Relevant No More?* Leege et al., *The Politics of Cultural Differences*; David C. Leege and Paul D. Mueller, "How Catholic is the Catholic Vote?" in *American Catholics and Civic Engagement: A Distinctive Voice*, ed. Margaret O'Brien Steinfels (Lanham, MD: Rowman & Littlefield Publishers, 2004), 213–250; and William B. Prendergast, *The Catholic Voter in American Politics: The Passing of a Democratic Monolith* (Washington, DC: Georgetown University Press, 1999).

29. James Davison Hunter, *American Evangelicalism: Conservative Religion and the Quandary of Modernity* (New Brunswick, NJ: Rutgers University Press, 1983); Dale McConkey, "Whither Hunter's Culture War? Shifts in Evangelical Morality, 1988–1998," *Sociology of Religion* 62 (Summer 2001): 149–174; Duane Murray Oldfield, *The Right and the Righteous: The Christian Right Confronts the*

Republican Party (Lanham, MD: Rowman & Littlefield, 1996); and Christian Smith, *American Evangelicalism: Embattled and Thriving* (Chicago: University of Chicago Press, 1998).

30. For more on the politics of the one-party South, see V. O. Key, Jr., *Southern Politics in State and Nation* (New York: Knopf, 1949); and Alexander Heard, *A Two-Party South?* (Chapel Hill: University of North Carolina Press, 1952).

31. A. James Reichley, *Faith in Politics* (Washington, DC: The Brookings Institution, 2002); and John Kenneth White, *The Values Divide: American Politics and Culture in Transition* (New York: Chatham House, 2003).

32. See Leege et al., *The Politics of Cultural Differences*, for a discussion of how race and cultural issues affected the electoral behavior of Southern whites and evangelicals.

33. Stanley B. Greenberg, *The Two Americas: Our Current Political Deadlock and How to Break It*, rev. ed. (New York: Thomas Dunne, 2005); Lyman A. Kellstedt, "Evangelicals and Political Realignment," in *Contemporary Evangelical Political Involvement*, ed. Corwin E. Smidt (Lanham, MD: University Press of America), 99–117; Andrew Kohut, John C. Green, Scott Keeter, and Robert C. Toth, *The Diminishing Divide: Religion's Changing Role in American Politics* (Washington, DC: The Brookings Institution, 2000); Layman, *The Great Divide*; Leege et al., *The Politics of Cultural Differences*; and Pew Research Center, *Trends 2005*.

34. John C. Green and James L. Guth, "Religion, Representatives, and Roll Calls," *Legislative Studies Quarterly* 16 (November 1991): 571–584; Geoffrey C. Layman and Edward G. Carmines, "Cultural Conflict in American Politics: Religious Traditionalism, Postmaterialism, and U.S. Political Behavior," *Journal of Politics* 59 (August 1997): 751–777; and Wade Clark Roof and William McKinney, *American Mainline Religion* (New Brunswick, NJ: Rutgers University Press, 1987).

35. Richard P. McBrien, *Catholicism*, new ed. (New York: Harper Collins, 1994); and David J. O'Brien and Thomas A. Shannon, eds., *Catholic Social Thought: The Documentary Heritage* (Maryknoll, NY: Orbis Books, 1992).

36. Brewer, *Relevant No More?*

37. Green et al., "The American Religious Landscape and the 2004 Presidential Vote,"; Kohut et al., *The Diminishing Divide*; and Pew Research Center, *Trends 2005*.

38. Nancy Tatom Ammerman, *Bible Believers: Fundamentalists in the Modern World* (New Brunswick, NJ: Rutgers University Press, 1987); and Wilcox, *Onward Christian Soldiers*, 2d. ed.

39. For more on what differentiates evangelicals from mainline Protestants, see David Bebbington, "Evangelicalism in Its Settings: The British and American Movements since 1940," In *Evangelicalism: Comparative Studies of Popular Protestantism in North America, the British Isles, and Beyond, 1700–1990*, Mark A. Noll, David W. Bebbington, and George A. Rawlyk, eds. (New York: Oxford University Press, 1994); Hunter, *American Evangelicalism*; and Wald, *Religion and Politics in the United States*, 4th ed.

40. Oldfield, *The Right and the Righteous*.

41. Shafer claims that the emergence of cultural issues in American politics is fundamentally about "the distinction … between traditionalistic and rationalistic values, between and inherited culture and a progressive one." Byron E. Shafer, "The New Cultural Politics," *PS: Political Science and Politics* 18 (Spring 1985): 221–231.

42. Robert Wuthnow, *The Restructuring of American Religion: Society and Faith Since World War II* (Princeton: Princeton University Press, 1988); and Wuthnow, *The Struggle for America's Soul*.

43. Balmer and Winner, *Protestantism in America*; Chip Berlet and Matthew N. Lyons, *Right-Wing Populism in America: Too Close for Comfort* (New York: Guilford, 2000); Marsden, *Fundamentalism and American Culture*; Oldfield, *The Right and the Righteous*; and Wald, *Religion and Politics in the United States*, 4th ed.

44. Robert Booth Fowler, Allan D. Hertzke, Laura R. Olson, and Kevin R. Den Dulk, *Religion and Politics in America: Faith, Culture, and Strategic Choices*, 3d ed. (Boulder, CO: Westview, 2004); Hunter, *American Evangelicalism*; Oldfield, *The Right and the Righteous*; and Wald, *Religion and Politics in the United States*, 4th ed.

45. Berlet and Lyons, *Right-Wing Populism in America*; Oldfield, *The Right and the Righteous*; Reichley, *Faith in Politics*; and Wald, *Religion and Politics in the United States*, 4th ed.

46. Hunter, *Culture Wars*; Hunter, *Before the Shooting Begins: Searching for Democracy in America's Culture War* (New York: Free Press, 1994); Wuthnow, *The Restructuring of American Religion*; and Wuthnow, *The Struggle for America's Soul*.

47. Nancy J. Davis and Robert V. Robinson, "Religious Orthodoxy in American Society: The Myth of a Monolithic Camp," *Journal for the Scientific Study of Religion* 35 (September 1996): 229–245; Nancy J. Davis and Robert V. Robinson, "Are the Rumors of War Exaggerated? Religious Orthodoxy and Moral Progressivism in America," *American Journal of Sociology* 103 (November 1996): 756–787; and Paul DiMaggio, John Evans, and Bethany Bryson, "Have Americans' Social Attitudes Become More Polarized?" *American Journal of Sociology* 102 (November 1996): 690–755.

48. Ibid.

49. John H. Evans, "Have Americans' Attitudes Become More Polarized?—An Update," *Social Science Quarterly* 84 (March 2003): 71–90. See also McConkey, "Whither Hunter's Culture War."

50. Phillip E. Hamond, Mark A. Shibley, and Peter M. Solow, "Religion and Family Values in Presidential Voting," *Sociology of Religion* 55 (Fall 1994): 277–290; Jonathan Knuckey, "A New Front in the Culture War? Moral Traditionalism and Voting Behavior in U.S. House Elections," *American Politics Research* 33 (September 2005): 645–671; Layman, *The Great Divide*; and Leege et al., *The Politics of Cultural Differences*.

51. James L. Guth and John C. Green, "Salience: The Core Concept?" in *Rediscovering the Religious Factor in American Politics*, eds. David C. Leege and Lyman A. Kellstedt (Armonk, NY: M.E. Sharpe): 157–174.

52. Brewer, *Relevant No More?*; Guth and Green, "Salience: The Core Concept?"; Andrew Kohut, John C. Green, Scott Keeter, and Robert C. Toth, *The Diminishing Divide: Religion's Changing Role in American Politics*, (Washington, D.C.: Brookings Institution Press, 2000); Layman, "Religion and Political Behavior in the United States"; Layman, *The Great Divide*; and Layman and Carmines, "Cultural Conflict in American Politics."

53. Charles Y. Glock and Rodney Stark, *Religion and Society in Tension* (Chicago: Rand McNally, 1965); Guth and Green, "Salience: The Core Concept?"; Lyman A. Kellstedt, John C. Green, James L. Guth, and Corwin E. Smidt, "Grasping the Essentials: The Social Embodiment of Religion and Political Behavior," in *Religion and the Culture Wars: Dispatches from the Front*, eds. John C. Green, James L. Guth, Corwin E. Smidt, and Lyman A. Kellstedt (Lanham, MD: Rowman & Littlefield Publishers, 1996): 174–192; and Kenneth D. Wald and Corwin E. Smidt, "Measurement Strategies in the Study of Religion and Politics," in *Rediscovering the Religious Factor in American Politics*, eds. Leege and Kellstedt, 28–37.

54. For a discussion of this matter, see Wald and Smidt, "Measurement Strategies in the Study of Religion and Politics." See also Andrew M. Greeley, *Religious Change in America* (Cambridge: Harvard University Press, 1989).

55. The religious salience index was created in the following manner. For church attendance, those attending every week were assigned a code of 3, those who attended almost every week or once or twice a month were coded 2, those who attended a few times per year were given a code of 1, and those who never went to services were coded 0. For guidance from religion, those who received a great deal were coded 3, those who responded quite a bit were given a 2, those who said some were coded 1, and those who said that religion was not important to them were given a 0. This results in minimum religious salience score of 0 and a maximum score of 6. In the interests of parsimony and greater sample sizes, the religious salience score was further collapsed, with those who scored 5 or 6 being coded as having a high level of religious salience, those with scores of 2, 3, and 4 coded as having a medium level of religious salience, and those who scored 0 or 1 coded as possessing a low level of religious salience. Altering the coding of scores to place scores of 4 in the high religious salience category and scores of 2 in the low category does not appreciably change the results generated using the religious salience index. Results available from authors on request.

56. Alan Abramowitz and Kyle Saunders, "Why Can't We All Just Get Along? The Reality of a Polarized America," *The Forum* 3 (Issue 2, 2005): 1–22. In their analysis of the 2004 presidential election, the Pew Research Center stated: "In fact, whether a person regularly attends church (or synagogue or mosque) was more important in determining his or her vote for president that such demographic characteristics as gender, age, income, and region, and just as important as race." Pew Research Center, *Trends 2005*, 26.

57. John H. Evans, "Worldviews or Social Groups and the Source of Moral Value Attitudes: Implications for the Culture Wars Thesis," *Sociological Forum* 12 (September 1997): 371–404; and Alan Wolfe, *One Nation, After All* (New York: Viking, 1998).

58. Morris P. Fiorina, with Samuel J. Abrams and Jeremy C. Pope, *Culture War? The Myth of a Polarized America* (New York: Pearson/Longman, 2005), 5. Other recent work skeptical of culture war claims include Wayne Baker, *America's Crisis of Values: Reality and Perception* (Princeton: Princeton University Press, 2005); and Geoffrey C. Layman and John C. Green, "Wars and Rumours of Wars: The Contexts of Cultural Conflict in American Political Behaviour," *British Journal of Political Science* 36 (January 2006): 61–89.

59. Peter L. Francia, Jonathan S. Morris, Carmine Scavo, and Jody Baumgartner, "America Divided? Re-examining the 'Myth' of the Polarized American Electorate." Paper presented at the annual meeting of the American Political Science Association, Washington, DC, September 1–4, 2005.

CHAPTER EIGHT

1. We are modeling our analysis in this chapter after that presented by Larry M. Bartels, "What's the Matter with *What's the Matter with Kansas?*" The paper was delivered at the annual meeting of the American Political Science Association, Washington, D.C., September 2005 and will appear in *Quarterly Journal of Political Science* 1, (March 2006): 201–226. We find the logic of his analysis very valuable for the issues we are examining here. His paper is available at www.princeton.edu/~bartels/kansas.pdf. For a rejoinder from Thomas Frank, see www.tcfrank.com/dismissd.pdf.

2. Even this slight rise in self-identified conservatism may not be all that meaningful. Erikson, MacKuen, and Stimson provide evidence that many Americans who identify themselves as conservatives in fact support liberal policy positions when asked about specific issues. Robert S. Erikson, Michael B. MacKuen, and James A. Stimson, *The Macro Polity* (New York: Cambridge University Press, 2002); and James A. Stimson, *Tides of Consent: How Public Opinion Shapes American Politics* (New York: Cambridge University Press, 2004).

3. Baker finds high levels of stability in the percentage of Americans holding "traditional" values over time. Wayne Baker, *America's Crisis of Values: Reality and Perception* (Princeton: Princeton University Press, 2005).

4. Herbert H. Hyman and Charles R. Wright, *Education's Lasting Influence on Values* (Chicago: University of Chicago Press, 1979); Herbert McClosky and Alida Brill, *Dimensions of Tolerance: What Americans Believe About Civil Liberties* (New York: Russell Sage, 1983).

5. Two changes to the questionnaire were made in 1990, and both probably increased the percentage saying they never attend services. From 1970 through 1988 the question about religious attendance followed a question about religious preference. Individuals were first asked their religious preference and then asked how often they attend services. Beginning in 1990, individuals were first asked about attendance and then their religious preference. First asking about religious preference (from 1970 to 1988) probably allowed individuals to indicate a preference when they really had no engagement. Having indicated some preference, they probably felt some need to indicate a degree of engagement. It may have been mildly embarrassing for an individual to express a preference, but no engagement, so many probably said they attended worship services several times a year even when they did not. The percentage saying they attended several times a year was 29 in 1986, 30 in 1988, and 15 in 1990. There was no change from 1988–1990 in the percentages saying they regularly attend services, but only in the percentage saying they never attend. The second change made in 1990 was to exclude certain forms of attendance as counting as religious attendance. In 1990 the language was changed to how often someone attended, "apart from occasional weddings, baptisms, or funerals?" Activities that were implicitly counted were moved to the category of non-attendance, increasing the percentage in that category.

6. This argument is central to Inglehart's claims of a post-material society. See Ronald Inglehart, *Silent Revolution: Changing Values and Political Styles among Western Publics* (Princeton: Princeton University Press, 1977); *Culture Shift in Advanced Industrial Society* (Princeton: Princeton University Press, 1990); and *Modernization and Postmodernization: Cultural, Economic, and Political Change in 43 Societies* (Princeton: Princeton University Press, 1997). For discussion of how the purported rise in post-materialism has affected American politics, see Jeffrey M. Berry, *The New Liberalism: The*

Rising Power of Citizen Groups (Washington, D.C.: Brookings Institution Press, 1999); and Steven E. Schier, *By Invitation Only: The Rise of Exclusive Politics in the United States* (Pittsburgh: University of Pittsburgh Press, 2000).

7. Bartels, "What's the Matter with *What's the Matter with Kansas?*" See also Mark D. Brewer, "Two Americas? An Examination of the Substantive and Group Bases of Electoral Polarization in the United States." Paper delivered at the annual meeting of the Northeastern Political Science Association, Philadelphia, Pa., November 2005.

8. E. J. Dionne, *They Only Look Dead: Why Progressives Will Dominate the Next Political Era* (New York: Touchstone, 1997). For an analysis of one of the architects of these efforts, see the *New Yorker* article on Karl Rove, "The Controller: Karl Rove is working to get George Bush reelected, but he has bigger plans," by Nicholas Lemann, "Profiles," *New Yorker*, May 12, 2003. It is available at www.bnfp.org/neighborhood/Lemann_Rove_NYM.htm.

9. An early statement of this approach is Kevin P. Philips, *The Emerging Republican Majority* (New Rochelle, N.Y.: Arlington House, 1969). See also William A. Rusher, *The Making of a New Majority Party* (New York: Sheed and Ward, 1975).

10. During the segregation era this was not a simple anti-government sentiment. The power of state government was used in the South to enforce segregation practices. The sentiment was against the federal government intruding to impose uniform national norms on the South.

11. Merle Black and Earle Black, *Politics and Society in the South* (Cambridge: Harvard University Press, 1987).

12. There are many books emerging now about the Republican strategy to attract conservatives to the party. A good overview is contained in John Micklethwait and Adrian Wooldridge, *The Right Nation: Conservative Power in America* (New York: Penguin, 2004).

13. Alan I. Abramowitz, "Issue Evolution Reconsidered: Racial Attitudes and Partisanship in the U.S. Electorate," *American Journal of Political Science* 38 (February 1994): 1–24; Alan I. Abramowitz and Kyle L. Saunders, "Ideological Realignments in the U.S. Electorate," *Journal of Politics* 60 (August 1998): 634–652; Alan I. Abramowitz, Brad Alexander, and Matthew Gunning, "Incumbency, Redistricting, and the Decline of Competition in U.S. House Elections," *Journal of Politics* 68 (January 2006): 75–88; and Gary C. Jacobson, "Party Polarization in Presidential Support: The Electoral Connection," *Congress and the Presidency* 30 (Spring 2003): 1–36.

14. A review of these changes is contained in Jeffrey M. Stonecash, "The Rise of Conservatives," in *The State of the Parties*, ed. John Green (Boulder, CO: Rowman and Littlefield, 2006). A longer-term view of the movement of conservatives to the Republican Party is contained in Nelson W. Polsby, *How Congress Evolves: Social Bases of Institutional Change* (New York: Oxford University Press, 2004); and Jeffrey M. Stonecash, *Political Parties Matter: Realignment and the Return of Partisanship* (Boulder, CO: Lynne-Rienner, 2006).

15. See, for example, Joel Brinkley, "Out of Spotlight, Bush Overhauls U.S. Regulations," *New York Times*, August 14, 2004,

16. Jeffrey M. Stonecash, "Parties and Taxes: The Emergence of Distributive Divisions, 1950–2005," manuscript, Maxwell School, Syracuse University, 2005.

17. In the analyses that follow, the coefficients are standardized OLS regression coefficients, which are more appropriate when the dependent variable is interval in nature. In these analyses the use of OLS regression coefficients is technically correct for party identification, but not for presidential voting, which is nominal in nature. Another approach is to conduct logistic analyses. We present the OLS regression coefficients because they are easier to interpret. To assure readers that the same results hold when logistic analyses are run, the tables below present results of logistic analyses for the same years and the same variables. The standardized logistic estimates indicate the same pattern: income has been a significant and enduring source of division since the 1980s, and abortion has steadily become an equally important source of division. We also did an analysis including non-whites. Including those respondents does not alter the patterns.

YEAR	Income	Religious Attendance	Abortion
Republican Presidential Voting			
1972	.07	.13	.08
1976	.16	.07	.04
1980	.15	.03	.03
1984	.22	.04	.18
1988	.11	.04	.17
1992	.18	.12	.23
1996	.20	.11	.36
2000	.17	.07	.38
2004	.16	.04	.44
Identification with Republican Party			
1972	.07	.01	.04
1976	.13	.04	.03
1980	.14	.11	.05
1984	.17	.02	.08
1988	.12	.07	.04
1992	.19	.07	.17
1996	.20	.09	.20
2000	.17	.08	.21
2004	.18	.07	.27

18. This technique also addresses the possibility of spuriousness, which exists when a simple look at a set of variables apparently shows a strong relationship, which is in fact caused by other variables overlooked in the analysis.

19. Morris P. Fiorina, with Samuel J. Abrams and Jeremy C. Pope, *Culture War? The Myth of a Polarized America* (New York: Pearson/Longman, 2005), 5.

20. In their analysis of opinions, they track overall the percentage supporting different abortion positions (35–37), how regions differ on this issue (38), and how religious traditions differ on the issue (39) and numerous other matters. They do not assess the partisan voting of supporters and opponents over time or how their party identification has evolved.

21. Herbert F. Weisberg and Dino Christenson, "Changing Horses in Wartime: The 2004 Presidential Election," presented at the annual meeting of the American Political Science Association, Washington, D.C., September 2005. Using the thermometer approach discussed earlier, respondents in NES surveys were asked their rating of Democrats and Republicans. They present both aggregate results and the correlation between results on p. 15 of their paper. The actual data are below.

Party Thermometer Means, Differences and Correlation Among Responses, 1972–2004

	1972	1976	1980	1984	1988	1992	1996	2000	2004
Democrats	66.4	62.9	63.9	62.1	61.5	59.0	58.8	59.0	58.7
Republicans	63.1	57.5	59.2	57.9	59.2	51.6	53.5	53.8	53.9
Difference	3.3	5.4	4.7	4.2	2.3	7.4	5.3	5.2	4.8
Correlation	.02	.01	-.23	-.40	-.39	-.27	-.42	-.34	-.48

22. Alan Abramowitz, "Is Polarization a Myth?" presented at the annual meeting of the Southern Political Science Association, Atlanta, Ga., January 2006.
23. Jacobson, "Partisan Polarization in Presidential Support," 26–32.
24. Stonecash, *Political Parties Matter*, 89–95.
25. In addition to Fiorina et al., other recent culture war skeptics include Baker, *America's Crisis of Values*; Geoffrey C. Layman and John C. Green, "Wars and Rumours of Wars: The Contexts of Cultural Conflict in American Political Behaviour," *British Journal of Political Science* 36 (January 2006): 61–89; and Gerald M. Pomper, "The Presidential Election: The Ills of American Politics After 9/11," in *The Elections of 2004*, ed. Michael Nelson (Washington, D.C.: CQ Press, 2005): 42–68.
26. David Cay Johnston, "Big Gain for Rich Seen in Tax Cuts for Investments," *New York Times*, April 5, 2006, A1.

INDEX

Note: notes, tables and figures are indicated by *n, t,* and *f* after page numbers, respectively

ABOUT THE AUTHORS

Mark D. Brewer is assistant professor of political science at the University of Maine, where he teaches courses in American government, parties and elections, and religion and politics. His research focuses on partisanship and electoral behavior at the mass and elite levels, the linkages between public opinion and public policy, and the interactions between religion and politics in the United States. Brewer is the author of *Relevant No More? The Catholic/Protestant Divide in American Electoral Politics* (2003) and coauthor of *Diverging Parties* (2003). He has published articles in *Political Research Quarterly, Political Behavior, Legislative Studies Quarterly,* and *Journal for the Scientific Study of Religion.*

Jeffrey M. Stonecash is professor and chair of the Department of Political Science at Syracuse University, where he teaches courses on American political parties, federalism and state politics, and quantitative methods. His research is in the area of political parties and their electoral bases, changes over time in electoral bases, and their impact on the nature of political debates in society. Stonecash is the author or coauthor of *Political Parties Matter: Realignment and the Return of Partisan Voting* (2006), *Political Polling* (2003), *Diverging Parties* (2003), *The Emergence of State Government: Parties and New Jersey Politics, 1950–2000* (2002), and *Class and Party in American Politics,* (2000), as well as editor of *Governing New York State* (2006).